HOW TO
cheat
IN
Adobe Flash CS4

The art of design and animation

Chris Georgenes

ELSEVIER

AMSTERDAM • BOSTON • HEIDELBERG • LONDON • NEW YORK • OXFORD
PARIS • SAN DIEGO • SAN FRANCISCO • SINGAPORE • SYDNEY • TOKYO
Focal Press is an imprint of Elsevier

Focal Press

Focal Press is an imprint of Elsevier
Linacre House, Jordan Hill, Oxford OX2 8DP, UK
30 Corporate Drive, Suite 400, Burlington, MA 01803, USA

First published 2009

British Library Cataloguing in Publication Data
Georgenes, Chris.
   How to cheat in Adobe Flash CS4 : the art of design and animation.
   1. Flash (Computer file)
   I. Title II. Adobe Flash CS4
   006.7'86—dc22

Library of Congress Control Number: 2009920393

ISBN: 978-0-240-52131-2

For information on all Focal Press publications
visit our website at www.focalpress.com

Typeset by Macmillan Publishing Solutions
(www.macmillansolutions.com)

Printed and bound in Canada
09 10 11 12   12 11 10 9 8 7 6 5 4 3 2 1

Contents

Foreword vii
How to cheat, and why viii
Acknowledgments x
How to use this book 1

1 Design styles 3

Drawing with basic shapes 4
The Brush tool 6
Mixing colors 8
Using gradients 10
Adding texture 12
The Pen tool 16
Trace Bitmap 18
Shading 1: line trick 20
Shading 2: shape it 22
Shading 3: paint selected 24
Shading 4: outlines 26
Realism with gradients 28
Spray Brush tool 32
Deco tool 34

Interlude: The new Flash interface 36

2 Transformation and distortion 39

Distorting bitmaps 40
The Envelope tool 42
Warping 44
Card flip 46
3D Rotation 48
Butterfly 50
Squash and stretch 52

Interlude: Being subtle 54

3 Masking 57

Rotating globe 58
Flag waving 60
Iris transition 62
Handwriting 64
Spotlight 66
Focus 68

Interlude: A moment of clarity 70

4 Motion tips and tricks . 73

The new Motion tween 74
The Motion Editor 82
Basic shadow 84
Drop shadow 86
Perspective shadow 88
Blur filter 90
Flying text 92
Combining effects 94
Blur filter (text) 96
Selective blurring 98
Background blurring 100

Interlude: Learning to be simple 102

Contents

5 Character animation 105

2.5D basics 106

2.5D advanced 108

2.5D monkey 110

Lip syncing (swap method) 112

Lip syncing (nesting method) 114

To sync or not to sync 116

Sync (Classic tween) 118

Sync (Motion tween) 120

Hinging body parts 122

Bone tool (Inverse Kinematics) 124

Closing the gaps 128

Bitmap animation (JibJab) 130

PSD Importer (JibJab) 132

Motion guides (JibJab) 134

Walk cycle 136

Advanced walk cycle 140

Anticipation 142

Drawing upon oneself 144

Looping backgrounds 146

Tradigital animation 148

Interlude: How did I get here? 152

6 Flash to video 157

Document setup 158

Ape Escape 160

Title and action safety 162

Safe colors 164

Safe colors (Kuler) 166

Keeping it all in sync 168

QuickTime Exporter 170

SWF2Video 172

Interlude: Graphics tablets 174

7 Animation examples 177

Super text effect 178

Page turn 180

Smoke with gradients 182

Smoke stylized 184

Full steam ahead 186

Fireworks 188

Soft reveal 190

Star Wars text 192

Color adjustments 194

Vertigo 196

Let it rain 198

Playing with fire 200
Winter wonderland 202
3D perspective 204
Bone and Spray 206

Interlude: From the inside out 208

9 Working with video ..227

Importing video 228
Flash Video (FLV) 230

Interlude: FLV tools and articles 232

8 Working with sound 211

Recording sounds 212
Audacity® 214
Adobe® Soundbooth® CS4 216
Adobe® Audition® 3.0 218
Sound in Flash 220
Dynamic sounds (AS3) 222

Interlude: Flash wasn't always 224
this good

10 Interactivity 235

Event handling 236
What a drag 240
Pausing the timeline 242
Loading images (AS3) 244
Loading images (AS2) 246
Toggling sound (AS3) 248

Interlude: Objects, objects everywhere 252

Contents

11 Extending Flash 255

Introduction to JSFL 256
Trace Bitmap and JSFL 258
AnimSlider Pro 264
Ajar extensions 266
iK'motion 268
Swift 3D Xpress 270
Flashjester 272
Toon Boom Animate 274

Interlude: Pimp my Flash 276

12 What's new in CS4 279

Motion presets 280
Motion and Classic tweens 282
Creating Motion tweens 284
Working with Motion spans 286
Editing Motion paths 288

Motion Editor properties 290
Custom easing 292
Motion tweens and 3D 294
3D Position and View 296
Basic bone armature 298
Complex bone armature 300
Joint rotation and constrain 302
Bone tool easing basics 304
Bones and shapes 306
Bind tool 310

Interlude: The History of Flash 312

Index 315
What's on the CD 321

Foreword

Flash originally became a member of Adobe Creative Suite 3 and is now a member of the various flavors of Adobe Creative Suite 4, sharing the suites with the likes of Photoshop, Illustrator, After Effects, and Acrobat. This exposes the tool to many new kinds of creative designers and developers, who will likely use Flash in ways the current Flash community hasn't thought of. Whether you're a new or existing Flash user, now is a great time to learn or use the software and get involved with the Flash community online.

Many years ago in a dimly lit basement, I started using Flash to create unpalatable, short, frame-by-frame animations – and discovered Flash was much easier than other tools I had been using to do the same thing. It's hard to believe what Flash has become over the years, from the relatively simple animation program it once was back then. For example, Flash now has a powerful programming language, a bucket full of filter and blending tools, and cross-product integration with tools like Illustrator, Photoshop, and Flex to help you make great animation, applications, or motion design.

One of the nice things about Flash is that it attracts so many different users, from inspiring and creative animators to hard-core programmers, and all sorts of people in-between. You certainly don't need to learn everything there is to know about Flash to be a master at the tool – you can choose to focus your talents on design or development, or challenge yourself from time to time by crossing over between graphics and code. But now that Flash is full of features and capable of so much, the tools can seem rather daunting to learn. But if you have helpful resources at your side, like this book, learning Flash doesn't need to be difficult. I believe the key to learning Flash is to keep it simple when you start out, take it slow, use the available resources (like books), and try to be patient. Learning Flash takes some time, but it is a lot of fun and very rewarding.

Flash is an incredible tool for expressing your creativity, style, and unique ideas. I hope that you use Flash with this book to get inspired, learn valuable new tricks and techniques, and create some wonderful animation. And of course, make sure to have fun with the software while you read and learn all about how to animate!

Jen deHaan
Instructional Designer, Web and DVA
Adobe Systems Inc.

How to cheat, and why

The truth about cheating

The word "cheat", in most cases, has a negative connotation. To "cheat" implies deception and trickery associated with a fraudulent act. In some ways this book will show you how you can trick your audience, not unlike a magician's "sleight of hand" technique where you can control not only what is being seen, but how the viewer sees it. But this book will certainly not teach you how to be a fraud.

To "cheat" in Flash is to find shortcuts to help you work more efficiently and economically. Time translates to money and if you can deliver a great looking project on time, that means you stayed within budget and everybody wins.

My philosophy

At the end of the day, if I didn't have any fun, then it's time to find another job. But I had to learn this lesson the hard way a few years ago while working with an animation company designing a network television series. I was designing the main characters for a show called *Science Court* (ABC), and there was a conflict between us and the network as to the choice of skin color for one of the characters. I liked green and the network preferred orange. I felt strongly that my color choice was the best and I admit I may have let myself become emotionally charged about the issue. One day I went to lunch with the animation director and we were casually talking about the color issue. It was something he said that changed my outlook on work from that day forward: *"We must have pretty cool jobs when the most stressful part of our day is whether or not a character looks too much like a frog."*

I stopped dead in my tracks, instantly realizing how right he was and how silly I felt about the matter. After lunch we returned to the studio where I immediately changed the character to orange and never uttered another word about it. I even ended up liking the orange more than the green. Since then, my philosophy has always been to have fun no matter how stressful my workday gets. My job, in comparison to all other possible occupations, is the best job even on the worst of days.

Workthroughs and examples

Each workthrough in this book is designed as a double-page spread so you can prop the book up behind your keyboard or next to your monitor as a visual reference while working alongside it. Many of the workthroughs are real-world client projects I have been commissioned to design and animate. Using these projects as examples has allowed me to provide you with a CD containing the source files for you to open and explore. Each chapter ends with an Interlude in which I talk about everything from my own experiences as a designer and animator as well as some relevant and useful information based on the topic at hand.

Flash terminology

Not much has changed when it comes to terminology in Flash. Symbols have been around since the beginning and so has the behavior any symbol can have (Graphic, Movie Clip and Button). The Timeline is essentially the same with a few new enhancements, namely the new Motion Editor and new Motion tween model. Nesting pertains to animations within symbols and remains as one of the strengths of Flash animation. If you already have a basic understanding of Flash then you will most likely be familiar with most of the terminology in this book. If there's anything that you come across that is unfamiliar, try searching the Flash Help docs or the reader's forum at **www.keyframer.com/forum**.

What's on the CD?

Lots of cool stuff so check it out! In almost all cases I have provided the actual FLA file for every tutorial in this book! But I didn't stop there. I have also included as many free extensions as I could find. There are a couple of cases where I was unable to provide the source file or some of the content had to be removed for copyright and distribution reasons. For full details as to what is included, refer to the chapter "What's on the CD" at the end of this book.

Going further

The official public discussion board for this book can be found by pointing your browser to **www.keyframer.com/forum**. Everyone is encouraged to register (registration is free) and discuss this book or Adobe Flash in general with the active Keyframer community. Keyframer.com is my Adobe Flash blog, resource and community portal where you will find many Flash related tutorials and useful learning resources as well as a very dedicated and active community of Flash animators. I welcome you to drop by and post a comment about this book or to simply say hello. It is a great place to exchange ideas and animations with other *Flashers*.

If you have any questions or concerns about this book requiring the attention of Focal Press, please visit the book's official website at **www.howtocheatinflash.com** where you can find out how to contact Focal Press and general information about this book.

Chris Georgenes

Acknowledgments

Now I finally understand why so many authors dedicate their work to their spouses. With the utmost love and respect, I dedicate this book to Rebecca, who has always supported me and my career of "coloring" things.

I am eternally indebted to:

Bobby, Billy and Andrea for being the greatest characters I have ever helped create.

Mom and Dad for encouraging me to choose my own path in life.

Marie Hooper and Georgia Kennedy of Focal Press for their support and providing me the opportunity to be a part of this wonderful series.

Steve Caplin for all of his knowledge, vision and kindness.

Buck DeFore for his invaluable input and attention to detail.

David Stiller of quip.net for his friendship and tireless contributions throughout this book and to the Flash community.

Fred Wessel and Dennis Nolan for giving me my greatest tool of all: the ability to draw.

Warm and fuzzy feelings to: Laith Bahrani, Karen Bresnahan, Joe Corrao, Jen deHaan, Mike Downey, Scott Fegette, Warren Fuller, Richard Galvan, Gary Goldberger, Jarred Hope, Kevin Kolde, Christine Lawson, Shine Lee, Stephen Levinson, Dave Logan, Kirk Millett, Eric Mueller, Ben Palczynski, Davendra Pateel, Adam Phillips, Benedetta Pontiroli, Puck, Waymaure Seuell, Todd Sanders, Tim Saguinson, John Say, Aaron Simpson, Colin Smith, Evan and Gregg Spiridellis, Ed Sullivan, Steven J. Tubbrit ("Sunchirp"), Urami, Jackie Watson, Lily Welch, Willo, Lynda Weinman and Vivek.

Adobe Systems Inc., and the entire Adobe Flash team for making such a cool product.

Thanks to the following companies for their approval to use their projects as examples for this book:

Abs Ale, Audacity, Cone Inc., Erain, Euro RSCG Worldwide, Fablevision, Flashjester, Frederator, istockphoto, Jib Jab Media, Leapfrog Innovations, New Balance, Pileated Pictures and Say Design.

Some of the photographic images used in this book are from the following royalty-free image sources:
Adobe Stock Images
www.istockphoto.com
www.iheartvector.com

In memory of Max Coniglio.

How to use this book

I am a digital animator – a *Digimator* if you will. I learned how to animate using a computer. Any animation program can have a mechanical feel to it since we work by selecting options from menus much of the time. The trick I have learned is how to make a software program like Flash feel more organic, as if it were a ball of clay, starting with a basic shape and pushing and pulling it into something unique. If this book teaches anything, I hope it teaches you to think differently as to how you approach Flash. Just because the Help docs, online resources or even other books tell you how something can or should be done, don't take that as carved in stone. Take it as carved in clay, meaning, you can continue to expand upon the ways the tools are used, even beyond what you may have read elsewhere.

The first few chapters focus on some of the basics of using Flash in real-world situations. I do not explain the rudimentary features of Flash, such as how to convert objects to symbols and what the differences are between Movie Clips and Graphic symbols. That is what the Help docs are for and are simply a keystroke away (F1). You bought this book to learn what goes beyond the Help docs and what can only be learned through the span of several years of experience using Flash. For you, this is the true essence of "cheating" because this book condenses those years into about 300 pages.

Any page that includes a CD icon means that the Flash file (FLA) is included on the CD. You can open these files and analyze how each file was designed but keep in mind just about all source files are protected by copyright or trademark, preventing them from being used commercially. However, I do hope they will provide a source of education and inspiration for you. All files can be opened in Flash CS3 and CS4. Some tutorials will include a "CS4" icon which means that Flash CS4 is required due to CS4-specific features. If you do not have Flash CS4, a free trial version is available from Adobe's website (**www.adobe.com/products/flash**).

You are not alone either. If you have a question or a technique you would like to share, visit the official book forum accessed through my Keyframer website:

www.keyframer.com/forum

There's no such thing as a dumb question and you may find yourself answering a few as well. I am easily accessible as the forum administrator and I welcome your comments and questions regarding this book and the Flash platform in general. It's a great way to meet other Flash users from around the world and keep yourself updated with the latest Flash news and events.

■No two snowflakes are exactly alike and the same can be said for artists and designers. A good drawing program will allow this individuality to be expressed without limitation.

1 Design styles

THE TECHNIQUES described in this book assume you have a reasonable working knowledge of Flash. In later chapters, we'll discuss workflows that involve symbols, timelines and various animation techniques. This first chapter will serve as a refresher course on the fundamentals of designing for animation and introduce a few cool drawing techniques along the way.

Later on, we'll go into more detail on how to work with symbols, Classic tweens, Motion tweens and Shape tweens, the Timeline and the Motion Editor.

Drawing with basic shapes

IF YOU PLAYED with Lego building blocks when you were a kid, you may find this drawing style familiar (or at least intuitive). You'll use several basic shapes and then connect them together. This technique requires breaking down each body part of the character into basic building blocks using the Rectangle and Oval tools. It's a fast and efficient way to simplify the character into manageable sections while achieving a very professional cartoon style.

Here, we will use shapes to cut in to other shapes. This is a very useful technique for cutting holes out of objects as well as altering the edges of shapes. Of course these techniques can be applied to background elements as well.

The key here is using simple shapes to build complex images suitable for Flash style animation, which we will get to in later chapters.

1 Here is my original pencil sketch that I have scanned and saved as a JPG file. I prefer to start with pencil on paper because I simply like the feel of this medium and the results are always a little more, shall we say, artistic.

2 After importing the scanned image, insert a blank keyframe on frame 2 and turn on the Onionskin tool. This allows us to trace the image in a new frame while using the original image as a reference.

6 To achieve the black outline, select the shape, copy it using ⌘ C ctrl C and paste it in place using ⌘ Shift V ctrl Shift V. While it's still selected, select a different color from the Mixer panel and scale it about 80% smaller.

7 The original shape is still present underneath your new shape. The trick is to position the new shape off-center from the original to achieve an outline with a varied weight.

3 Using the Oval **O** and Rectangle **R** tools allows us to quickly achieve the basic forms of our character. The Selection tool is great for pushing and pulling these basic fills into custom shapes based on our sketch.

4 Turn on the Snap option (magnet icon), and drag corners to each other so they snap together. This process is not unlike those Lego building blocks you played with when you were a kid.

5 Next, click and drag the sides of your shapes to push and pull them into curves. This is a fun process as your character really starts to take shape.

8 The parachute uses a slightly different technique I like to call "cutting in". Let's start with the Oval tool for the parachute's basic shape.

9 You can cut into this shape using different colored shapes such as this blue oval. position it over the area you want to cut into, deselect it, then select it and hit the Delete key *Delete*.

10 Once your shape is the way you want it, you can use the Ink Bottle tool **S** to quickly add an outline to it.

The Brush tool

THE BRUSH TOOL is probably the most versatile of all the drawing tools, especially when combined with a pressure-sensitive tablet. Drawing with the Brush tool is essentially drawing with shapes. It's the tool that feels the most natural due to the support of pressure sensitivity and tilt features.

Wacom makes a series of popular tablets that work great with Flash. Wacom tablets can work in conjunction with your existing mouse, or replace your mouse completely. Many digital designers use a tablet with any number of graphics editors including Adobe Photoshop and Adobe Illustrator.

When to use the Brush tool is really a matter of style and preference. For this character, I wanted to achieve a loose, hand-drawn feel, so the brush was a perfect choice.

1 The first adjustment you will want to make when using the Brush tool **B** will be the amount of smoothing you want applied. This option appears as a hot text slider in the Properties panel when the Brush tool is selected. The right amount of smoothing to use depends on personal preference. The higher the number, the smoother the line (and vice versa). For this character, we'll choose a low amount of smoothing to maintain an organic quality to the line work.

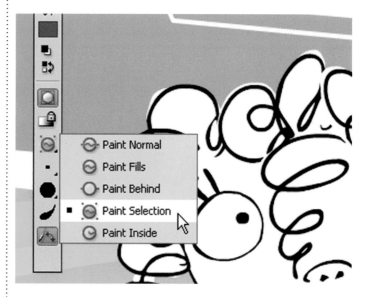

3 To remain consistent with the loose drawing style, you may want to add a fill color that bleeds outside of the outlines a little. There are several ways to achieve this by painting on a new layer below the outline art or setting the brush to "Paint Behind" and painting on the same layer. If you turned on Object Drawing mode **J**, then each object you draw will reside safely in a container.

2 Always design your characters with the intended purpose in mind: animation. Form follows function and the animation style can often dictate how a character is designed. If you are a perfectionist like me, you'll want the hair to look as much like individual curls as possible. To do this, avoid designing the hair as one large flat object. Instead, draw individual sections of curls to keep them as separate objects so they can be moved independently of each other. Turn on Object Drawing mode (subselection of the Brush tool). Object Drawing mode allows you to draw shapes as separate objects. These objects can be drawn over each other without them being merged together. You can select each Object Drawing with the Selection tool **V** and then convert each one to a symbol.

4 The final result represents the loose hand-drawn style we were after. The line quality feels natural and reflects the imperfections the human hand is capable of. We are not trying to achieve a slick design style here, but rather to convey a looser line quality representative of hand-drawn artwork. This style lends itself well to a child character as the integrity of the line is similar to how a real child would draw.

Mixing colors

COLOR IS POWERFUL. It can be used in a variety of ways to suggest the tone of your graphic design or mood of an entire animated scene. Let's take a look at how to adjust color values using the Color Mixer's HSB sliders. Using the drop-down menu,

change the color mode from RGB to HSB. Now the sliders next to each swatch can be used to adjust your colors based on their hue, saturation and brightness.

1 You can convert your colors to gray scale by picking the colors with the Eyedropper tool and then dragging the saturation slider all the way down to 0%. This will lower the saturation but maintain its hue and brightness.

2 Change the hue of your colors by adjusting the amount of hue with the slider. Type a new value directly into the input field if you prefer or copy and paste color values from other sources into these fields.

3 Here's another example where the hue for each color has been easily adjusted using the hue color value. This technique can be very effective for providing an overall tone to your website design or matching an existing color scheme.

4 You can experiment by adjusting two or more values to create unique contrasts in color. The lower the saturation, the less contrast there will be between colors. You can achieve that nice "pastel" color scheme by fine-tuning these values.

5 Adjust the sturation value to create a strong contrast between colors. The saturation will determine the intensity of a specific hue.

SHORTCUTS
MAC WIN BOTH

9

Using gradients

G RADIENTS CAN BE very effective when you want to break away from the flatness of solid color fills. They can be used to add a sense of depth and dimensionality to your characters, backgrounds and graphics in general. Gradients can also work against you due to their ease of use, resulting in generic and often lackluster images. When in the right hands, both linear and radial gradients can contribute to a very effective and sometimes realistic design.

1 A simple radial gradient is used to fill most of the shapes that make up the monkey. The trick here is providing the illusion of a 3D object in a 2D environment. Four colors are used for this gradient. The critical color for this illusion is the fourth color (far right). It represents a light source coming from behind the sphere, suggesting the sphere is truly round.

4 To make the ear look concave, mix another radial gradient going from darkest in the center to a lighter value on the outer edge. Fill the shape with this gradient and position it off-center so that only half of the gradient is shown. Since darker colors will recede and lighter colors will appear closer to us, this otherwise flat shape now gives us the impression it is concave.

7 For those classic cartoon "ping-pong" eyeballs, mix a radial gradient the same way using white and gray colors. Color theory teaches us that to show light, you must show dark. Apply this technique to the eyes by placing them in front of a darker shape. This will help add some contrast, making the eyeballs *pop*, thereby adding depth.

2 Edit the gradient to conform to the shape using the Gradient Transform tool **F**. Use the handles to rotate, scale and skew the gradient so it is slightly larger than the shape. Select the center control point and drag the entire gradient and position it slightly off-center from the shape.

3 Click and drag the focal point tool so that the highlight is positioned between the center of the shape and its edge. By doing this you are suggesting that the light source is at more of an angle. Notice the fourth color of our gradient is showing along the bottom and right edge. This implies light wrapping around the sphere from behind.

5 The hair is a shape filled with another radial gradient. Most of this shape will be hidden behind other graphics, so you only need to concern yourself with how the outer edge looks when the character is fully assembled.

6 The hands are really not hands at all. A few strategically positioned spheres with the same radial gradient as the face and body are used to suggest hands.

8 The nose is a combination of spheres filled with radial and linear gradients. To create the nostrils, use a linear gradient and edit it so that the darker color is above the lighter color. By themselves, the spheres are just shapes. But placed against the radial sphere, they become holes.

9 Good designs are consistent in technique. When each element is comprised of the same graphical style, the overall result will typically be consistent and fluid. Don't deviate from your plan; choose a technique and stick with it.

Adding texture

1 The first task is to design your textures. A digital camera is a very handy device for this purpose. Take a walk around your neighborhood and you'll quickly find an unlimited supply of interesting textures that can be used for your designs. Use Photoshop to adjust the color, add filters and crop your images. Remember to keep the image small enough for Web output.

BITMAPS CAN BE a very effective way to add texture to your designs. Since any image could be a potential texture, the possibilities are endless. For this frog character, I wanted a slightly more sophisticated look while still maintaining a cartoon feel. Instead of using solid color fills and some spot color shading, the use of imported bitmap textures added that extra sense of depth and richness.

4 You can use the Bucket tool to fill your shapes with the different bitmaps you imported, broke apart and picked with the eyedropper.

2 Select the imported bitmap and break it apart ⌘ *B* *ctrl* *B*. Click on it using the Eyedropper tool. It will now be added to the Color Mixer as a swatch.

3 Using the Brush tool, draw your shapes using the bitmap as the fill color.

```
// AS2 looks like this:
_quality = "BEST";

// AS3 looks like this:
stage.quality = "BEST";
```

5 Most likely the bitmap fill will need to be scaled, rotated or re-positioned. Select the Free Transform tool *F*, and edit your fill using the various handles around the bounding box.

6 The final step is to convert all parts to symbols and add a slight amount of dark tint to the instances behind the character. This helps separate similar bitmap textures from each other and adds a touch of depth.

SHORTCUTS
MAC WIN BOTH

Adding texture (cont.)

BITMAPS DON'T ALWAYS have to look flat. Introducing "Grotto", a character made almost entirely of bitmap fills and some carefully placed Flash gradients to provide the illusion of form, volume and, most of all, texture.

Here we'll look at how to give otherwise flat bitmap textures a bit more depth using some basic gradients and alpha.

1 The first step is to create your texture in Adobe Photoshop, import it into Flash, break it apart and then select it with the Eyedropper tool 🖋. I created the shape for Grotto's body with the paint brush and the bitmap swatch as my fill "color". Select the body shape and convert it to a Graphic symbol.

4 Sometimes the devil is in the details, which is evident here with the additon of some subtle highlights to the lip. On a new layer use the Brush tool to paint some shapes and then fill them with a linear gradient containing 30% white to 0% white. Use the Fill Transform tool **F** to edit the gradient as necessary.

2 Edit the symbol by adding another layer above the shape layer. Copy ⌘ C ctrl C and paste in place ⌘ Shift V ctrl Shift V the body shape into this new layer. Fill it with a radial gradient with two colors: black with about 30% alpha and black with 0% alpha.

3 The mouth/lip symbol was made the same way by layering a radial gradient over the bitmap fill shape. Use the Fill Transform tool to position the gradient so it forms a shadow along the bottom half of the shape.

HOT TIP

You may also want to adjust the properties of the imported bitmap (double-click the bitmap icon in the document library) and select "Apply Smoothing". This will apply anti-aliasing to your image and make it appear smoother.

5 The nostril is another example of layering various gradients over the original shape containing the bitmap fill. Here I used a linear gradient for the inner nostril shape and a radial gradient to provide some shading for a more realistic effect.

6 When all these subtle details are combined, they can add up to a very sophisticated image. The shapes that make up Grotto are simple yet convincing simply by layering some basic gradients over our textures.

SHORTCUTS
MAC WIN BOTH

The Pen tool

S O FAR IN this chapter we have looked at several ways of achieving different styles of drawing. From the basics of snapping simple shapes together forming bigger, more complex shapes, to using bitmaps as textural fills. Most of the time the design process demands a combination of tools and techniques to get the job done. For this character design I went from a rough pencil sketch to a fully rendered vector drawing using the Pen tool and basic shapes. The Pen tool, in combination with the Selection tool, offers infinite flexibility when it comes to manipulating strokes and shapes.

1 Start with a scanned sketch or draw directly into Flash. Create a blank keyframe on frame 2 and turn on the Onionskin feature. Using the sketch as reference, trace the hair using the Pen tool by clicking and dragging each point as you go. This will automatically create curves with Bezier handles, allowing you to manipulate the stroke each time a point is made.

5 A linear gradient can be applied to a path without having to convert it to a shape like in older versions. For this gradient I chose to mix 3 colors: a light, mid and dark tone. With this gradient selected in the stroke color swatch in the Color panel, click on the path using the Ink Bottle **S** tool to apply it. Edit the gradient using the Gradient Transform tool **F**.

COLOR

Type:	Radial
Overflow:	
	☐ Linear RGB

R:	254
G:	198
B:	69
Alpha:	100%	#FEC645

HOT TIP

Go to Edit > Preferences > Drawing and make sure the "Show Pen Preview" option is checked. This will allow you to see a preview of what your lines will look like as you are drawing with the Pen tool. Hold down the Shift key to snap your lines to 90 and 45 degree angles as you draw. To designate a control point as the end of your line, hold down the Ctrl/ Command key while clicking.

2 Using the Subselection tool **A**, modify the contours of the hair by clicking an anchor point and adjusting its Bezier handles. Once this shape is complete, temporarily cut and paste it to a new layer and lock it to avoid editing it unintentionally.

3 To add an anchor point, hover the Pen tool over the path until you see the "+" symbol appear and click. Remove an anchor point by hovering over and clicking it.

4 Once you have closed the path, fill it with a color. Here I have mixed a radial gradient to provide a sense of volume to the shape.

6 The Pen tool is clearly a useful tool for drawing paths, but in some situations the Oval and Rectangle tools are a better and faster alternative. The Selection tool **V** can be used for basic editing of paths made with the shape tools.

7 The final result is a combination of shapes and paths created with the Pen, Oval and Rectangle tools. Editing of these paths and shapes was the result of using the Selection, Subselection and Pen tools.

SHORTCUTS

MAC WIN BOTH

Trace Bitmap

P HOTOGRAPHIC IMAGES CAN be used to add a measure of realism to any Flash project. They can be imported and used in their original state, or they can be simpified for a unique, stylized look. The obvious approach to vectorizing photographs is to import the image into Flash and use the drawing tools to trace it by hand. But that can be very time-consuming depending on the complexity of the image.

The trick here is to average down the amount of colors in your image, and Adobe Photoshop makes this an almost effortless task. Combine that with the Trace Bitmap engine in Flash, and you won't even have to select one single drawing tool!

1 Start with a good quality image that has enough color contrast. Open it in Adobe Photoshop and save it as a PSD file. Now may be a good time to adjust the contrast, saturation, colors or whatever else you prefer to edit. Save for Web using ⌘ Shift ⌥ S ctrl Shift alt S and select GIF as the file format. Select Grayscale from the Color Reduction drop-down menu and limit the number of colors to two or three depending on the image and number of colors you prefer to keep. Click Save and name your new GIF image.

4 Select the entire image and go to Modify > Shape > Optimize to open the Optimize Curves panel. With Preview selected use the slider to adjust the amount of smoothing desired and click "OK".

2 Import the optimized GIF into Flash ⌘ R _ctrl_ R. Make sure it is selected and go to Modify > Bitmap > Trace Bitmap. In the Trace Bitmap dialog panel, you can adjust individual settings that will ultimately dictate the level of complexity your image will have when converted to vectors. The proper setting will vary depending on your image and personal preference.

3 Once the trace is complete, your image will be all vector and fully scalable. The resulting image of this dog is now only 12kb but we can get it even smaller by using Flash's built-in Optimize engine.

5 Flash CS4 now offers Advanced Smooth and Straighten panels that provide more control over how your vector image is optimized.

6 End result is an image that is very lightweight for the Web, weighing in at only six kilobytes. It is also easy to change its color scheme using the Paint Bucket tool K and the Color Mixer.

SHORTCUTS
MAC WIN BOTH

19

Shading 1: line trick

1 Start with a basic shape that contains a fill and outline. This technique will work just as well with shapes that have no outlines.

2 Select the Line tool **N** and make sure the Snap to Objects tool is also selected in the toolbox. I also recommend turning off Object Drawing mode **J**.

THERE ARE ALWAYS several ways to achieve the same result in Flash. With all the various tools at our disposal, I am constantly finding different ways of using them to achieve various effects.

Cell shading is commonly referred to as "toon shading". This style of shading is popular with comic book style artwork and classic Disney films. I have discovered four different ways to achieve cell style shading for you to choose from.

6 An alternative way to mix colors in Flash is to click the color wheel button in the upper right corner. This will open the color palette mixer that is native to your operating system. Mix your new color and click "OK".

3 Draw a diagonal line inside the fill of your shape. Use the Selection tool **V** to drag each end point of the line so they snap to the edge of the fill.

4 Use the Selection tool to bend the line so that its arc reflects the shape of the oval.

COLOR

Type: Solid

H: 35°
S: 68%
B: 94%
Alpha: 100%

#EFAD4B

5 With the fill color selected, mix a slightly darker color using the Color panel mixer.

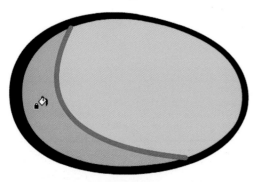

7 Use the Bucket tool **K** to fill the shape you created with the Line tool.

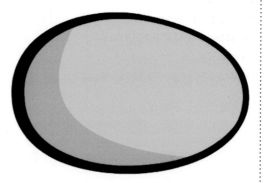

8 Select the line and delete it. Easy, right? If it still isn't perfect, you can continue to use the Selection tool to edit the edge of the new fill you created.

SHORTCUTS
MAC WIN BOTH

Shading 2: shape it

1 Using the Rectangle tool **R**, draw a box inside your shape that contains a darker fill color (no outline).

2 Use the Selection tool **V** to pull the corners until they snap to the edges of the shape (make sure the Snap feature is turned on).

HERE'S ANOTHER VARIATION on cell style shading in Flash. This technique involves the Rectangle tool and allows for more complex shading. This may be preferable if your shapes require more complex shadows.

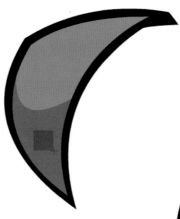

5 Let's take this technique one step further by adding more shading for a more realistic effect. Repeat the above procedure using an even darker color inside the shaded area.

6 Use the Selection tool to pull the corners until they snap to the edges of the shaded shape.

3 Fill the gap area created after snapping the corners to the edge of the shape.

4 Use the Selection tool to bend the edge of the darker fill color so that its arc reflects the shape of the oval. Having used the Rectangle tool, you have an extra corner to play around with. This can be useful for creating more complex shading such as with the ear shape.

7 Fill the gap area created after snapping the corners to the edge of the shape.

8 Use the Selection tool to bend the edge of the darker fill color so that its arc reflects the contour of the shape.

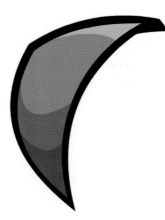

9 You can repeat this procedure as many times as you like. The more color values you add, the more realistic the image will be.

SHORTCUTS
MAC WIN BOTH

Shading 3: paint selected

1 Start with a shape.

- ■ ⊖ Paint Normal
- ⊖ Paint Fills
- ○ Paint Behind
- ⊕ Paint Selection
- ⊖ Paint Inside

2 Select the Brush tool **B** and then from the brush mode subselection menu, select Paint Selection. This will restrict any paint to selected fills only.

WE ARE ALL different and we tend to find different ways of using the same tools. We get used to certain techniques because they become familiar to our workflow and we become comfortable in our own individual habits. Here is yet another technique for creating cell style shading that you may prefer over the previous versions. It lends itself well to the designer who likes a more hand-drawn feel to their work.

6 Next, simply fill the space created by the new fill you just painted.

7 *Voila*! Now you've got a convincing cell style shading for the leg.

3 Use the Selection tool **V** to select the fill color you'll be adding the shade color to. Now use the Brush tool and adjust the amount of smoothing desired for the shape you'll paint. Next, paint inside the selected fill.

4 Don't worry about being sloppy. Once you release the brush, the painted fill will exist only inside the selected area you intended.

5 Sometimes the area may be too large to paint entirely by hand. In this situation, just draw the contour of the edge for the shaded area.

8 The face shading can be drawn the same way. Remember the direction your light source is coming from and paint a crescent fill.

9 Fill the space created by the new fill and you are done.

10 Cell shading can add that extra dimension to your designs, giving them depth and realism.

Shading 4: outlines

T HIS VARIATION ON cell style
shading works well for simple
shapes and very complex shapes. If
you have line work that is very loose
and hand-drawn looking, this may be
the technique for you. You will use
the Ink Bottle to create a line around
your fill. Then you can reposition
this line off-center and fill the space
created with a darker shade of color.

1 Start with the Ink Bottle tool and a stroke color that doesn't exist
anywhere in your design. Set the stroke height to around 3 or 4 point. Click
anywhere within the fill to outline it with a stroke in the color you chose. Don't
worry about how it looks because you will eventually delete this line entirely
after you are done.

4 For this character's outfit, I
applied a stroke outline to the
overalls as well.

5 The stroke is selected and
repositioned based on the same
light source as in the previous example.

2 Select the line by double-clicking on it with the Selection tool. Next, use the arrow keys to nudge it away from the original shape in the direction of your light source. Fill the area created between the stroke and the original edge of your shape with your shade color.

3 Delete the entire stroke by pressing the (Delete) key. If your stroke has been deselected, select it by double-clicking on it with the Selection tool. Double-clicking the stroke will select the entire stroke while single-clicking on it will select a segment of it if it contains multiple points.

6 A darker shade of color is mixed and filled to create the illusion of form and realism.

7 With the stroke still selected, delete it. In some cases, the resulting shape created may need some tweaking.

8 Use the Selection **V** tool to further refine your shading based on your needs and design sense.

Realism with gradients

F LASH IS MUCH more than a tool for designing cartoon characters. Its full array of vector drawing tools is suitable for many styles of illustration. Here we will go step by step creating a realistic flower illustration. Flowers are always appealing to draw and at the same time challenging due to the subtle variations of color they often contain.

The main tools to be used for this example are the Pen tool and Gradients. The Pen tool has been greatly improved in Flash CS4 and if you are familiar with Illustrator's Pen tool, you will notice some similarities. Flash has adopted the core functionality of Illustrator's Pen tool including identical shortcut keys and hot key modifiers – not to mention identical pen cursors as well. Integration is bliss.

One particularly cool Pen tool trick is to hold down the spacebar to redirect the current point while drawing. Another nice feature in CS4 is that the auto-fill when completing an enclosed shape with the Pen tool has been removed for consistency reasons.

The more you experiment with the new Pen tool the more I think you'll like it. In fact, I think it's better than Illustrator's Pen tool.

1 The first step is to outline the basic shape of the flower's petal with a stroke color that is high in contrast to the original image. Be as precise as you want, but I recommend using the original image as a guide, simplifying where needed along the way.

2 The Pen tool **P** is perfect for this task simply because it is quick and easy to manually trace the contour of the petal by clicking and dragging along the contour of the image.

6 The initial gradient will provide the overall hue and tonal range of the flower petal. Flash lets you apply up to 15 color transitions to a gradient.

7 Fill your shape with your radial gradient and then use the Fill Transform tool **F** to edit its size, position and rotation. You can delete the stroke at this stage as it is no longer needed.

3 To close the path, position the Pen tool over the first anchor point. A small circle appears next to the Pen tool pointer when positioned correctly. Click or drag to close the path.

4 Use the Subselection tool **A** to refine your path if you desire. To adjust the shape of the curve on either side of an anchor point, drag the anchor point, or drag the tangent handle. You can also move an anchor point by dragging it with the Subselection tool.

5 Next we need to mix some radial gradients. Flash's color picker can grab colors from anywhere on your screen if you click on any of the color swatches found in the Color Mixer, Properties panel or the toolbox and drag to the area containing your desired color.

HOT TIP

If you prefer avoiding multiple layers, turn on Object Drawing mode **J** to avoid having overlapping objects "cut-in" to each other.

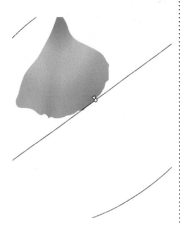

8 Copy ⌘ C ctrl C and Paste in Place ⌘ Shift V ctrl Shift V this shape to a new layer as you will be layering several gradients on top of each other to create a realistic effect. The following gradients contain varied amounts of alpha to create subtle transitions in color.

9 Fill the duplicated shape with your new gradient and use the Fill Transform tool to create the suggestion of subtle undulations within the shape. Repeat the process of copying and pasting in place this shape to new layers for each new gradient.

10 You can manipulate each new gradient using the Free Transform tool to create soft shadows and highlights. In almost all cases, you will only use partial gradients to create subtle transitions of light and shadow.

SHORTCUTS
MAC WIN BOTH

Realism with gradients (cont.)

11 It's always convincing to position soft shadows where the edge of the shape contains an imperfection. The combination of gradient colors and irregular contours makes for a very convincing imperfection.

12 This is the end result of using several variations of layered radial gradients, producing beautiful undulations of color.

15 To achieve the effect of depth in the center of the stigma, drag the little white arrow in the radial gradient's center to move the focal point towards the edge.

16 Here's what the flower image looks like once all the petals and stigma have been illustrated. But you don't have to stop here. Let's have some fun with Flash's filters. Convert the entire flower to a Movie Clip symbol.

13 Repeat the same procedure for each petal of the flower image. To keep your main timeline layers to a minimum, convert each layer to a group or an object drawing and convert each petal to a symbol.

14 The center of the flower, technically named the stigma, was created with a donut-shaped fill containing a radial gradient.

17 From the Filters panel, add a Drop Shadow. Set the blur, alpha and distance to your desired amount. You may want to also add a Blur filter to soften the overall image of the flower.

18 Duplicate the instance of the flower movie clip. Scale and rotate them to create an appealing floral arrangement. It's almost hard to imagine this style of illustration can be made entirely in Flash, right?

SHORTCUTS
MAC WIN BOTH

Spray Brush tool

FLASH CS4 PROVIDES us with a new design tool called the Spray Brush. The name describes its function accurately, as this tool will create a customizable spray pattern in seconds.

You can customize the Spray Brush to suit your needs by assigning any Movie Clip symbol from the Library to use as your spray object. The advantages to using your own custom movie clips are limited only by your imagination.

1 Here we will create a simple outer space scene and populate it with "stars". Start by making a background graphic the size of the stage using a simple linear gradient with dark colors.

2 Use the Spray Brush tool **B** to create the stars. Customize its properties by selecting white as the color and selecting Random scaling.

1 The Spray Brush tool is assigned a circle shape by default, but you can swap this for any Movie Clip or Graphic symbol you have in the document's Library. Here I've created a 5-pointed star using the PolyStar tool and converted it to a movie clip.

3 Click to create short bursts of "spray" using the default object (which is just a simple vector circle). You can click and drag across the stage to produce a continuous spray pattern.

4 With random scaling selected, the pattern (or lack thereof) produces a convincing galaxy-like effect. Throw in a planet or two and a dog in a space suit and your scene is complete.

2 Select the Spray Brush tool **B** and then click Edit in the Properties panel. The Swap Symbol panel opens to display all Movie Clip symbols in your Library. Here I've selected my "star" movie clip.

3 Click or drag to create a random pattern using the Star symbol. For this example I sprayed stars around the character's head to suggest it may have suffered a head injury or has become dizzy. The point is, the Spray Brush tool can make short work of repetitive tasks such as this.

HOT TIP

You can take this effect even further if you create an animation inside the Movie Clip or Graphic symbol you select with the Spray Brush. Open the file "SprayBrush-2. fla" from the source disk and test the movie to see the effect in action.

SHORTCUTS
MAC | WIN | BOTH

33

Deco tool

THE DECO TOOL is actually several tools in 1; Vine Fill, Grid Fill and Symmetry Brush, all providing ways to quickly create simple or complex patterns that would otherwise be too time consuming to design manually.

This a true designer's tool, in that it can be used to create repeating patterns commonly found in some design work. You can create a complex pattern using any graphic shape or object.

1 Using the Deco Tool **U** is very easy. Select it and then simply click anywhere on the stage to create a pattern using the default options. As seen here the default options will create a vine pattern based on the default shapes. You can easily customize this pattern by creating your own graphics and converting them to symbols.

4 The Deco Tool comes with additional drawing effects such as the Grid Fill. Click anywhere on the stage to create a perfectly drawn grid of black squares (default). You can edit your grid further by using the options from the Advanced Options drop-down menu. Change the amount of space between the objects horizontally and/or vertically as they scale.

5 Just like the Vine Fill option, you can edit the grid by swapping the default shape for any symbol in the Library. Here I have also applied a grid pattern to a fill color simply by clicking inside of it.

2 Open the file "deco_tool.fla" located on the source disk from the back of this book. In the Library you will find a few custom symbols to play with. Deselect "Default" in the Properties panel and selected my custom drawn star and flower symbols. I also clicked on the color swatches to change their colors.

3 What could be better than a custom tiled background? An animated tiled background of course! Select the "Animate Pattern" option in the Advanced Options menu and then click on the stage. Sit back and watch Flash CS4 create an animated background pattern for you.

6 Use the Symmetry Brush to arrange symbols symmetrically around a central point represented by a set of handles that appear when you click on the stage. Use the handles to control the symmetry by increasing or decreasing the number of symbols.

7 **Rotate Around Point Rotates** the shapes in the symmetry around a fixed point that you designate. To rotate the object around its center point, drag in a circular motion. **Reflect Across Line** flips the shapes an equal distance apart across an invisible line that you specify. **Reflect Around Point** places two shapes an equal distance apart around a fixed point that you specify. **Grid Translation** generates a grid pattern using the shapes in the Symmetry effect. Adjust the height and width of the shapes using the X and Y coordinates defined by the Symmetry Brush handles. **Test Collisions** prevents or allows shapes in the Symmetry effect to overlap with each other.

35

The new Flash interface

FLASH IS GROWING UP. It started out a long time ago in a galaxy far far away. A simple Web animation tool was created, and, for all intents and purposes, has grown to become a worldwide development platform. Let us take a brief step back in time to compare the two interfaces, i.e. the very first version and what Adobe has delivered in the most recent version of Flash. The interface originally called "*FutureSplash Animator*" was comparatively much simpler if not shockingly primitive compared with the current version. It merely consisted of a stage, timeline, some drawing tools and a Library. ActionScript hadn't even been invented and its development team consisted of only 10 people. It didn't even have

the Flash Player and animations were exported to the "SPL" (FutureSplash Player) format. At least with the current "SWF" format we have been lovingly referring to our exported files as "*Swiffs*" for years. Imagine what our Flash ancestors sounded like when they referred to their animations as "*Spills*". What you saw (above) is what you got – just enough tools to make something move.

Today, Flash's interface has progressed dramatically from its earliest incarnation. Upon initial inspection you'll notice the look and feel has been streamlined in keeping with the Adobe suite of tools. Icons are now shared across programs and integration has been implemented. As always, you can customize the workspace and save your layouts. Below is a typical setup, which optimizes the interface for animation.

One of the coolest new features in CS4 is the variety of workspace layout presets that are easily accessible from a drop-down menu to the right of the menu bar. Not only can you still customize workspaces in almost unlimited ways, but each workspace can be assigned a keyboard shortcut. This makes it quick and easy to switch workspaces if you use Flash for a variety of tasks. The Tools panel can also

be oriented in various ways by undocking and resizing it as you would a browser window.

As you read through the following chapters, you will learn more about the new interface, drawing and integration features Adobe CS4 has to offer.

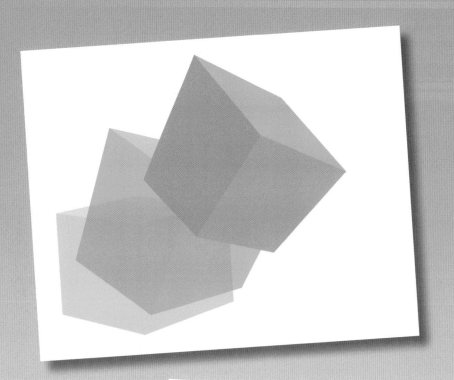

■ The most basic of objects, the cube, can be brought to life using just the Free Transform tool. With a little rotating and distorting, you can easily create an animation that gives an otherwise boring subject some life and personality. The same techniques can be applied to almost any object – including characters.

2 Transformation and distortion

SQUASH, STRETCH, BULGE, warp, distort, rotate, skew, deform – what do all these transformations have in common? Hint: it's not how you felt after that second baked bean burrito you know you didn't need to eat. Answer: it's the Free Transform tool, the single most efficient and versatile tool Flash offers, and it will prove to be one of the most used tools in your daily animation workflow.

With the release of Adobe Flash CS4 comes two new powerful tools: 3D Rotation and 3D Translation. We can now transform and animate objects in a true 3D space natively in Flash! Transforming and distorting objects is now more powerful than ever!

Distorting bitmaps

AS A DESIGNER and animator, I find that one of the most frequently used tools in Flash is the Free Transform tool. It is the most multifaceted tool in the toolbox and will prove to be critical to the transformation and distortion of objects and then some.

Free Transform is the tool to use when you want to scale, rotate, shear and distort your images. Free Transform is also used to edit the center point of instances of symbols. You can use Free Transform to transform imported bitmaps or graphics created with the Flash drawing tools.

There are a variety of modifier keys to be used with the Free Transform tool that allow you to transform objects in different ways, as we will discuss here.

1 Enter Free Transform mode by selecting the Free Transform tool in the toolbox or by pressing the keyboard shortcut **Q**. Let's start by transforming an imported bitmap image.

2 Break apart your imported image **⌘ B** **ctrl B** before transforming it. If you want you can convert it to a Drawing Object (Modify > Combine Objects > Union).

6 Position the cursor outside the bounding box between the handles and drag to shear the object. Hold down **⌥** **alt** to shear based on the center of the object.

7 Hold down **⌘ ⌥ Shift** **ctrl alt Shift** and drag a corner handle to distort the object's perspective equally on both sides. Unfortunately Flash does not distort the image but, rather, crops it.

3 When you drag any of the four corner handles, you will scale the object. The corner you drag will move while the opposite corner will remain stationary. Hold down the Shift key to scale based on the object's center.

4 If you grab any of the four center side handles, you will scale the object horizontally or vertically. This is great for squashing and stretching the object.

5 Grab one of the corner handles to rotate the object. Hold down *Shift* to constrain the rotation to 45 degree increments. Hold down *⌥* *alt* to hinge the object at the opposite corner.

HOT TIP

Some of the Free Transform tool features cannot modify instances of symbols, sounds, video objects or text. If you want to warp or distort text, make sure you break apart the text field into raw shapes first.

8 Hold down *⌘* *ctrl* to distort the object in a freeform manner. But unfortunately again, Flash doesn't truly distort a bitmap image but, rather, crops it.

9 Select the Envelope tool (sub-selection of the Free Transform tool). The Envelope modifier lets you warp and distort objects.

10 Drag the points and tangent handles to modify the envelope. Changes made to the envelope will affect the shape but not the bitmap image itself.

SHORTCUTS

The Envelope tool

WHEN USING THE free transform tool with raw vector objects, the Distort and Envelope subselection tools become available. This is where you can really have some fun warping and deforming shapes as if they were clay. Think of how your reflection looks in a fun house mirror and you'll start to get an idea as to what these tools are useful for. If you need to be precise with how your images are scaled, rotated or skewed, use the Transform panel to type in your values for the respective transformation.

1 Enter Free Transform mode by selecting the Free Transform tool in the toolbox or by pressing the keyboard shortcut **Q**. Select the Distort subselection tool at the bottom of the toolbox. Click and drag any of the corner handles to distort your shape.

TRANSFORM			
↔ 100.0%	↕ 100.0%		
⊙ Rotate			
△ 0.0°			
○ Skew			
0.0°		0.0°	
3D Rotation			
X: 0.0°	Y: 0.0°	Z: 0.0°	
3D Center point			
X: 54.5	Y: 41.5	Z: 0.0	

4 The Envelope modifier is great for warping and distorting shape. When you select the Envelope subselection tool, you will notice multiple handles attached to the bounding box. Manipulating these handles will affect the shape contained within. Click and drag a corner handle to start warping your shape.

2 The Distort tool is useful for manipulating the perspective of a shape by clicking and dragging the corner handles.

3 Hold down the **Shift** key while dragging a corner handle to constrain the adjoining corner an equal distance and in the opposite direction from each other. Think of it as tapering your shape.

HOT TIP

Holding down
⌘ ⌥ ctrl alt
when dragging a
corner point will
lock the tangent
handles to their
current position.
Holding down
the same keys
while dragging
one of the side
handles will
constrain that
entire side and
all its points.

5 Drag any of the eight tangent handles to warp your shape in almost any direction. These tangent handles are located at each corner and along both horizontal and vertical sides as well.

6 You can move any of the points to a new location to further warp your shape. But be careful; once you click outside of the selected shape, the transformation will end. You can select it again and continue to warp and distort it, but the previous point and tangent positions will be lost.

Warping

T HE ENVELOPE TOOL can help shave some time off your production schedule. In this case, the Envelope tool was used to deform the head of the Evil Mime character to represent the effect of being hit by a self-imposed uppercut. Sure, the entire head could have been drawn, but not often do we have the luxury of time to start from scratch when a deadline is looming. It was much easier to start with the head already drawn and warp it to suit our needs.

1 Duplicate the artwork of the head by creating a new keyframe in the head symbol. Select the entire head and the Free Transform tool **Q**, then select the Envelope subselection tool.

2 Using the Envelope tool, you can move the handles to deform the relative area of the head.

6 Here's the hand drawn in Flash using the Line tool. You may find the need for a variation of this same illustration and need to make it quickly.

7 Using the Envelope tool allows you to quickly distort the drawing into a different shape.

3 Continue to push and pull the Envelope's anchor points and control handles to deform the shape to your liking.

4 You can start the envelope process over by deselecting the artwork and selecting the Envelope tool again. This will reset the anchors and handles, which will allow you to further distort your image.

5 Don't be afraid to manually go back into the artwork and adjust your linework using the Selection tool. Don't rely purely on the tools; often it's your own eye that is the best tool.

8 Here's the foot in its default state. Depending on your animation, you may need several feet in different shapes.

9 Once again, the Envelope tool gets the job done, quickly and efficiently.

10 Don't rely completely on the tools. In most cases, they can only go so far. You may want to further refine the details of your image manually.

SHORTCUTS
MAC WIN BOTH

Card flip

A POPULAR ANIMATION REQUEST appearing on the Flash public forums is how to animate a flat card rotating or flipping 360 degrees. What makes this animation difficult for many to understand is the approach to actually making it. It is easy to assume, since Flash is a two-dimensional program, that adding a third dimension simply is not possible unless the object is redrawn manually one frame at a time. But with Flash, it's all in the approach, and it doesn't have to be taken literally. Two dimensions are plenty to work within for this animated effect.

1 Start with a simple rectangle with no stroke around it. Add a second keyframe on frame 10. Select the Free Transform tool **Q** and then the Distort subselection tool.

2 Hold down the *Shift* key and pull a top corner point away from the shape. With the *Shift* key still pressed, pull a bottom corner in the opposite direction.

5 New to Flash CS4 is the ability to apply a shape tween from the context menu in the timeline. So go ahead and apply one.

6 Now that you have the first half of the animation, you need to create the second half. Select frame 11 and insert a keyframe.

10 Let's add some shape hints to correct the problem. Select the first frame in the faulty tween and then go to Modify > Shape > Add Shape Hint ⌘ *Shift* **H** *ctrl* *Shift* **H**.

11 Drag the red "a" hint to one of the corners of your shape until it snaps.

3 Click outside the shape to end the transformation. Select it again, hold down the **Shift** key and drag the bottom middle handle upward. The **Shift** key will constrain the shape vertically.

4 Turn on the Onionskin tool so you can see the previous frame. Position the newly transformed shape so that it is centered over the original shape seen through the onionskin.

HOT TIP

While writing this topic, I experienced a common weakness with shape tweens in Flash. Due to the nature of vectors and how Flash tries to calculate what it thinks you want to achieve, sometimes the tween implodes or twists in ways we never anticipated. Shape hints exist for this very reason and they are easy to learn about in the Flash help docs. An alternative solution for this example would be to convert frames 1–10 to keyframes, copy and paste them in frames 11–20 and then reverse them.

7 Modify the shape in frame 11 by flipping it vertically.

8 Select the keyframe in frame 1 and copy the frame **⌘** **C** **ctrl** **alt** **C**. Next, select frame 20 and paste the frame **⌘** **V** **ctrl** **alt** **V**.

9 Apply a shape tween to the latter half of your frames. You may experience a misbehaving tween like I did when writing this topic. Let's fix it.

12 Go to the last keyframe in your tween and drag the green "a" hint to the same respective corner. Repeat this procedure again for the opposite corner.

13 The final visual effect is to mix a slightly darker version of the color of the card and then use it to fill the shapes in frames 10 and 11.

14 The card will not only tween its shape, but also its color from light to dark. This color change makes for a convincing three-dimensional effect.

SHORTCUTS

MAC **WIN** **BOTH**

3D Rotation

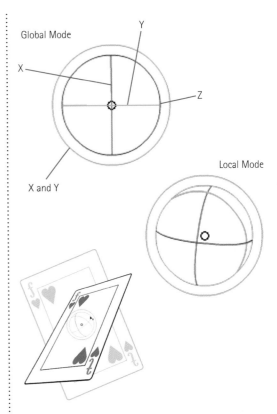

Global Mode

Y

X

Z

X and Y

Local Mode

THE PREVIOUS CARD flip example demonstrates how to transform a vector shape with the Free Transform tool and "Classic Tweens". Adobe Flash CS4 introduces new tools to simplify the same process. I debated whether or not to leave the previous "Card flip" example in this book as it could be regarded as a deprecated technique along with its use of the Distort tool. In the end, I decided to include it for a couple of reasons: not everyone will be upgrading to Flash CS4, the Free Transform tool and its subselection tools are still Flash CS4 features and remain relevant and Classic Tween is still an option in Flash CS4. Moving forward, let's take a look at an exciting new feature that finally introduces 3D space in Flash at authortime!

1 The 3D Rotation tool **W** rotates movie clip instances in 3D space. A 3D rotation control appears on top of selected objects on the Stage. The X control is red, the Y control is green, and the Z control is blue. Use the orange free rotate control to rotate around the X and Y axes at the same time.

The default mode of the 3D Rotation tool is global. Rotating an object in global 3D space is the same as moving it relative to the Stage. Rotating an object in local 3D space is the same as moving it relative to its parent movie clip if it has one. To toggle the 3D Rotation tool between global and local modes, click the Global toggle button in the Options section of the Tools panel while the 3D Rotation tool is selected. You can temporarily toggle the mode from global to local by pressing the **D** key while dragging with the 3D Rotation tool.

2 The first thing to do is to right-click over the movie clip and select Create Motion Tween. Flash CS4 will automatically insert frames based on the document frame rate to achieve a full second in the timeline. This document is set to 24 fps, and therefore the duration of my motion tween is 24 frames.

3 Position the frame marker on frame 12. Select the 3D Rotation tool **W**. Click on the instance of the card and notice the 3D rotation controller that appears on top of the symbol. Click inside the 3D control and drag along the "Y"-axis to rotate the card in 3D space. Notice that Flash has inserted a keyframe automatically for you.

4 Position the frame marker on the last frame and continue to rotate the movie clip along its "Y"-axis in 3D space until it is 180 degrees from its original orientation. Repeat these steps as often as needed depending on the number of rotations you want to animate.

HOT TIP

Press the **D** key to toggle between global and local mode.

5 If you want to extend the motion tween in the layer without effecting the existing keyframes, simply hold down the **Shift** key while dragging the right edge of the tween. Another way to do the same thing is to click on a frame further down the timeline and press the F5 key to insert frames up to the selected frame.

SHORTCUTS
MAC WIN BOTH

Butterfly

IN THE FIRST
edition the
butterfly's wings were
animated using the Distort tool
(subselection of the Free Transform tool).
With the new 3D tools in Flash CS4 it is much
more efficient to use the 3D Rotation tool for
the flapping wing animation.

Here I have converted the original wing
graphic to a Movie Clip symbol and applied a
motion tween using the new Motion Model.
The advantages of using the 3D Rotation
tool for this animation are faster results and
a smaller file size. The smaller file size is on
account of using motion tweens and several
instances of the same symbol. In the previous
CS3 model, the resulting animation was a
frame-by-frame animation using raw vector
art for each keyframe – this leads to a
larger file size since each frame contains
all new data that need to be loaded
sequentially when viewing it
online.

1 Convert the wing into a Movie Clip symbol twice so you
end up with a movie clip inside a movie clip. You will
want to animate the wing inside a symbol so a 2nd instance
can be used for the other wing later.
Select the 3D Rotation tool **W**. Click on the instance of the
wing and notice the 3D rotation controller that appears on
top of the symbol. Reposition the controller by dragging it
to a new location. The controller's position determines its
center point. Right click over the symbol and select Create
Motion Tween. Flash CS4 will automatically insert frames
based on the document frame rate to achieve a full second
in the timeline. This document is set to play back at 30 fps,
and therefore the duration of my motion tween is 30 frames.
This can be easily changed by dragging the right edge of the
motion tween left or right.

4 To separate the wings and add some depth to the
butterfly, move the back wing to the right a few pixels
and skew it slightly. You can also move the front wing to the
left and skew that a little also.

2 Position the frame marker about mid-way between frames 1 and 30 (frame 15 will work). Click inside the 3D control and drag along the "X"-axis until the wing is 180 degrees from its original position. Notice that Flash has inserted a keyframe automatically for you.

3 Position the frame marker on the last frame in the tween. Drag along the "X"-axis inside the 3D control until the wing is back in its original position. Play back your timeline by pressing the *Enter* key to see the wing flapping along the "X"-axis.

HOT TIP

Double-click the center point of the 3D control to move it back to the center of the selected movie clip.

5 Copy and paste *ctrl C* *ctrl V* *⌘ C* *⌘ V* the movie clip containing the wing animation to use as the 2nd wing. Select it and, using the Tint color effect in the Properties panel, darken it slightly to provide a sense of depth.

6 All that's left is to create a body shape, align the wings to it and publish your movie to see the butterfly take flight.

Squash and stretch

SQUASH AND STRETCH is a traditional animation technique that is widely used to give animations more realism and weight. When a moving object comes in contact with a stationary object, it will deform on impact, unless it is completely rigid. One thing that is important to remember is that no matter how much an object squashes or stretches, it always maintains the same amount of volume. The amount of squash and stretch depends on how much flexibility your object should have. Traditional animation usually contains exaggerated amounts of squash and stretch. A good example of this is a bouncing ball. When it hits the ground it actually deforms and gets squashed. It will then become stretched as it propels itself upwards. With a little motion tweening and frame-by-frame animation in Flash, we can achieve convincing realism with relatively little effort.

1 Start with the object in its highest position. Convert it to a symbol and then edit its center point using the Free Transform tool. Move the center point to the center of the bottom edge.

2 Insert a second keyframe further down your timeline and position the ball vertically just above the horizontal guide. Apply a motion tween with Easing set to "-100" (ease in).

6 Start the ball's ascent by inserting yet another keyframe and removing all transformations. The Transfrom panel has a Remove Transform button to make this a one-click solution.

7 Copy the first frame and paste it as your last frame. This will position the ball at the end of your timeline in the exact same position as it started. Apply a motion tween and set the Easing to "100" (ease out).

3 In the next frame, insert a keyframe and turn on the Onionskin tool. Use the Free Transform tool to scale the ball so it becomes wider and shorter. It's important to keep the volume of the ball consistent.

4 Insert another keyframe about four or five frames further down the timeline. Squash and stretch the ball even more. Apply a motion tween and set the Easing to "100" (ease out).

5 Insert another keyframe a few frames down your timeline and transform your ball in the opposite direction. Make sure it still has some deformation applied to it.

HOT TIP

As you create various animation examples from your day-to-day workflow, it's a good idea to keep them all in a single FLA document. This serves as a great way to quickly reuse animations using the Copy Motion feature in Flash CS4.

8 Flash CS3 and CS4 offer ways to reuse animations. Copy Motion allows a Classic tween, its frames and symbol information to be pasted to another object. Select all the frames in your squash and stretch animation. Select Edit > Timeline > Copy Motion.

9 Insert a new layer and create (or drag from the Library) a new symbol to the stage. Select this new symbol and go to Edit > Timeline > Paste Motion. Your additional symbol will now have the exact same span of frames, motion tweens, easing and transformations. Thanks to Joe Corrao for contributing the character above (joecorrao.com).

SHORTCUTS
MAC WIN BOTH

Being subtle

ANYONE WHO HAS EVER heard me speak publicly about Flash and what led me to this industry might recognize the term "moment of clarity". As an artist, there have been several of these moments – the most memorable transpired long before Flash was around.

It was spring of 1989 and after four fulfilling years at the Hartford Art School, I was finally about to receive my BFA degree. My drawing style during this time could best be described as hyper-realistic. I was illustrating images that looked like actual photographs. Sometimes the illustrations would fool even a well-trained eye into thinking they were real – at least at first glance. Objects caught in motion as if snapped by some high speed camera shutter, and foreshortened as if they were literally flying out from the page and about to hit you square between the eyes. I can only imagine this style represented my excitement as a young artist having this ability to push the limits of light and dark onto a two-dimensional surface, with only the best professors looking over my shoulder. I spent so many hours trying to master this drawing style that I would often have to use my left hand to pry the fingers of my right hand off of the pencil.

Most of my work was large in scale, 18" × 24" and even as large as 30" × 40". A large majority of it was lithographs and etchings that took weeks and often months to create. One afternoon I had a leftover piece of copper plate that I was about to discard. It was small, about 3" × 7", and tiny compared with what I was used to. For no particular reason I drew a rough study of a figure of a woman. I spent no more than 10 minutes on the drawing before throwing it in the acid bath so it could be etched. I rolled some ink into it and printed about six copies of it. It was a simple drawing, loose in line style, and very much the opposite of the hyper-realistic style I was known for, and for this reason I didn't think it was a very impressive piece. I contemplated tossing the print and the copper plate in the trash and going back to my much larger and more realistic pieces. But something told me to hang on to it, at least for a little while. So I slid it between the pages of a book in my backpack.

Like all graduating seniors, we were celebrated with our own showing in the school's gallery. While setting up my show, I carefully chose my biggest and most realistic drawings and prints. While hanging the last piece, the small etching of the girl slipped out onto the floor. I reluctantly decided to include it in my show next to the light switch in the darkest corner of the room.

The night of the show was a success and, a few days later, my illustration professor, Dennis Nolan, who was unable to attend, asked to see my work before it was to be taken down. He was one of the professors I most admired and to this day I adore his skill and dedication as an illustrator. He quietly perused each lithograph, etching, watercolor and pen and ink illustration. When he finished, he turned to me and asked, "Want to know what is your best piece?" Confident he was going to point to the largest and most realistic piece, I was shocked when he turned and pointed to the small etching next to the light switch. My heart sank and for a moment I felt as though I might be insane.

He explained to me that its simplicity and essential quality provoked an emotion within him, and compared it to Rembrandt or Da Vinci. He told me it was a milestone not only in my career, but in any artist's career to draw like that. It was subtle, and that subtlety made more of an impact than any of the other pieces I had done in my four years as a student. The world of art changed for me that day and, in some ways, the way I looked at life changed as well. It took four years and that very moment for my eyes to be opened as an artist. I was changed forever. It taught me more than I ever thought I would be able to know and it's a lesson I carry with me to this very day. Being subtle is powerful.

■ The hula hoop appears to be around the girl's waist, or is it? In the original image, above, the hula hoop is clearly in a layer above the girl. By creating a mask for the hula hoop, we can hide that portion of it that overlaps the girl's waist, making it appear to be around her.

3 Masking

MASKS ARE POWERFUL. They can be used in myriad ways to achieve limitless results. Masks can make your daily workflow easier, less time-consuming and, in most cases, become your most indispensable tool.

Having the ability to control the way two or more layers interact with each other through the use of masks is vital to your abilities as a designer and animator. The coolest thing about using masks in Flash is that not only do they help you to create stunning images, but they can also be animated – a very powerful concept that can be mastered quite easily.

Rotating globe

1 First step is to create the continents. A quick online image search will yield plenty of examples. Import the image into Flash and leave it as a bitmap or use the Trace Bitmap feature or manually trace it using Flash's drawing tools. Convert it to a symbol.

WHENEVER I WORK with masks, I feel like a magician. Masks provide the ability for you to create illusions, much like a magician's "sleight of hand" technique. It's all about what the viewer doesn't see and you, as the designer, have the ability to control that.

One of the more popular animation requests from Flash users is how to make a rotating globe. The first thought is that a globe is a sphere and to animate anything rotating around a sphere requires either a 3D program or painstaking frame-by-frame animation. Not so if you can use a mask. Remember, it's not what you see, but rather, what you don't see.

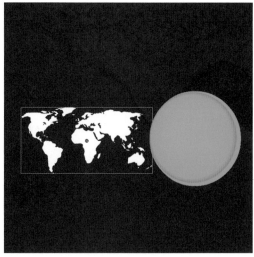

4 The next step is to create a mask layer using yet another copy of the circle in the bottom layer. Create a new layer above your continents, paste in place the circle and then convert this layer to a mask layer. This will prevent the continents from being visible outside this circle. All you need to do now is motion tween the continent symbol across this circle.

2 Create a new layer and move it below your continents. Draw a perfect circle using the Oval tool **O** while holding down the **Shift** key. Select this circle and copy it, then paste it in place on a new layer above your continents.

3 Mix a radial gradient similar to the one shown and fill the circle in the layer above your continents. Make sure you mix enough alpha into each color so the continents will show through. Using the Gradient Transform tool **F**, edit your gradient so that the highlight edge is off-center to one side.

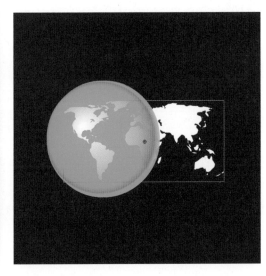

5 To avoid too much of a delay in the animation between the first and last frames, you can add a new masked layer with a new instance of your continent symbol. The best way to make this looping animation as seamless as possible is to copy the first frame of the continents and paste it in place into the last frame of your timeline. Then work backwards in the timeline and position the continents outside of the circle to the right.

6 Since the first frame is exactly the same as the last frame, and each frame in between represents a slightly different position for the continents, select the symbol in the last frame and use the arrow keys to nudge it over a few pixels. This will avoid the two-frame "hesitation" in the movement of the continents every time the playhead returns from the last frame to frame 1.

HOT TIP

You can always move your entire animation into a Movie Clip symbol so that it can be easier to position, add multiple globes and/or target with ActionScript. To do this, drag across all frames and layers to highlight them in black. Right-click or Command-click over them and select "Copy Frames" from the context menu. Open your Library and create a new Movie Clip symbol. Right-click or Command-click over frame 1 of this new symbol and select "Paste Frames".

SHORTCUTS
MAC WIN BOTH

Flag waving

1 You will begin by making a nice long repeating ribbon shape. Start with a simple rectangle with any color fill and no outlines. Make it a little wider than it is taller.

4 Repeat step three by pasting your new shape and flipping it vertically. Then attach it to the side of the shape again. See the ribbon pattern taking shape? But your ribbon is a solid color and lacking some depth, so let's continue by adding some shading.

7 Create a mask layer above the ribbon layer. Using the Rectangle tool, make a shape big enough to cover a section of the ribbon as shown. It helps to use a high contrast color.

THE WAVING FLAG is a popular "how do I...?" request in the Flash community. To be honest, it plagued me for quite some time as to how best to achieve this animation. My initial reaction was to use shape tweens and frame-by-frame animation – but that proved time-consuming and had unconvincing results. Then one day, out of the blue, it hit me: if I slide the right shape across a masked area, I could create the illusion of a flag waving without having to kill myself animating it in a traditional way. It suddenly became so easy anyone can do it.

10 Test your movie using ⌥ ctrl Enter to see the effect of the flag waving as it passes through the mask. But let us not stop there. Let's animate the mask using shape tweens to further emphasize the left and right edges of the flag waving. Use the Selection tool to bend the left and right edges. Create a keyframe further down the mask layer.

2 Use the Selection tool **V** to bend the top and bottom edges slightly so they have a nice arc to them. You will want to repeat this shape to create a pattern, so select it and copy it.

3 Paste your shape and then flip it vertically. Use the Selection tool to drag it so that it connects to the original shape. Once these shapes are joined together, select it and copy it.

5 Mix two colors and add them to the Swatch panel. Mix a linear gradient with several color pointers alternating between these two color values. Fill your ribbon shape with this gradient and edit it so that the darker tones are in the concave sections of the ribbon shape.

6 Once you have the ribbon the way you want it, select it using `⌥A` `ctrl A`, copy it using `⌥C` `ctrl C` and then paste it using `⌥V` `ctrl V`. Align it edge to edge with the original shape to essentially double its length. Convert it to a symbol.

8 Next, create a keyframe somewhere down the timeline and reposition the ribbon to the left of the mask shape. Apply a motion tween.

9 To create a seamless loop of the ribbon, copy and paste in place a new instance to a second masked layer (using the same mask). Motion tween it so that it follows the original ribbon shape without creating any gaps.

11 In this new keyframe, bend the left and right sides of the mask shape in the opposite direction. Apply a shape tween. Repeat this procedure until the last frame is reached. The animated mask adds an extra animated touch to the overall flag waving effect. Presto! You are done.

12 Don't forget to add a flag pole and sky background for an even more convincing illusion. Try placing this animation in a Movie Clip symbol and drag a few instances of it to the stage. Scale them and arrange them in perspective for the ultimate flag waving effect.

HOT TIP

This is a looping animation. For best results make sure the first and last frames are identical. To do this, use copy frames – paste frames or copy the object in the first frame and paste it in place in the last frame.

SHORTCUTS

MAC WIN BOTH

Iris transition

T HERE ARE USUALLY several ways to go about creating the same animations and effects in Flash. Animated on the timeline or dynamically generated animation using ActionScript, allows us to work within our own comfort zones. A simple iris transition is an example of an effect that could be done several different ways. I personally wouldn't know where to begin coding this kind of animation, but give me a timeline and some keyframes and I am in my element. Using a mask for this example provides us with even more options; we can easily control the direction and focus of the iris itself, where it starts and where it ends. This can be a nice touch to your storytelling if you want to focus the viewer's attention to a very specific area of the screen.

1 First step is to create a simple circle using the Oval tool (**O**). The fill color is insignificant. Hold down **Shift** while dragging to constrain its proportions. Do not convert this shape to a symbol, but rather convert the layer to a Mask layer.

4 Add a new layer and drag it over the mask layer so it becomes linked to it as a "masked" layer. This is the layer where your content will reside. If your content requires multiple layers, then make sure they are all masked or move all content into a new symbol and drag an instance of the symbol to the masked layer.

2 In frame 1, scale this circle as small as possible. Open the Scale and Rotate panel using `⌥` `alt` `S` `ctrl` `alt` `S`, type in a percentage and click OK. Use the Align panel using `⌥` `K` `ctrl` `K` to center the circle to the stage.

3 Create a keyframe a few frames down your timeline in the same mask layer. Scale the circle so that it covers the stage completely. Convert the shape to outlines so you can see the stage underneath it. Apply a shape tween so the circle grows from small to large, filling the stage completely.

5 Create a new layer (not masked) below all the other layers and create a black rectangle the size and shape of the stage. The color can be anything you choose, but black typically works well for this type of effect. At this stage you can reverse the animated mask by copying keyframes in reverse order and applying another shape tween.

6 Since you are creating the iris effect with an animated mask, you can easily control what area of the stage the iris focuses on. In the last keyframe, position the circle in the last frame over the character's eye. When the animation plays, the iris will animate and close in on the eye – a typical technique used in several cartoons.

Handwriting

THIS IS ONE of my favorite animated effects because I am asked frequently how it can be achieved, yet it is quite simple in technique. Every time I demonstrate how to make text "write" itself, the reaction is almost always the same: "Oh wow! That's all there is to it?" The example here uses an animated mask which yields a very small file size, ideal for large blocks of text.

Hand writing

1 The first step is to type some text on the stage. It doesn't matter what it says; just choose a font and start typing. By default, text fields in Flash are set to Dynamic. In some situations this may be fine but when an effect is added to the text field, the text may not render correctly in the Flash player. Such effects include masking, alpha, rotation and scaling. If you need to use Dynamic text, embed the font outlines.

Hand writing

3 Add a new layer above your text layer and convert it to a mask layer. The text layer will automatically be linked to it as a "masked" layer. In frame one, draw a rectangle just to the left of your text, making sure it is as tall as the text itself.

Hand writing

5 Now just apply a shape tween in between these two keyframes. Lock all layers and play your movie or test your movie to see the effect of your text writing itself.

2 If you choose to change the behavior of your text field to Static, the font will be embedded in the compiled SWF and the Flash player will render it correctly – even with an effect added to it. Another option is to break apart the text until it becomes raw shapes. This will insure the text renders correctly but also creates a larger file size and it will be harder to edit the text if need be in the future.

4 In this same layer, create a keyframe further down the timeline and scale the shape horizontally so that it spans the entire width of your text.

6 If you need to use Dynamic text, you must include the font outlines so that the text renders correctly in the Flash player. To do this, select the Dynamic text field and then click the "Embed..." button in the Properties panel. The Character Embedding panel will appear, allowing you to choose the range of characters used in your animation. Try to select the minimum number of characters because embedding all characters can increase file size significantly.

HOT TIP

If you want a more realistic technique to make text look like it is writing itself, check out the frame-by-frame method in Chapter 10.

SHORTCUTS

MAC WIN BOTH

Spotlight

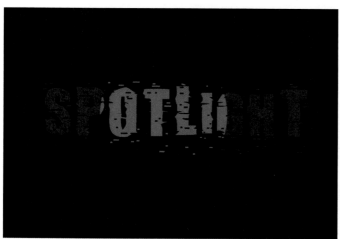

A NIMATED MASKS, as we've seen, can provide an interesting dimension to your animation. It really doesn't take much effort to create various visual effects using an animated mask, such as this spotlight effect for a client's logo.

1 The first thing you need is some text or other image to "shine" a spotlight on to. Convert it to a symbol. The background should be dark if not completely black. In order to show light, we first need to create darkness. This technique wouldn't have the same effect if the background was very light.

2 Create a new layer above your image layer and convert it to a mask layer. The image layer will automatically be linked to it as a "masked" layer. Draw a shape using the Oval tool **O** while holding down the *Shift* key to constrain its proportions. Convert it to a symbol.

3 Add a keyframe further down the timeline and position the mask shape to the opposite side of the image. Apply a motion tween so that the mask shape passes across the image.

4 The key to making this technique convincing is to copy and paste in place the image to a new layer below the original layer. Make sure it is a normal layer (not masked). Select the symbol and tint it to a dark color. This layer will not be affected by the mask .

HOT TIP

Don't be afraid to add more keyframes in your mask layer and position the mask symbol in various positions relative to the image it is revealing. You can also animate the mask getting larger and smaller by scaling it. Be creative and change the shape of the mask to say two circles side-by-side to suggest we are looking through binoculars.

5 Test your movie to see your animated mask pass over the original image layer while the darker instance remains unmasked and visible throughout the animation.

SHORTCUTS
MAC WIN BOTH

Focus

ONE OF THE most exciting features in Flash CS4 is the PSD and AI importer. Flash has wonderful integration between Photoshop and Illustrator alike. For this example we will edit an image in Photoshop, save it as a PSD file and import it into Flash via the PSD Importer wizard.

We will also add a slight touch of ActionScript for some added interactivity. If you suffer from ActionScript-phobia, don't panic, this will be painless with only a couple of lines of simple code. If I can do it, you can as well. The code simply will hide the cursor in the Flash player and allow us to drag a movie clip around the stage. The trick here is the mask itself, allowing us to see the sharper image through the mask shape only. Open wide and say "Ahhhh". This won't hurt a bit.

1 First you need to start with an image, of course. This might be a good time to browse your hard drive or grab your digital camera. It doesn't have to be a raster-based image or even a photograph. It can be vector art drawn in Flash or imported from a different program. Whatever image you choose, you will need two versions, the original and a blurred version of the original.

4 Once the import process is complete, your Flash document should contain both images on different layers. Make sure the blurred image is below the sharper image.

5 Create a new layer above the sharper image and convert it to a mask layer. The image layer below will be automatically linked to it. Draw a shape in your mask layer and convert it to a Movie Clip symbol. Lock these two layers to see the mask work.

2 Open your image in Photoshop and duplicate the layer it is on so you have two copies of the same image. Apply a Gaussian Blur to one of your images. Save the file as a PSD file.

3 In Flash, import the PSD file you just created. The PSD Importer wizard will appear and prompt you with a variety of options. The left panel will display all the layers of the PSD file. Click on them to display options for each. You will also want to convert layers to Flash layers, place layers at original position and set your Flash stage to the same size as your Photoshop stage.

HOT TIP

The shape of your mask doesn't have to be a circle. It can be as simple or as complex as you wish to make it. Experiment in Photoshop with image effects beyond blurring. There's enough to choose from to keep you busy for a while. I particularly like the Glass filter (Filter > Distort > Glass...).

ActionScript 1.0-2.0:
Mouse.hide();
startDrag("focus", true);
For ActionScript 3.0:
Mouse.hide();
focus.startDrag(true);

6 You are almost done! Lock all layers to see the effect. It works but it is pretty boring as the mask just sits there. Time to add some functionality.

7 Use the Selection tool **V** to select the Movie Clip symbol containing the mask shape. In the Properties panel, type in an instance name. I chose "focus" for this example. With the movie clip still selected, open the Actions panel and type the following ActionScript exactly:

SHORTCUTS
MAC WIN BOTH

69

A moment of clarity

I REMEMBER THE MOMENT WELL, as I should, since it was the moment when I realized what I needed to do as an artist to make my mark in the world. What I wasn't sure of was how big a mark I could make. What made the moment even more significant was that it took me over 6 years to figure it out.

It began in 1989 when I graduated from the Hartford Art School (Connecticut) with a major in printmaking and a minor in Art History. I took enough Illustration classes to constitute a double major. The result: a portfolio filled with static lithographs, etchings and a multitude of illustrations of varied mediums. Animation didn't exist in the curriculum and therefore was never an option. I never considered animation as a skill I would even be good at.

After graduating, I pounded the pavement with portfolio in hand, knocking on as many doors as I could. With the exception of a handful of interviews, having no experience did not get me very far. The Internet didn't really exist back then – at least not as we know it today. The term "home PC" hadn't been invented yet, and I was stuck with a book filled with analog images that represented four hard years as an artist – and hardly anyone to show it to.

After 6 years of countless random jobs (jeep mechanic, restaurant manager, Boston Water & Sewer Collections Dept, etc....), I became aware of a local education software company that was producing a new animated series on Comedy Central. On a Monday morning I walked in the front door of this software company, gave my portfolio to the receptionist and told her I'd be back on Friday to pick it up. I turned around and walked out the door.

A month later, they hired me to work on an animated pilot for DreamWorks. At that time, the company used an old DOS-based animation program called Animator Pro (Autodesk) that soon became obselete. We turned to Flash and little did I realize the impact it would have on my career. Initially we were using Flash to animate for broadcast shows. We didn't have a clue how to use it for the Web – until we got a deal to produce an animated series for shockwave.com (now atomfilms.com). I was put in charge of this project and had to ramp up my knowledge of Flash very quickly. During this time, my contact at

Shockwave asked if I could speak at the Flash Forward conference in New York City. I agreed without knowing exactly what that meant.

I drove the 3 hours from Boston to NYC the day of my session. I shared the stage with two brothers, Gregg and Evan Spiridellis, who had just started a small company in NYC called JibJab (ever heard of it?). We became fast friends and remain so even to this day.

That evening was the Flash Forward Film Festival, held in a huge theater with a very large screen that displayed the best use of Flash in several

categories. Awards were being given and the excitement in the air was palpable. I never anticipated that a software program could generate such a buzz. I was witness to a culture being born, an entire society of Flash users who shared a common bond as if it were some secret handshake or cryptic language. And there I was, standing in the middle of their nest, surrounded by the frenetic buzzing and energy derived from this program.

It was my first experience seeing the best of the Web being celebrated on a huge stage and it suddenly all made sense to me – why I was there, what I was involved with, and what I had to do. It was my first moment of clarity.

To descibe the image of me standing in the back of the theater, watching this phenomenon transpire, recall the scene from The Blues Brothers film where John Belushi is in the church chanting "The band!" as he is struck by a holy beam of light through the church window. That was me. I knew from that moment on what I needed to do. I drove home as my head was spinning with ideas about how I was going to display my art with Flash for the world to finally see. It was a 3-hour drive and I never even turned on the radio the whole way.

■ The Yahoo! Super Messengers, in a classic superhero pose. The above version is a bit lackluster if not completely boring. Below is the same shot with the help of some simple motion effects. The difference is an animation with a bit more punch (sorry, pun intended).

4

Motion tips and tricks

LET'S FACE IT, Flash is about motion. In some cases, the more motion, the better. Motion can emphasize the intensity of an action sequence and can add a measure of realism to your animations. Whether it is making text fly around a website or animating a character in an action sequence, providing convincing motion effects can be critical to their success visually.

In this chapter we will look at the new Motion tween method and Motion Editor as well as what I consider to be some of the most valuable motion effects you can use in your everday life as a Flash designer and animator.

The new Motion tween

ANYONE WHO HAS EVER used Flash for animation is familiar with tweens. Tweening has always been a very straightforward and simple process. The tween essentially interpolates animation between two keyframes. This interpolation is based on changes to the object's properties (position, scale, color effect, etc). Until CS4, Flash has always offered one kind of tween, appropriately called the "motion" tween. Now we have two tweens: "motion" and "classic". So what has changed? Well, the new "motion" tween is nothing like the old tween. To avoid confusion, the old way of tweening is now called "classic" in Flash CS4. Take all of what you know about the "classic" tween and put it up on a shelf for a moment.

Adobe has completely rewritten the animation core. The new Motion tween is object-based, not frame-based. This is the major difference between the two tween methods and it provides more options that Classic tweens do not support. What is limiting about the Classic tween is that it is frame-based, hindering the ability to control multiple properties over the span of the tween.

Motion tweens enable additional properties to be controlled independently while reducing the number of steps required with the "classic" tweening method. Let's take a look at a simple example of the new Motion tween method in Flash CS4.

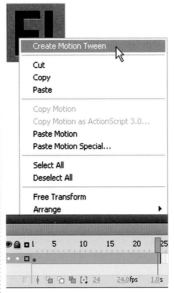

1 Draw or import an object to your stage. Convert it to a symbol and then right click over it and select Create Motion tween. Flash CS4 will create a motion span in the object layer that spans a total duration of 1 second. If your document's frame rate is 24 fps, then this span will be 24 frames long. It's easy to adjust this later.

2 Place the playhead in a frame where you want to move the object. Using the Selection tool **V** drag the object to a new position on the stage. Flash will create a path between the original and new positions. You will also notice that Flash has inserted a property keyframe in the motion span as well.

PROPERTIES

Motion Tween

▽ EASE

Ease: 100 out

▷ ROTATION
▷ PATH
▷ OPTIONS

6 Drag the path to a new location on the stage using the Selection tool **V**.

7 Select the motion span in the timeline to bring up the easing options in the Properties panel. Here you can use the hot text slider to add a basic ease across the entire span.

3 The easiest way to edit the motion path in order to change the position and direction of the object is to place the playhead on a new frame and drag the object to a new position on the stage. The motion path will be updated and Flash will continue to automatically insert the appropriate property keyframe in the timeline.

4 The new motion tween supports the 3D transformation tool **W** as well as the Free Transform tool **Q** and various other properties.

5 The motion path can be reshaped using the Selection tool **V**, Subselection tool **A** and Free Transform tool **Q**. Drag a straight path using the Selection tool to create a curved path. Use the Subselection tool to expose the path's Bezier handles and control points. The path can be scaled using the Free Transform tool.

8 You can even draw your own path using the Pen **P** or Pencil **Y** tools and apply it as the motion path of your tween. In a different layer or Flash document, draw a stroke path and shape it as you prefer. Copy the new path to the clipboard, select an existing tween span and and paste it. The original path will be replaced by the newly pasted stroke and your target object will now animate along this new path. You can perform the opposite by copying and pasting the motion path as a stroke to a new layer or document.

Motion tween (cont.)

S O HOW DOES the new motion tween apply to a marionette style character animation? Let's take a look at how the new Motion tween stacks up against the Classic tween from an animator's perspective, shall we? In this example the character is comprised of several flat shapes converted to symbols. Each symbol has had its center point positioned to simulate "hinging" in a relatively natural way. See Chapter 5 for a more detailed example of how to "hinge" body parts by editing the center point of a symbol.

The motion technique here relies on a simple process called "cutout" animation, where flat objects are moved about the stage in a very two-dimensional way. One of the best known modern day examples of cutout style animation is the popular series South Park. While production relies now on Maya and Corel Draw software, some of the earliest episodes actually used real paper cutouts.

1 This particular character is already prepared for animation. Each body part has been converted to symbols and distributed to layers. Since this will be a looping animation, I have posed the character in its starting position. Select all symbols and then right click over them. Select "Create Motion Tween" from the context menu. The document is set to 24 fps; hence 24 frames have been inserted automatically by Flash.

4 To complete the looping animation, the 1st pose must be identical in the last frame, in this case frame 24. When working with the new Motion tween, to select keyframes, hold down the `ctrl` `⌘` key and click or drag across multiple keyframes. Here I have selected all the keyframes in frame 1 by holding down the `ctrl` `⌘` key and dragging from the bottom layer to the top layer.

2 Position the playhead on a frame where you want the next gesture of your character to reside. Here I have chosen frame 12 because it is the midpoint between frame 1 and frame 24. Select one or more symbols and use the Free Transform tool **Q** to rotate it/them. If you have more than one symbol selected, you can still edit their center point collectively (indicated by the red arrow).

3 Here's the character in its final pose mid-way through the animation. The idea is to create the 2nd of 2 gestures to complete the loop. Since this new Motion tween is object-based, working with keyframes in the timeline is very different from what we've been used to when working with what is now named Classic tweens. Selecting, moving, copying and pasting keyframes is handled differently.

5 Next, with all keyframes in frame 1 still selected, hold down the *alt* ⌥ key and drag these keyframes to the last frame in the tween spans. Holding down the *alt* ⌥ keys duplicates the keyframes that you click and drag. When you release, the character's pose in frame 1 is now duplicated in the last frame, creating a seamless looping animation.

6 To further refine areas of the animation, repeat the same process of Ctrl-clicking a keyframe or a property keyframe and then Alt-clicking and dragging it to duplicate keyframes in the motion span. Then you can edit the symbols on the stage that reside in these keyframes.

Motion tween (cont.)

7 For this particular animation, I want the feet to remain planted on the ground longer and then rise quickly later in the span. Duplicating their keyframes allows me to create this effect within the span. Here I held down the *alt* ⌥ key while dragging the keyframe in frame 1 to frame 8. This insures the firmly planted foot in frame 1 remains planted through frame 8. From frame 8 to frame 12 is when the foot rises.

8 One of the strengths of using the new Motion tween is having the ability to scale your animations easily. Drag the left or right edge of a tween span to increase or decrease its duration. Any keyframes within the span will be re-interpolated. This is a feature many animators have requested for years.

11 Just as arcs provide a more natural and continuous flow, applying some easing to your animation has its natural advantages also. Motion tweens and easing are approached differently when compared to Classic tweens and easing. The properties panel has a hot text easing slider that is applied to the entire motion span, which can be limiting if you need to apply easing between individual keyframes.

12 My personal taste is to apply easing in and out between certain keyframes, which eliminates the previous step. To create more sophisticated tweens in a tween span you'll want to use the new Motion Editor. Select a tween span and open the Motion Editor (Window > Motion Editor).

9 Another advantage of using the new Motion tween is having the ability to animate objects along a curved path. Using the Selection tool **S** you can bend the motion path so that the object moves in an arc. This is useful to prevent the hand from becoming dislocated from the arm symbol when the character swings his arms back and forth.

10 The same technique of animating on an arc is repeated here with the head. In fact, you should always try to animate objects on an arc – especially characters. Arcs are more natural and remove that robotic feel your animations will have if tweened in a linear fashion.

HOT TIP

Dragging the edge of one span into the frames of another span replaces the frames of the second span. To extend a span without re-interpolating any keyframes, Shift-drag either end frame of its tween span. Flash adds frames to the end of the span without tweening those frames. You can also select a frame after the tween span in the same layer and press F5.

13 The Motion Editor lets you view and edit all tween properties and their keyframes. You can really control and fine-tune your animations from within this panel. The Motion Editor displays only the properties of the currently selected tween; you can't select multiple spans and edit them together in this panel. Once you have created a tween in the timeline, the Motion Editor allows you to control the tween in several different ways. You can set the value of individual property keyframes as well as add or remove property keyframes for individual properties. You can copy and paste a property curve from one property to another, which I especially find useful. Turn to the next page to become more familiar with this powerful panel.

SHORTCUTS
MAC WIN BOTH

Motion tween (cont.)

WELCOME TO THE new motion editor. Let's put the Motion Editor to work by creating a custom tween, applying it to a property as well as copy and paste the tween curve to other tween spans.

14 Select a tween span in the timeline and open the Motion Editor panel. One of the first things I do is use the hot text sliders in the lower left corner to adjust the width of the timeline on the right side so I can see all 30 frames.

15 Click on the "+" icon in the Eases property row and select Custom from the drop-down menu. A new custom ease row will be added to the Motion Editor. Click on this row to expand it vertically.

18 Next, apply your custom curve to the Basic motion properties using the drop-down menu.

19 On the stage you will notice the tween path will update to reflect the new ease curve you just applied to it.

20 Return to the Motion Editor and in the custom ease property curve area, right-click and select Copy Curve.

16 The easing effect we will create for the caveman animation example discussed on pages 76–79 will add easing in and out between keyframes within the tween span. Let's start by adding a keyframe on frame 15 in the Motion Editor to match the main timeline's frame 15 keyframe.

17 Using the Selection tool **S**, click and drag the control points in the ease curve until the Bezier handles appear. Use the handles to shape the curve similar to curve in the screenshot above.

HOT TIP

It is helpful to have both timeline and Motion Editor panels open while switching between them.

21 Select the next tween span in the main timeline and then return to the Motion Editor. Create a new custom ease by clicking on the "+" symbol as you did in step 2. Right-click over the property curve area and select Paste Curve. Use the Basic motion property drop-down menu to select and apply the custom curve to your 2nd tween span.

22 Repeat this procedure for every tween span you want to apply the custom ease to. It is helpful to have both timeline and Motion Editor panels open while switching between them. This is where having a 2nd monitor can be very useful.

SHORTCUTS
MAC WIN BOTH

The Motion Editor

WELCOME TO THE NEW MOTION EDITOR. At first glance this new panel will probably provoke 1 of 3 reactions:

1: An overwhelming sense of dread that there's a seemingly complicated new set of tools to learn.

2: Sweet! I don't know how to use it or what it does but I can't wait to dive in and find out.

3: Aha! I've used After Effects before and this looks familiar! Whatever your reaction is, the Motion Editor will prove helpful when creating complex animations.

Use this drop-down menu to select your custom ease and have it applied to the relative property.

Click here to add and remove keyframes. The arrows on both sides of the gold diamond will bring you to the next or previous keyframe in the timeline.

The property row expands when you click on it. Click it again or select a different property to collapse it.

Each property value is represented as a hot text slider, easily edited by dragging or typing in a new property value.

Use these controls to change the width and height of the property rows and timeline width.

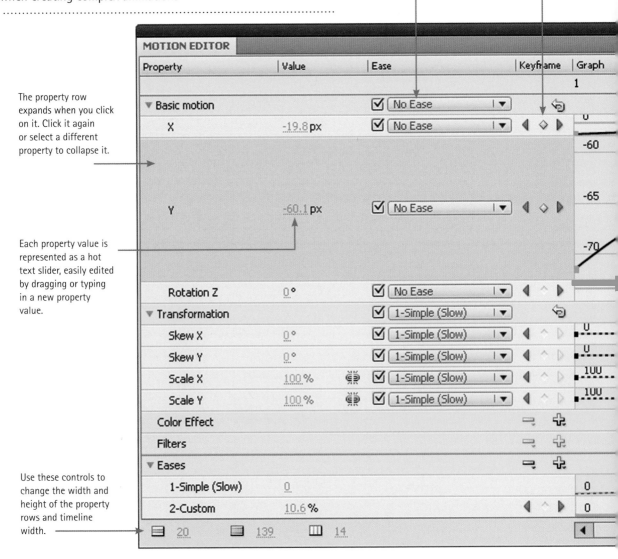

The timeline playhead is directly related to the plahead in the original timeline. Scrubbing the Motion Editor will playback the animation on the stage.

This is the property curve manager. This is where you can edit the curve that affects the property of your object.

5   10

Basic shadow

SHADOWS CAN ADD depth to your project. This is the most basic way to add a shadow to an animated character. Its simplicity does have its limitations, however. In this chapter you will learn more advanced shadow techniques with greater flexibility – but some may not be supported in older versions of the Flash player. Depending on your target audience and your clients' technical requirements, you may need a technique that will allow you to publish to older player versions. This is one such technique.

1 For the best result, place your character animation inside a symbol – this is commonly referred to as "nesting". The next step is to simply copy the symbol of your character using ⌘ C ctrl C. Create a new layer and move it below the character layer. Paste the copy of the symbol using ⌘ V ctrl V into this new layer.

4 With the Free Transform tool **Q** still selected, click and drag horizontally outside the bounding box in between the handles to skew the shadow.

2 Next, apply a tint to the symbol instance you just pasted. The tint needs to have a strength of 100% to completely hide the character's details. The color of the tint should also be a darker color value than the background.

3 Position the shadow instance and with the Free Transform tool, scale it vertically to suggest some perspective of it being cast against the ground.

5 You may want to scale your shadow slightly smaller to suggest more depth. Play around with its position relative to the original character for the best results. Because the shadow symbol is a duplicate of the original animated character symbol, it will also animate in sync with the character. This will result in a convincing shadow effect. Since you have not used any special filters, this shadow effect is supported by all versions of the Flash Player.

SHORTCUTS
MAC WIN BOTH

Drop shadow

SEPARATION BETWEEN CHARACTER and background can be critical to the overall impact of your animations. There are several ways to approach adding shadows for characters but, with animation, the approach can seem a bit daunting at first. Flash CS4 makes this as easy as possible with the use of filters.

For this example we will take a look at the Drop Shadow filter in its purest form. The technique that follows this one will provide a cool way to use the same filter that adds more depth and perspective.

1 Filters can only be applied to movie clips. If your animation is not in a movie clip, you'll need to remedy this by selecting the entire range of frames and layers and then Copy Frames from the right-click context menu.

2 Create a new Movie Clip symbol from the Library panel. Select the first frame of this symbol and, from the right-click context menu, select Paste Frames.

5 If you have a complex background, set the opacity to around 30–40%. This will allow the background values to show through the shadow itself for a realistic effect. I usually spend most of my time adjusting the angle and distance of the shadow relative to my light source. Test your movie to see the movie clip and shadow animation.

3 Drag an instance of this movie clip to a new layer on the main timeline. Delete all the original frames and layers as they are no longer needed. Select your new Movie Clip instance and from the Properties panel, select the Drop Down filter from the Filters category.

4 Adjust the amount of blur, opacity, angle and distance to achieve your desired results. You can also select the color of the shadow by clicking on the swatch color.

6 Select the Hide object feature to hide the movie clip. The drop shadow will remain on stage. Test your movie to see just the shadow animation. Experiment with some of the other options, such as Knockout and Inner shadow. Here I have placed an image of a blackboard behind the character,

adjusted the filter and played with 3D perspective using the 3D Rotation tool (see pages 48–51) to create a "chalk" effect. Using Flash CS4's filters and 3D tools, this entire effect took less than 1 minute to create. The best part is, the effect is applied to the entire animation inside the movie clip.

Perspective shadow

S O FAR WE'VE LOOKED at how to add a Drop Shadow filter to an animated character using a movie clip and the Filters feature. But the drop shadow can be a little limiting in some situations. To place a character in an environment that has more depth and perspective to it, the drop shadow will not work very well since it tends to flatten the perspective. You may need a shadow that provides the illusion of perspective and depth.

1 Select your Movie Clip instance and copy it using ⌘ C ctrl C. Create a new layer below it and paste it in place using ⌘ Shift V ctrl Shift V.

2 Lock the top layer to avoid editing it. Select the instance in the layer below it and, using the Free Transform tool Q, edit its center point so that it is positioned on the bottom edge.

5 With the symbol still selected, apply a Drop Shadow filter to it.

3 Scale the symbol downward by dragging the handle in the top center. Notice that the center point positioned on the bottom edge limits that edge from scaling.

4 Next, skew the symbol by dragging in between the handles outside the top edge.

6 The "cheat" to this technique is to select the Hide object feature. Now all you'll see is the Shadow filter itself.

7 Play around with the options provided. You can adjust the amount of blur, opacity, quality, angle and distance. You can even change the overall color of the filter itself.

SHORTCUTS

Blur filter

1 The billiard ball is simply a circle with a radial gradient. The trick is mixing the gradient using 5 colors: highlight, midtones, shadow and then a lighter value to the far right. This is the most critical color as it suggests light coming from behind the shape, creating the illusion that it is three-dimensional. Use the Gradient Transform tool to edit the center point as well as the scale and rotation.

THE BLUR FILTER is a very handy tool for creating a more realistic motion blur compared to just a linear gradient. Filters can only be applied to Movie Clip symbols, so you will need to plan ahead if your animation relies on several nested animations that need to be in sync with each other. With a combination of motion tweens and some basic ActionScript, you can control what each movie clip does and when it should do it – not unlike the director of a movie.

4 To add a realistic blur effect to the ball as it is motion tweened across the stage, select it and in the Filters panel drop-down menu, select the Blur option. Since the ball is traveling horizontally, we do not want any vertical blurring. So click on the little magnet icon to unlock the blur constraint. Set the amount of blurring in the X dialog. The Y dialog box should be set to "0".

```
1  ball1.gotoAndPlay("rollStop2");
2  ball3.gotoAndPlay("rollStop1");
```

7 When two or more balls collide, you must target each instance and tell them what to do. On the main timeline you can control what they do with keyframes and motion tweens. The nested animations must be targeted with ActionScript since a movie clip's timeline is independent of the main timeline. Both movie clip timelines are controlled with one line of code each. The nested animations then play until they reach a Stop action.

2 Convert your sphere to a Movie Clip symbol. All of the ball animations are nested in this symbol, consisting of a starting roll, rolling to a stop and a continuous roll. Check out the source file on the CD to see how these animations were made using a mask and motion tweening the symbol "8" across the sphere.

3 Copy and paste, or drag multiple instances from the Library, of this symbol to the stage – each on its own layer. Select them one at a time and type in a unique instance name in the Properties panel. This will allow you to target them individually.

HOT TIP

Locate the file named "8ball. fla" from the CD included with this book. Double-click one of the ball symbols to see how it was animated using motion tweens and a little masking. You can add to this timeline by creating additional ball rotations. The illusion here is that the ball never rotates at all; the white circle with the number 8 inside it is what actually moves across the surface of the circle shape. For similar illusions made with masks, see Chapter 3.

5 The technique is to use motion tweens and the Blur filter to provide the illusion that these balls are moving at an extreme velocity. Once a ball makes contact, its speed is dramatically reduced, at which point the Blur filter is removed by adding a keyframe and clicking the "-" symbol in the Filters panel.

6 To synchronize the nested animations to the main timeline, add a blank keyframe where you want to target your movie clip(s). Make sure the keyframe is selected and with the Actions panel open, type in the Movie Clip instance name you want to target, and then tell it what to do. Here the movie clip "ball1" is being told to go to the frame label "rollstop1" and play.

8 You can use _currentFrame to start or stop the ball on whatever the current frame happens to be. This is particularly handy when the timing of the animation changes on the main timeline and you don't want to constantly have to update the nested animations. When this script is called, whatever the current frame is inside the targeted movie clip, its playhead will simply stop.

SHORTCUTS
MAC WIN BOTH

Flying text

REMEMBER THE FIRST time you learned to use a mouse? Or to tie your shoes? These tasks seem so simple now, but some things are just plain easier after someone shows you how. It's the "not knowing where to start" that can be frustrating.

Well, consider this your start. I'm going to show you how simple it is to achieve some basic cool motion effects in Flash CS4 – effects that look really difficult to build, but, once you know how, are not so hard to create. Specifically, you'll make objects appear to move very fast using an animation effect known as motion blur.

1 First, you need to create the two objects used for this effect: text and a linear gradient. The linear gradient should have at least three colors, the middle color should be a value similar to the main color of the object and the left and right colors should be the same color as your background. If you have a complex background, mix these two colors with 0% alpha so the blur blends into the background.

3 About three to five frames down your timeline, add a new keyframe (F6). Holding down the Shift key, use the right arrow key to move the gradient across the stage. Position it wherever you like; just make sure it remains on the stage entirely (do not position it off the stage).

flying text

5 This effect is not limited to a horizontal format. Rotate the gradient 90 degrees.

6 Align the text below (or above) the gradient using the Onionskin tool to help guide you.

2 To create the animation for this effect, convert the linear gradient to a symbol and place it about halfway off of one side of your stage. You might want to start the animation on a frame other than frame 1 to provide a moment for the viewer to anticipate the action.

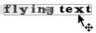

4 Apply a motion tween to make the gradient symbol move across the stage. Next, create a blank keyframe in the frame after your second keyframe and drag your text symbol to the stage from the Library panel ⌘ C L. Turn on the Onionskin tool so you can see the previous frame and where the linear gradient is positioned. Align your text to the right of the gradient. Play back your animation.

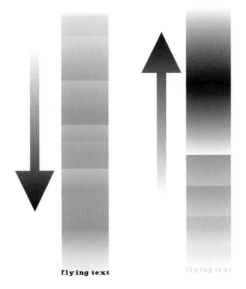

7 Repeat the same procedure as you did for the horizontal effect. Motion tween the gradient vertically from outside the viewable stage area. Then, in the frame after the tween, add a blank keyframe and position and align the text below the gradient. Reverse the procedure to make the text fly out and off the stage. I'm sure you will have a lot of fun with this effect as it is one of the easiest to master – yet it looks so good!

Combining effects

1 Type out your text using the Text tool. This particular font is pretty complex and already suggests movement. Your text, however, can be hand-drawn graphics depending on the style of project you might have.

THERE ARE SOME animated effects that look so advanced, it's difficult to determine how they were actually made. It is often assumed the skill level necessary to create such advanced motion graphics is well out of the reach of the average Flash user.

Not true in most cases. When we watch animated motion graphics, if the frame rate is fast enough, the human eye may not be able to see everything that is happening. As a result, our mind fills in what may not even be there. The good news is, we can use this natural shortcoming of the human eye to our own advantage when creating "advanced" motion effects. In my experience I have discovered that the most visually appealing animations are a combination of multiple techniques happening at the same time.

3 With every letter still selected, right-click over one of them and select Distribute to Layers. This will create a new layer for every letter and each letter will be placed into its own layer for you. A true time saver if ever there was one. Now is a good time to convert each letter to a graphic symbol.

5 Next, to create the effect of each letter fading in one after the other, you will stagger each motion tween to overlap the one below it. Starting with your second letter, select the range of frames in the motion tween, then drag them down the timeline a few frames. You can also select a frame before the tween and press F5 (Insert Frames) to push each motion tween down the timeline.

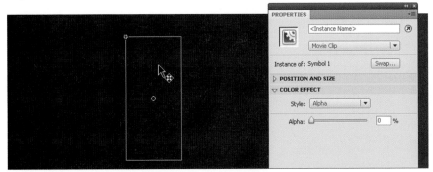

2 With the text field still selected, break it apart using ⌘ C ctrl C once. This will split the text field into individual text fields per letter. This retains the properties of the font and you have the ability to edit each letter as such. If you wish, you can break it apart one more time to convert the font into raw vector shapes.

4 On each layer, add a keyframe about three to four frames down the timeline. Now go back to the first keyframe containing your letter, select the letter symbol on the stage and apply some alpha via the Properties panel. Drag the alpha slider all the way down to 0%. Repeat this procedure for every letter. Apply a motion tween for every letter so that they all fade in when you play back your timeline.

6 The final step is to select the first frame of each animation and use Shift while pressing the left arrow key. This will position each letter with 0% alpha to the left and on playback will create the motion of each letter flying into position while fading in at the same time. Once again, there is nothing particularly difficult about this effect. All you have done is used motion tweens with some alpha fades. This is still a very basic Flash animation technique. The only difference is the timing of each letter relative to each other. Throw in a slight amount of movement and suddenly you have what looks like an advanced animated text effect.

Blur filter (text)

1 It is usually a good idea when creating animated effects to work backwards. Start with the final frame, insert frames to extend your entire timeline and then add keyframes to the last frame.

SOMETIMES YOU MAY need a blur effect that is more realistic than the linear gradient method. The Blur filter is perfect for creating realistic blurs – even animated ones. Filters were introduced in Flash 8 and to create the same blur effect in older versions, we had to export the object from Flash as a PNG file, open it in Photoshop (or any graphics editor of choice) and apply the motion blur. Then we would have to export from Photoshop as a PNG file and import back into Flash. Thankfully, those days are long gone with the ability to not only apply filters, but to animate them as well.

3 In frame 1, select a Movie Clip symbol on the stage and apply a Blur filter from the Filters panel. Click on the small black magnet icon to unlock the blur constraint. Use the slider to adjust the amount of blur for the X-axis only.

5 For objects that fly in vertically, limit the amount of blur to the Y-axis. Remember to use your Shift and arrow keys to maintain alignment between keyframes – unless of course you want to have your object travel at an angle.

2 Go back to frame 1 and begin the animation process by positioning the objects that will animate into view off the stage. Hold down the *Shift* key while pressing the arrow keys to maintain alignment and move the object incrementally ten frames.

4 Drag the keyframe in your last frame closer to the first keyframe and apply a motion tween. The symbol will animate from outside the stage into its original position. The Blur filter will also be motion tweened from the amount of blur in the first frame to no blur in the last frame.

6 Objects that appear as if being focused from thin air use an equal amount of blurring for both the X and Y axes. Use the hot text sliders to blur both the X and Y axes to a value of 255 – the maximum allowed.

97

Selective blurring

H ERE'S ANOTHER COOL TRICK to suggest
movement between two keyframes.
Open the "cowboy.fla" from the included
source CD and play back the animation. The
technique being used is basically a mixture of
frame-by-frame animation with a variation
of blurring and stretching. Look closely at the
movement of the cowboy's arm when he reaches
for the gun. There's only two frames where
this effect is used and at 24 fps it's almost
impossible to see. Yet the effect is still visually
effective as it really smooths out the motion
of his arm through the gesture of reaching and
drawing his weapon.

1 The first step is to add a little anticipation (refer to the "Anticipation" topic to
learn more). Rotate the arm into a position that suggests he is about to grab
something (refer to the "Hinging" topic to learn more about rotating body parts
based on a custom center point). I also added some "itchy-finger" animation to
build up the anticipation and focus the attention on his hand.

4 The next frame is similar to the previous frame. I used the Brush tool again
to draw new shapes using the same colors. Turn on the Onionskin tool to
see the previous frame as a reference.

2 Replace the arm with some very simple shapes drawn freehand style with the Brush tool. The fill for the arm is a mixture of black and about 30% transparency. The fill that represents the hand is the flesh tone mixed with some transparency as well.

3 You can mix in a little alpha by typing in a percentage manually or using the handy slider bar. Add this new color to your Swatch panel using the upper right corner drop-down menu.

5 After two frames of blurring, it is time to bring the original arm back to the animation and in a new position. You will notice I also added some brush strokes behind the arm to suggest the arm is still moving but decelerating.

6 When a gun is fired, the resulting action is referred to as "recoil". We have Sir Isaac Newton to thank for showing us that every action has an equal and opposite reaction. This law of physics is critical for us to understand and, when necessary, incorporate into our work.

HOT TIP

The selective blurring technique works best when it is barely seen. If it stays on stage long enough for the viewer to notice it as an object, it has performed a disservice to your animation effect. In essence, this technique should enhance the motion as a whole, not introduce an additional component to it. It should be subtle and used sparingly for a greater overall effect.

99

Background blurring

I F YOU WATCH animated shows on television then I'm sure you've seen the motion blur technique, where the characters remain relatively still while the background is being blurred. This provides the illusion that the character is flying through air at incredible speed. Visually it's a very dramatic effect and can be used in myriad ways during an action sequence.

The illusion here is that the background is actually moving through the shot – but in fact it doesn't have to be and in most cases never really moves at all. In this example the shapes that represent the motion simply wiggle slightly in a very short loop. What makes this effect convincing is a combination of color, line work and of course the character itself.

1 Start with a radial gradient as the undertone of your shot. Use the Gradient Transform tool **F** to position the gradient in the lower left corner. It is where the character will fly in from and helps provide some needed depth to the scene.

4 Select all lines and convert them to a graphic symbol. Edit this symbol by adding several keyframes on the same layer. This duplicates the lines for each added keyframe. Select a keyframe and click the "Smooth" tool a few times. Make sure the amount of smoothing is different for each keyframe. The idea is to create an oscillation between frames. Flash CS4 introduces the Advanced Smooth panel ctrl alt Shift M ⌘ alt Shift M that provides fine tune controls for smoothing.

2 Create a new layer and use the Line tool with a stroke color high in contrast to your gradient colors. Draw some lines to use as directional guides.

3 Create a new layer above your guidelines and using the Brush tool **B** and a large brush size, hand draw some thick lines that taper slightly towards the lower left corner.

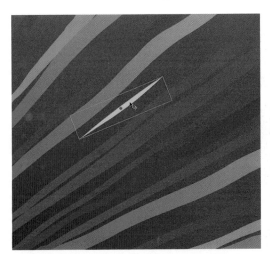

5 On the main timeline I added some random shapes flying through the shot in the same direction as the background lines. This helps emphasize the speed and direction the character is moving.

6 The final touch is to add your character. This effect works best when your character is drawn in a way that reflects the speed and wind resistance they would encounter.

7 You can emphasize the dramatic effect by motion tweening the character from off the stage into its final position. Combine this effect with some of the motion blur effects previously learned in this chapter and you'll have a killer action sequence.

HOT TIP

With the background as a nested looping animation, you can easily re-use it for other similar shots that need to imply very fast motion. As a symbol you can transform it by scaling, skewing and even tinting it based on the design of your shot.

SHORTCUTS

101

Learning to be simple

ONE OF THE MOST DIFFICULT challenges for me as an artist was to learn how to simplify my drawing style. Early in my career my work consisted of large scale lithographs depicting weeks of painstakingly complicated imagery. Spending days and often weeks on each print wasn't uncommon for me. But if you asked me to whip up a simple cartoon character, I wouldn't even know where to start.

Fact is, simplifying my drawing style didn't come easily. I was literally thrown into the world of cartoon animation when asked to join an animation

team at a local production company. They already had an established series on a popular cable network channel (*Dr. Katz, Comedy Central*), and my job was to design and animate a pilot for DreamWorks. It was a nice way to get thrown into the world of animation, resulting in a very diverse artistic direction for me. I embraced the challenge.

The next several years provided me the experience of designing and animating several successful television series and animated content for the Internet. We used Flash for everything, including storyboards, animatics, character and background design and, of course, animation. We were a paperless studio and Flash was our Swiss army knife of software tools. As Flash matured with each version, my skill level using it was maturing also.

Strict deadlines and cut-throat delivery dates meant working fast. Working fast meant keeping the drawing style simple, which I became very good at through practise. Not unlike a classical musician ending up performing children's pop music, it was my fine art training that helped pave the road to cartoon animation.

Ironically today, I am considered a cartoonist and character animator as opposed to a fine artist. The ability to draw with simple shapes and lines did not come easily to me. Admittedly, I continue to find it a challenge creating graphics that are iconic in style. To break down an image into a few simple shapes and have it still be appealing and even the least bit amusing is a daunting task. Sometimes I can nail it in a few minutes of sketching, other times it can take a few hours of pushing and pulling shapes until I think they work together. All too often my efforts get tossed aside and spend the rest of their lives stored onto a cold and dark back-up hard drive. Being asked to author this book has granted me the opportunity to choose some of the more successful designs as feature topics for the sole reason that they help make the book more visually appealing. What you don't see are the hundreds of failed attempts and design blunders I have created to reach this level in my career. There does exist an island of misfit characters where the majority of habitants are the result of my own handiwork.

Michelangelo was once quoted as saying "I saw the angel in the marble and carved until I set him free." As modest as he may have been, his perspective on design is timeless. Apply this thinking to your own approach when designing anything from a character, logo, background or even a website. All the best details are there in front of you; it's everything else that needs to be removed.

■ From concept sketch to finalized animated body parts – just how does a Flash animator get from point A to point B? What is the workflow when it comes to animating characters in Flash? This chapter looks at several real world examples of actual characters and how they were built, and why.

5 Character animation

IT IS TIME to get down and dirty. In previous chapters we looked at how to achieve a wide variety of design styles, transformations and motion effects. But the concept of how to bring all these techniques together to create a successfully animated character can remain a mystery. When is it advantageous to nest certain animations and why? How can swapping symbols be effective? What exactly does the Sync feature do? What is the most effective way to synchronize a character's mouth and lips to a voice-over soundtrack?

These questions and more are explained in the following pages. So roll up your sleeves and get ready for a fun ride into the world of Flash character animation.

5

2.5D basics

TWEENING IS A GREAT WAY to add quick and simple animation to your Flash movie. But what if you could push the tweening method to its limits and give more realism to your character? What if you could harness its simplicity and make it work in ways not too many other Flash users have thought of? What if you have learned everything there is to know about tweening, go back to the first 10% of that knowledge, and take a left turn? Where would that take you?

In this example, I'm going to reveal a truly killer Flash animation technique that will actually create a 3D optical illusion that has fooled even the most discerning eye. The cool thing is you never leave the Flash environment and remain in the 2D realm. You are now in a dimensional limbo. If it's still 2D but looks like 3D, then what exactly is it? Welcome to what is commonly referred to as "2.5D animation".

1 Let's start with a few basic shapes that resemble eyes and a mouth on a face. You can add some horizontal and vertical guides to help keep these objects aligned with each other. Before you start editing these shapes, insert keyframes a few frames down the timeline across all layers. You will see why this is useful later.

4 Move the other eye over as well but scale it slightly wider as it gets closer to the middle of the head. This is where, if it were truly mapped to the surface of a three-dimensional sphere, it would be at its widest – the point where it is closest to us.

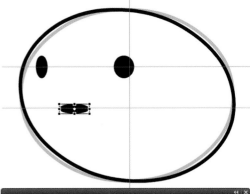

5 Next, move the mouth over in the same direction and scale its width slightly smaller like you did for the first eye. You might want to push the mouth closer to the left edge to provide more space between the mouth and the right eye. This will help make it feel as if the mouth is truly wrapping around the head like the left eye is starting to do.

2 Insert keyframes across all layers between the first and last frames of your timeline. Start with the head symbol by skewing it with the Free Transform tool. Since you will be creating the illusion of the head turning to the left, skew this shape by clicking and dragging just outside the bounding box in this direction.

3 Next, select the left eye symbol and position it close to the left edge of the head shape. Use the Free Transform tool to reduce its width slightly, creating the illusion of the eye moving away from us around the surface of the head.

6 Now all you have to do is apply motion tweens to all the layers. Drag across all layers to select them and apply a motion tween from the context menu or Properties panel. Remember when you added keyframes to the final frame in step 1? Now all you need to do is apply motion tweens to the latter half of your timeline to return the head to its original position.

7 Repeat the same procedure but in the opposite direction to make the head appear to turn to the right. Experiment by making the head move from left to right by removing the keyframes in the middle of the timeline.

HOT TIP

Don't be afraid to push the limits of this technique. I see my students attempt this style of animation and all too often they hardly move the features across the face enough to make the illusion convincing. Play back your animation frequently to test the overall effect. You can always add or remove frames if the animation is too slow or too fast. Add a little easing to make it look even more realistic.

SHORTCUTS

MAC WIN BOTH

2.5D advanced

LET'S APPLY THE same technique, as explained in the previous example, to a more sophisticated character. This character is comprised of several individual objects, all of which were designed and composed with this animation technique in mind. The spacial relationship of each object to each other is important as they will all need to move, skew and scale together, but at varied amounts. The effect is based on the whole being greater than the sum of its parts. There's nothing overly sophisticated about creating this technique but the result can look very complex on the surface.

1 The first step is to make sure all objects have been converted to symbols and you have edited their center point to your desired location (check out the "Hinging body parts" topic on page 122). For this technique to be successful, it's often useful to design your characters in three-quarter view as opposed to a profile view or facing us directly.

4 Next, skew the hair to the right from its bottom edge. Since you want to convey this object coming around the front of the character's face, move it over to the right and scale it horizontally to make it slightly wider than it is in the first frame. This creates the illusion that it is moving not only across the face, but also slightly towards us as well.

2 If you want to create a seamless loop by making the head eventually return to this same exact position, select a frame (across all layers) somewhere down the timeline and add a keyframe (F6). It pays to think ahead because you have avoided having to copy and paste the keyframes from frame 1 later. Select another frame (across all layers) an equal distance between your first and last keyframes.

3 This middle frame is where you will edit your character. Start by using the Free Transform tool **Q** to skew the symbol instances. Here I have skewed the hat, which is comprised of two separate symbols, a front and a back. Selecting and skewing them together insures that they remain aligned which each other. It's helpful to lock all other layers temporarily while you do this.

5 Repeat this process for each object, combining various amounts of skewing, scaling and positioning. The smaller symbol representing the hair on the right side is the only symbol, in this example, that gets positioned to the left. Moving it behind the head emphasizes the illusion that the head is a sphere that objects can seemingly "wrap" around.

6 The final touch is to add easing using the Custom Ease panel. The straight path represents no easing. The "S"-shaped path represents easing in and out within a single tween.

HOT TIP

Character design is critical for this effect to be successful. Keep it simple and stylized because the more anatomically correct your character is, the harder it will be to animate in this style.

SHORTCUTS

2.5D monkey

T HE KEY TO REALISM lies within the shading. The same 2.5D animation technique is being used here, but this time the graphics are drawn using gradients to promote an even more convincing faux three-dimensional effect.

1 Start with the character at a three-quarter angle in frame 1. Let's call this "point A".

2 In your last frame, create what we'll call "point B". The challenge is getting from point A to point B through the use of tweens.

6 The ears play a pivotal role in this effect. At this new angle, we can see more of the left ear and less of the right ear.

7 Once the head symbols are transformed and positioned where you want them, lock their layers, select all the body parts and rotate them.

8 Next, adjust the legs and tail individually by selecting and rotating them.

3 Using the Free Transform tool, rotate, skew and move each symbol into it's "point B" position. Here the mouth symbols are transformed first.

4 Next, trasform the nose, eyes, pupils and eyebrows. Pay close attention to the spacial relationship between each of these objects and our perspective at this new angle.

5 The head and hair symbols are rotated and positioned accordingly. At this angle, we see more of the hair from the left side and less on the right.

9 Select everything except the arms and hands and move the monkey over using the right arrow key. Hold down Shift to move in 10-pixel increments.

10 Rotate the arms so they align with the monkey's new position. Their center point is positioned where the hands grab the vine to make this even easier.

11 Apply motion tweens to each layer and play back your animation. Final adjustments are usually necessary at this stage.

Lip syncing (swap method)

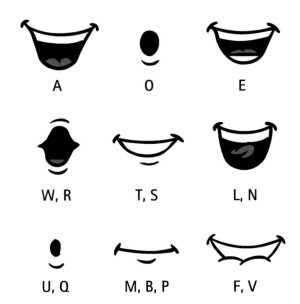

A O E

W, R T, S L, N

U, Q M, B, P F, V

LIP SYNCING IS AN ART form in its own right. It is the art of making a character speak to a pre-recorded vocal soundtrack. This technique involves the creation of various mouth shapes and matching them to the appropriate dialog. This technique can also be very time-consuming, especially if your dialog is very long. You can be as simple or as complex as you want. There's a big difference between South Park and Disney style animation when it comes to matching mouths to sounds. There are two basic methods of lip syncing in Flash which we will look at here.

1 Here are the standard mouth shapes to use as a guide. Each shape corresponds to a specific sound or range of sounds. Each sound is noted below each shape. For most animation styles, you do not need to create a different mouth for each letter of the alphabet. In most situations, certain mouths can be reused for a variety of sounds.

4 The next step is to import your sound into Flash. Sound formats supported are WAV , MP3, Aiff and AU. Go to File > Import to Stage and locate the sound file on your hard drive. Once imported, create a new layer in your timeline and select a frame. Using the Sound drop-down menu in the Properties panel, select the sound you just imported. Next, set the sound from the default "Event" to "Stream".

When you name each mouth symbol, include a description of what dialog sounds it should be associated with. This simplifies the process of choosing the appropriate symbol by allowing your eyes to scan down the list of names in the Library without needing to select each symbol to see the thumbnail.

2 Using the standard mouth shapes as your guide, draw your character's mouth shapes, taking into consideration the design and angle of your character. After drawing each mouth, convert each one into a Graphic symbol.

3 Based on the design of your character, you will likely want to have your mouth symbol on its own layer. This makes it easier to edit it for animation.

5 On the main timeline where your character resides you can animate the mouth talking by creating keyframes and using the "Swap Symbols" method via the Properties Inspector. The Swap Symbol panel will open, allowing you to scroll through your Library.

6 Click once to preview each Library item and click OK to replace the instance on the stage with this symbol. It helps to name your mouth symbols starting with the same three letters as they will be sorted by name in the Swap Symbol panel, making it easier to find the mouth you want.

7 Click "OK" to swap the symbol instance on the stage with this new symbol from the Library.

SHORTCUTS
MAC WIN BOTH

Lip syncing (nesting method)

THROUGH YEARS OF ANIMATING in Flash, I have developed what I think is an even better and faster way to lip sync a character. A few years ago I was working in a full production environment with teams of animators producing several series for television and the Web. Most of these episodes were 22 minutes in length with several characters and plenty of dialog. Lip syncing quickly became the most dreaded of tasks. Using the Swap Symbols method is certainly a useful approach, but when you have 22 minutes of lip syncing to do and only two days to finish it, finding a faster method becomes a production necessity.

The Swap Symbols method requires a minimum of four mouse clicks for each swap.

1. Select the symbol instance.
2. Click the "Swap" button.
3. Select the new symbol.
4. Click "OK".

Over the course of thousands of frames and symbol swaps, those clicks can add up to an enormous number. Shaving off just one click per mouth shape can, over time, save valuable production costs (not to mention an animator's sanity).

This is where "nesting" really shows its strength and versatility. By nesting all your individual mouths into a single symbol, you can control the instance of this symbol with the Properties panel. This method eliminates the need to swap symbols and also saves time.

1 The first step is to place all your mouth shapes into a Graphic symbol. I recommend editing an existing symbol on the stage to help you align your additional mouths to the character on the main timeline. Double-click the mouth symbol on the stage to enter Edit Mode. Create a blank keyframe for each additional mouth. If your mouths already exist as symbols, open your Library ctrl L ⌘ L and drag each mouth to its own keyframe. Use the Onionskin tool to help align each one.

5 The convenience of nesting is obvious when you transform (rotate, scale, flip horizontally or vertically, etc.) your character; all nested assets are transformed as well.

6 Often you may need a custom mouth animation – for example, a mouth that whistles. Right-click over your mouth and select Duplicate Symbol. Give it a descriptive name.

2 Back on the main timeline, open the Properties panel and select your "mouth" symbol containing all of your mouth shapes. As a Graphic symbol, the Properties panel will allow you options to control the instance.

3 Add a keyframe to the mouth layer, select the mouth instance and in the Properties panel select Single Frame. In the Frame input box, type in the frame number that corresponds to the mouth shape needed.

4 Scrub the timeline (drag the playhead back and forth) to hear the next sound. Repeat the same process by adding keyframes, and typing in the corresponding frame number for the mouth shape needed.

HOT TIP

When designing your character, it's important to conceptualize how the character's features may work. Some mouths are designed so that they are independent of the jaw and nose, while other mouths are an integral part of these features. So ultimately your mouth may be drastically different in terms of design, yet follow these basic standards.

7 Remove the unneeded symbols by selecting them and choosing "Remove Frames" from the right-click context menu. Keep the symbol that closely represents a "whistle" shape.

8 Animate the whistling mouth as a short loop. Here I used the Envelope tool to distort my original mouth shape after breaking it apart.

9 On the main timeline, add a keyframe and select the "whistle" symbol containing your new animation. In the Properties panel select "Loop" from the drop-down menu.

To sync or not to sync

T O SYNCHRONIZE A NESTED ANIMATION inside a Graphic symbol with the main timeline, select the Sync option in the Property Inspector. Sync is a feature that is available when a motion tween is applied. Select a keyframe with a motion tween to find the Sync option in the Properties panel. What this means for nested animations is that the nested frames will be synchronized with the main timeline.

In Flash CS3, Sync was inconsistently on or off depending on how you applied a motion tween: If you applied a tween from the drop-down menu in the Properties panel, then Sync was UNCHECKED. If you applied a motion tween via the right-click context menu, then Sync was CHECKED. The Sync feature was indicated on the timeline when a keyframe was followed by a vertical line.

Flash CS4 consistently turns on the Sync feature by default no matter how the motion tween is applied.

So when would you use Sync? When would you want to avoid it? Let's first take a look at a situation where Sync would not be useful.

1 In order for you to see the effectiveness of the Sync feature, you need a nested animation to work with. A mouth symbol with several mouths on diferent keyframes will do just fine. Thumbnail views of each frame were selected using the Frame View drop-down menu in the upper-right corner of the timeline panel (to the right of the frame numbers). This is a handy way to see the contents of each frame.

5 When you apply a motion tween and want the ability to control the frames nested inside graphic symbols, select a keyframe in the tween and turn off the Sync feature via the Properties panel. Note that this only applies to Classic tweens in CS4 and not the new Motion Model.

2 The Frame View drop-down menu offers several choices for you to customize the way your timeline looks. My personal favorite is the "Short" setting, which lowers the overall height of each layer.

3 You can take lip syncing a bit further by tweening the mouth on the main timeline. This adds a second layer of animation since this mouth symbol contains nested mouths as well.

4 Using the Free Transform tool, scale and/or skew the mouth depending on the vocal sound and apply a motion tween. The Sync option becomes a factor when motion tweens are applied.

HOT TIP

Check out the "Extending Flash" chapter, specifically the AnimSlider Pro by Warren Fuller and the FrameSync extension by Justin Putney. They are very useful extensions for controlling nested graphic symbol animations and, personally, my favorite tools for Flash.

6 In the timeline, the top image indicates a keyframe with Sync turned on. The bottom image indicates a keyframe with Sync turned off.

7 Having the ability to assign a specific frame number is critical for lip syncing. If Sync is selected, you will not be able to edit the current frame number. Once Sync is turned off, you are free to change the frame number pertaining to the nested animation.

SHORTCUTS
MAC WIN BOTH

5

Sync (Classic tween)

ONE DAY THE CLIENT asks for you to animate their company's character logo across their website splash page. You use several keyframes and motion tweens to animate their character (nested inside a symbol) along a motion guide and deliver the final version to your client and await their feedback. Unfortunately the client changes their mind and asks if you could change the bee character to a dog with a jet pack instead. Do you have to do the entire animation over again? No, because you can always swap out the bee symbol for another symbol. But you have to swap out each instance of the bee for every keyframe you made in the animation. What a drag! The more keyframes on the timeline, the more monotonous and frustrating this task can be.

Sync to the rescue!

1 Let's start with a simple animation involving a nested character animation in a Graphic symbol motion tweened along a guided path. Apply a Classic tween using the Tween drop-down menu in the Properties panel. The Sync option will be turned on by default. Nothing too complex going on here. The bee symbol contains some nested animations (wings flapping, eye movements and the bee sneezing).

4 You just about finish the animation when the phone rings and your client informs you that they want to change the bee to a totally different character. Thanks to Sync, your time and hard work will not be wasted. Go to File > Import > Open External Library and navigate to an FLA containing the replacement symbol and click Open. You can also click the New Library panel button to open the Library of an FLA already open in Flash. A new Library panel will open displaying the symbols and assets contained in the selected FLA. Click and drag the preferred symbol from the external Library to the Library of your current document.

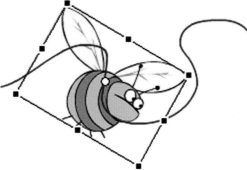

2 Insert a keyframe somewhere in the motion tween. Use the Free Transform tool **Q** to rotate the symbol. Feel free to scale or skew the symbol as well. Because the first keyframe is "Synced", all subsequent keyframes will have Sync turned on by default as well.

3 Continue to insert keyframes every few frames and transform your symbol by rotating and scaling. The idea here is to make this simple motion tween relatively complex for the example purposes.

HOT TIP

Use the Sync option to control different symbols within the same motion tween. Turn off Sync for certain keyframes if you want to swap to another symbol for that keyframe. Turn on Sync to keep the same symbol in sync with the main timeline. This method will not work with Movie Clip symbols. Use only Graphic symbols because only Graphic symbols can be synced to other timelines using the Sync feature. Movie clips have timelines that are independent of all other timelines and need actionScript to be synced to other timelines.

5 Select the bee character in the first frame of your motion tween. In the Properties panel click the Swap button and locate the new symbol you just added to your Library and click OK.

6 Since every keyframe in the motion tween has the Sync option selected, your entire animation will be updated across all keyframes. Crisis averted, go and make yourself another cup of coffee, catch up on your email overflow and get back to your client in a little while. Make sure to sound out of breath when you call them to tell them the changes have been made (just kidding).

SHORTCUTS

Sync (Motion tween)

THE NEW MOTION TWEEN changes everything when it comes to tweens and what we can do with them. If you remember one thing about them, remember this: the new Motion tween is *object-based* while the Classic tween is *frame-based*. This means much of what we used to do in previous versions was in the timeline when it involved animation: creating and removing keyframes, applying tweens, creating and applying motion guides, copying and pasting frames, etc.

With motion tweens most tasks are applied to the object on the stage while Flash does most of the work for us. For this particular animation, the joke is always on the dog. Each of his meals are dropped into his dish and each time the meal is different (as well as revolting and inedible). Knowing this scene will be reused countless times, it was critical to build it in a way that made it easy to swap out the object that falls into the bowl. If you thought using the Sync feature to swap symbols across animations couldn't be easier, think again.

1 The first step is to draw the object that is to land in the bowl and convert it to a symbol. Position the symbol above the bowl and almost off the top edge of the stage. Since the motion tween is *object*-based, right-click over the symbol and select "Create Motion Tween". Flash will automatically create a motion span in this layer and insert a duration of frames equal to a full second based on the document's frame rate. This will likely be plenty of time as this animation won't last beyond 1 second.

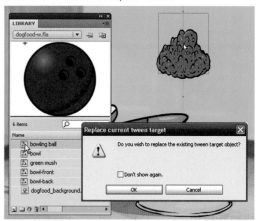

4 Once you have the animation complete, swapping out the current symbol for an alternative symbol is surprisingly easier than using the Sync method from previous examples. Thanks to the new Motion tween, all you need to do is open the Library panel, find the symbol you wish to use in place of the current symbol and drag it to the stage (make sure the layer with the motion span is selected). Flash will prompt you to confirm that you want to replace the existing tween target object. Click "OK".

2 Insert some time before the animation actually starts, which was always a bit cumbersome when using "classic" tweens. With the new Motion tween all you need to do is click and drag the left edge of the motion span and drag it to a new frame. Position the frame indicator somewhere around frame 15, hold down the *Shift* key and drag the symbol vertically so it ends up inside the dog bowl.

3 To provide the illusion of weight to the dog food, additional keyframes and positions were added as well as some squashing and stretching (see page 52). To make the effect even more convincing, the dog bowl itself can be animated as if it is reacting to the impact of the food.

5 Your new object has now been applied to the entire motion span, replacing the original object across all keyframes and properties. Using this technique has obvious advantages over the Sync method: instead of selecting the first keyframe in a classic tween and swapping out the symbol from the Library, the Motion tween method is a simple case of dragging a new object to the stage containing the animation.

6 You can even select the span and press the *Delete* key to remove the object entirely from the animation. All of the motion tween data are retained, allowing you to drag a new object to the stage or copy and paste a new object into the existing span.

HOT TIP

To remove frames or cut frames from within a span, Ctrl-drag (Windows) or Command-drag (Macintosh) to select the frames and choose Remove Frames or Cut Frames from the span context menu.

To extend the presence of a tweened object on Stage beyond either end of its tween, hold down Shift key while dragging either end frame of the tween span. Flash adds frames to the beginning or end of the span without tweening those frames.

SHORTCUTS MAC WIN BOTH

121

Hinging body parts

W ITH FREE TRANSFORM, we can edit the center point of a symbol instance, thus editing the point on which the symbol rotates or "hinges" itself. Any simulation of inverse kinematics is purely coincidental. This technique does not allow you to link objects together in a chain like the Bone tool does (see page 124), but can be useful for manipulating objects individually.

1 Select the Free Transform tool **Q** and then click on one of your symbols on your stage. The center point of the symbol is now represented by a solid white circle. Simply click and drag this circle to a new location. In my example, I moved the center point of the arm to where the shoulder is (approximately).

4 You can select multiple symbols across multiple layers and hinge them as if they were one single object. With the Free Transform tool still selected, hold down the *Shift* key and click on multiple symbols on the stage. The center point will now be relative to the center point of all the symbols selected.

2 With the same tool rotate the arm symbol. It will "hinge" based on its new center point, making it easier to position each arm movement in relation to the body symbol.

3 Repeat this process for each body part you want hinged. As you can see I even hinged the ear symbol as well. Now you can start animating by creating additional keyframes and apply motion tweens throughout your timeline.

To select multiple objects, it is often easier to click and drag with the Selection tool across the objects on stage. Make sure you set the center point for each symbol on frame 1 of your timeline. If the center point is different between keyframes where a motion tween is applied, your symbol will "drift" unexpectedly.

5 This can be very useful for hinging the head of a character which may contain multiple symbols (eyes, mouth, nose, hair, etc).

6 The center point for each individual symbol will be retained but the center point representing multiple selected symbols will not be remembered once they are deselected.

SHORTCUTS

123

Bone tool (Inverse Kinematics)

INVERSE KINEMATICS (iK) is an exciting new tool for animating an object or a series of objects in relation to each other using what is commonly referred to as an armature or a chain. This new tool is called the Bone tool in Adobe Flash CS4.

Not unlike a marionette puppet, the Bone tool allows symbol instances and shape objects to move in a chain-like fashion. It made sense to me to introduce this feature using an actual chain example for simplicity's sake.

I have included a folder named "CS4 Bone tool examples" on the source CD included in the back of this book. This folder contains several examples that showcase the Bone tool.

1 To create a chain you need 2 or more objects. Here I have created 2 simple chain graphics using the rectangle tool and a stroke color. They were converted to Movie Clips and have a Bevel filter applied to them for a touch of realism.

2 I have duplicated these 2 symbols several times and configured them to form a straight vertical chain. Now that the objects are configured, it is time to create the chain.

6 Insert some frames in the armature layer your chain now resides in. Position the playhead in the last frame.

7 Drag the chain again in the opposite direction. A 2nd keyframe has been automatically added. Now you can play back your animation and watch the chain move from left to right.

3 Select the Bone tool **X**, and start with the top-most symbol. This will be the root or parent symbol. Drag from the top of this symbol to the top of the next symbol in the chain. A solid bone will be displayed between both objects.

4 Repeat this procedure until all objects are linked together to form a chain. The exact location over the object where you release the mouse is where the bone will be attached. An object can have only one single attachment point.

5 Click the last object in the chain (in this example it is the bottom-most chain link graphic) and drag it to the left. All the other links in the chain will follow in a realistic fashion.

8 To create a seamless looping animation, right-click over the keyframe in frame 1 and select Copy Pose.

9 Insert more frames in the armature layer by clicking on an empty frame further down the timeline and pressing the F5 key. Right-click over the last frame in the span and select Paste Pose.

10 Select a frame in the span and select one of the easing presets from the drop-down menu in the Properties panel. Use the hot text slider to control the strength of the ease.

HOT TIP

You can apply different types of easing in between different sets of keyframes throughout the same span. Just select a frame in between a span, set the type and strength of the ease and repeat.

Bone tool (cont.)

HOW DOES THE bone tool work with a character? Now we're getting into some fun new territory with Flash CS4. Here's a great character design from talented character designer Steven J. Tubbrit, founder of Sunchirp (**http://sunchirp. blogspot.com**).

This character is a perfect next step for learning about Inverse Kinematics. It is a relatively simple design with only a handful of moveable parts yet complex enough to keep our attention.

1 The first step is to convert all body parts to Graphic or Movie Clip symbols and arrange them roughly in their default positions. They can either be on the same layer or different layers. Using the Bone tool **X**, click and drag from one symbol to another. The first symbol in the chain becomes the root (sometimes called the parent) symbol of the entire chain. It appears with a circle around the head of the bone.

4 Simply select the object you want to arrange and right-click over it, and select Arrange and then the desired stacking order relative to the other symbols. Send to Back will place the object behind all other objects. Send Backward will position the object behind the next object directly below it.

2 This armature is different from the previous "chain" in the previous example. Instead of linking one object after another, here it is best to link the next object from the same starting point as the root bone you made in step 1. The reason for this is because the body of the dragon is simply too large to link other body parts any other way. Each bone will need to originate from the same point.

3 Repeat the process of linking body parts with the Bone tool by dragging from the same starting point. You'll notice, as you link objects, they will swap depths with each other. You will have to stack them again in the right order after your armature is created.

5 Click and drag any of the bones to manipulate your character. Position the playhead on a different frame and create a new pose by manipulating the armature.

6 Continue to position the playhead on different frames and adjust your character's pose. When you play back the timeline you will see the character animate from pose to pose.

SHORTCUTS
MAC WIN BOTH

Closing the gaps

F ORM FOLLOWS FUNCTION in Flash. The more stylized the design, the more flexibility you will have when it comes to adding motion. On the other hand, the more anatomically correctly your character is designed, the less you can get away with when the time comes to animate it.

Sometimes a project comes along where the design style demands realism. As a result, the animation technique demands attention to detail, which can be limiting to a certain degree. One particular issue is bending arms and legs at their respective joints, and the unsightly gap between them that is often created. The solution: "caps". At least that's what I like to call them. An elbow cap for the arms and a knee cap for the legs can solve the dreaded gap problem.

1 The Evil Mime character for the Yahoo! Super Messengers project was designed in a very anatomically correct style. This caused some problems during the animation process – specifically the joints between limbs. When the arms or legs are in their original positions (as they were drawn originally), there's no gap.

5 The leg, like the arm, works quite well when in a straight position. The upper thigh blends perfectly into the calf and shin.

6 The problem arises when these body parts are pushed to their anatomical limit when rotated and bent at the knee (or lack thereof).

2 Once the arm is bent, the gap appears between the forearm and upper arm symbols. This is a problem inherent with this style of line work.

3 The solution is to add a new symbol in the form of an elbow. This new "cap" can be used as "filler" to hide that ugly gap between limbs when rotating.

4 Use the Free Transform tool to skew the cap symbol so it aligns with both arm symbols – bridging the gap between them, so to speak.

7 Once again, adding a knee cap symbol solves this problem quite nicely.

8 Position the knee cap in between the upper and lower leg symbols and align as necessary. Use the Free Transform tool **Q** to skew and scale the knee so that it fits properly.

9 It may seem like a lot of work to add elbow and knee caps, and subsequently more layers to your Flash document. But in the end, the results of your hard work and attention to detail will not go unnoticed.

Bitmap animation (JibJab)

J IBJAB MEDIA gained widespread notoriety for its election year shorts "This Land" and "Good to be in DC", which featured George W. Bush and John Kerry during the 2004 Presidential campaign and were viewed online more than 80 million times.

The JibJab team uses both Photoshop and Flash to create the majority of their animation, and the process involves sketching, photography, Photoshop collage and, of course, Flash animation. In this tutorial, you'll be instructed on how to make a President Bush dance cycle. You'll need a photo of President Bush's head, a camera and an understanding of tweens, guide layers and the basics of character animation.

Special thanks to Aaron Simpson (**www. coldhardflash.com**), and Gregg and Evan Spiridellis (www.jibjab.com) for their generous contribution to this book. This is Flash animation gold.

1 For this type of animation, you should define the proportions and the action your character will be executing. Start by drawing the first pose for your character.

2 Sketch the second pose and when you're finished, you should have a clear idea of the photos you'll need to animate with.

6 You should only build one arm, as we'll flip these assets and reuse them on the opposite side. Here the arm was cut out using another Quick Mask.

7 The arm looks too thin at the shoulder area. Press ⌘ ctrl T to enter Transform mode and click the Warp icon, then manipulate the Bezier handles to impart a cylindrical shape.

3 Photograph a front view of a jacket, shirt and tie and then a separate photo of a fist. In this situation, you can reuse the arms as legs, and create a vector foot.

4 Open your photograph file in Photoshop. Press **Q** to enter Quick Mask mode and, using a hard edge brush, select the area you want to animate separately.

5 Here's the body section after cutting it out with the Quick Mask feature. Make sure the background is transparent.

8 Next, select a circle where you want the elbow joint to be and save that selection in a new channel.

9 Here is the lower arm graphic after being cut out from the overall arm.

10 Here the upper arm receives a little more transforming with the Warp tool for good measure.

HOT TIP

Check out Steve Caplin's *How to Cheat in Photoshop CS4* for some of the best tips and tricks for how to extend your Photoshop knowledge. it's a great companion book to have next to this one.

SHORTCUTS
MAC **WIN** **BOTH**

PSD Importer (JibJab)

ONE OF THE coolest features in Flash CS4 is the PSD Importer. You have the ability to import PSD files straight into Flash! This is a great feature that integrates Photoshop and Flash seamlessly.

1 This is how the layers look in the Photoshop file. Many of the images have transparent backgrounds. Transparency is one of the many features preserved when importing.

2 In Flash, go to File > Import and navigate to your PSD file. The PSD Importer wizard will launch automatically. Besides having a convenient thumbnail preview of each layer, you can also select or deselect which ones get imported. Other options include maintaining editable layer styles, conversion to movie clips, compression and how layers are distributed in the timeline (layers or frames).

6 The shoulder should rotate where it meets the torso, and the forearm should rotate at the elbow.

7 The image of President Bush is easily found by doing an image search on the Web. Assets like the hands can be shot with your own camera and edited in Photoshop.

8 Reuse the arm assets for the legs by copying and pasting them to new layers. Then scale and stretch the copied version and align it to your character as the thigh and calf.

3 Flash also offers a PSD Importer preference panel that allows you to set your own defaults for each option. Just go to Edit > Preferences and click on the PSD File Importer category in the left column.

4 You may prefer to convert your images to symbols after importing. Keep your library organized by using symbol names the same as the names of your images.

5 Edit the center point of each symbol using the Free Transform tool **Q**.

9 The pelvis area was created with a shape and a bitmap fill from one of the imported bitmap images. Use the Gradient Transform tool **F** to scale it to show only the blue fabric.

10 In frame 1, pose your character based on your initial sketch. You can choose to have your sketch to the side or directly underneath your symbols. Whichever way you prefer, the main objective is to position your character in this same gesture. In your second keyframes, pose your character in its final state using your sketch as a guide. You can't flip your symbols horizontally or you will ruin the motion tween.

133

Motion guides (JibJab)

MOTION GUIDE LAYERS let you create paths along which you can tween instances of symbols, grouped objects, or text blocks. You can link as many layers as you want to a Motion Guide layer and have multiple objects follow the same path. A normal layer that is linked to a Motion Guide layer becomes a guided layer.

Motion guides are useful because, without them, a normal motion tween is linear, meaning it moves in a straight line only. If your object needs to move along a curve, a Motion Guide is necessary.

1 Create a Motion Guide layer for the left hand by selecting the hand layer and clicking the Motion Guide layer button in the Timeline panel.

2 The hand layer will automatically be linked as a guided layer. Draw your desired path using the Pencil or Pen tool.

6 Add a motion guide for each additional object you need to animate along an arc and draw the appropriate path needed.

7 Using a combination of motion guides, paths, transformation and tweens, you can animate any object in any direction you prefer.

3 Make sure Snap is selected (magnet icon) and drag your symbol until it snaps to your motion guide.

4 Add additional keyframes as necessary and snap your object to the path. Use the Free Transform tool to rotate your symbol as well.

5 In your last frame, snap your symbol to the end of your motion guide and add your final transformation.

HOT TIP

Test your work often by using Ctrl + Enter. Flash will generate an SWF file and play it for you within the Flash authoring environment. This SWF can be found in the same directory where you saved your FLA file.

8 The legs and feet do not need to be guided along a motion path since they only move in linear directions.

9 The final step is to place your character in its intended environment by adding a background. The American flag shown here was edited in Photoshop and imported into a layer below all the other layers.

SHORTCUTS
MAC WIN BOTH

Walk cycle

1 Design your character in three-quarter view. At this angle the character is simply easier to animate – especially when it comes to walk cycle animations. Next, convert your entire character and all its parts into a Graphic symbol. You will be working entirely inside this symbol to create your walk cycle.

2 Let's concentrate on just one leg for now. In fact, turn all other layers off so only one leg of your character is visible. This character's leg is made up of three different symbols: an upper thigh, a lower leg and a sneaker. This is a straightforward setup with enough flexibility for a simple walk cycle.

4 Notice that I didn't use the same sneaker for every frame. Depending on the position of the leg, I duplicated the original symbol, gave it a new name and edited its shape to reflect its new position. This is the type of detail I love to add to my animations and I really feel, as subtle as it may be, that it adds a lot to the overall look and feel of the character's movements.

8 Feel free to experiment with the number of frames between each of your leg positions. You can have more frames for when the foot is sliding back along the ground (so it travels slower) and fewer frames while the leg is off the ground (so it travels quicker), returning it rapidly to its initial position. This can create the illusion that the character is heavy, or perhaps carrying something heavy. If you do the opposite and have the foot slide quickly across the ground and slower when off the ground, it may suggest your character is on a slippery surface, such as ice.

LET'S FACE IT, as an animator you are eventually going to be faced with the task of making somebody or something walk. For whatever reason, newcomers to animation regard walk cycles as being extremely difficult. Why? I won't lie to you, they are. Well, in an anatomically accurate way, they can be very challenging. As an animator, you will find it nearly impossible to avoid the walk cycle, so it may be best to face your fear head-on right now. You just might learn that walk cycles aren't all that difficult to accomplish. There are several ways to make the task of animating a walk cycle very difficult or relatively easy. Let's examine the easy way.

The best way to create a walk cycle in Flash is to animate the character walking in place, as if on a conveyor belt. The main idea here is to drag an instance of this looping walk cycle animation to the stage and use a motion tween to animate the character walking across the scene. We'll get more into that after we tackle the actual walk cycle.

3 Position the leg into several major walk positions using keyframes. Start with the leg planted firmly on the ground. The next position is the foot still on the ground but bent so the heel is up off the ground. Then create another keyframe and position the leg just before it is lifted off the ground. Next, position the leg completely off the ground and in its most rearward position. The final keyframe shows the leg is in its most forward position off the ground. Use the Free Transform tool to rotate each leg symbol until it

is in the desired position. Notice there are several slightly different shapes to the sneaker based on the amount of weight (or lack of) being placed upon it. When it is fully compressed on the ground its bottom edge is flat. Just before it's lifted off the ground, it is bent just after the toe. When it is entirely off the ground, its bottom edge is slightly rounded. These may seem like very insignificant details, but in the grand scheme of things, they can make all the difference.

5 Turn on the Onionskin tool and adjust the playhead brackets so you can use your established leg positions as references. Create keyframes across all layers that contain your leg symbols.

6 Use the Free Transform tool **Q** to rotate and move each leg symbol into an intermediate position relative to the keyframes you already created. The number of frames between the major leg positions will determine the characteristics of the walk cycle.

7 Experiment with the frames between each leg position. Adding more frames when the foot is sliding back along the ground will create the effect of the character gripping the surface. Add fewer frames while the leg is returning to its initial position.

9 Play back your animation constantly so you can get real-time visual feedback as to your process. This type of animation work is trial and error and depends on your personal animation style to get the walk cycle to look and feel good to you. Don't get frustrated, it simply takes practice. Sometimes it helps to not think of it as an actual leg. Try to imagine it's not a leg at all but some kind of mechanical assembly like a basic pulley or lever system. This thought process make animating less daunting and a lot more fun.

Open the "**leg_simulation.fla**" from the included source CD. This FLA contains an example of a walk cycle experiment. I made it to show how a walk cycle can be thought of in mechanical terms. It was a fun experiment because it removes the intimidation factor that is associated with animating a walk cycle.

SHORTCUTS
MAC **WIN** **BOTH**

Continued...

Walk cycle (cont.)

ONCE YOU ARE finished creating enough keyframes and leg positions, and you are satisfied with the movement of your leg, we can now move on to the other leg. Since you already animated one leg, there is no reason to start from scratch with the second leg (unless the other leg is designed differently). Therefore, delete the other leg entirely from the stage. Seriously, go ahead and delete it. We don't need it any more. Trust me.

10 Hold down the *Shift* key to select multiple layers and drag them to the trashcan icon or click on the trashcan icon to delete them from the timeline.

11 Select the entire range of frames and layers of the leg you previously animated. Right-click (Control + click) over the highlighted area and select "Copy Frames" from the context menu.

15 Select this entire range of frames and layers by clicking and dragging across all of them.

16 Click and drag this entire range of frames and layers to the left until they start on frame 1. Remove the residual frames by selecting them and "Removing" them from the right-click context menu.

20 As we did with the leg animations, animate just one of your character's arms and then copy and paste its keyframes into a new layer(s) to achieve the second arm. Select the first half of your arm/hand animation and place it after the latter half of the animation.

21 Select and drag the entire arm/hand animation so it starts again on frame 1 and remove the residual frames that are left behind.

12 Add a new layer below your existing leg, select the entire range of frames, right-click over them and select "Paste Frames" from the context menu.

13 Lock all layers except these three you just copied and pasted. Select the first half of this duplicated leg animation by clicking and dragging across layers and frames.

14 Click and drag the entire section of highlighted frames down the timeline and place it after the latter half of the animation.

17 Using Edit Multiple Frames, select the new leg symbols and use the arrow keys to nudge them to the right and up slightly. This will help separate the two leg assemblies.

18 Apply a color tint to the leg symbols using black with approximately 30% strength. This gives the illusion the back leg is in shadow and helps create a sense of depth.

19 Animate the arm and hands by rocking them back and forth. You can use frame-by-frame or motion tweens depending on your needs.

HOT TIP

Be careful when using the Edit Multiple Frames feature. Make sure only the layers you want to edit are unlocked and all other layers are locked to avoid accidents.

22 Turn on Edit Multiple Frames again and select this entire range of arm/hand symbols. Click on them once with the Selection tool and apply the same color tint as the legs.

23 With Edit Multiple Frames still turned on, use the arrow keys to nudge them up and to the right slightly.

24 You can add to your walk cycle animation by adding some motion to its head and body. It comes down to personal preference and your individual animation style.

SHORTCUTS
MAC WIN BOTH

5 Advanced walk cycle

Contributed by Ben Palczynski
www.hiylea.com

THIS IS AN EXAMPLE of a traditional walk cycle animation where each frame is drawn completely by hand. What makes this particular animation "advanced" is that it requires not only drawing skills, but a sense of rhythm and timing. Ben makes it look easy, but with some dedication and practice, you can achieve great results.

One of the most well known and highly praised resources for character animation is *The Animator's Survival Kit* (Richard Williams). Williams explains everything you could ever want to know about all kinds of walk cycles and it's a reference no animator should be without. It's one of those books that should be next to your workspace at all times.

1 Pick a starting point to draw. The initial step as the front foot contacts the ground will do. It helps to use a horizontal guide to help keep things aligned and level.

2 Now draw the halfway position where the standing leg is straight and central. Turn on the Onionskin tool to use the previous drawing as your reference for scale and alignment.

5 Turn onionskinning on over the whole animation so you can look for the arcs of motion to check that things are generally lined up. If something is jittering in your animation this can help you spot where it is.

8 Drag this nested walk cycle to a new layer on the main timeline and motion tween it across the stage.

9 The head "turn" uses the same "globe" technique as shown in Chapter 3 (Masking).

3 Continue drawing the key main poses using the Onionskin tool to reference your previous keyframes.

4 Now do the poses in between these positions. The more keyframes and poses you add, the smoother and slower your animation will be. Experiment with frame rate and number of keyframes for your walk cycle.

6 Next, center the drawings so you can create a nested loop. Combine any layers you have for each frame, turn on Edit Multiple Frames and span all keyframes using the Frame Indicator brackets. Use the Align panel to center them all.

7 Place these keyframes in a symbol if they aren't already. Draw your character or drag pre-made body parts from the Library into a new layer above your walk cycle. Align each body part according to each sketch for each keyframe.

HOT TIP

When animating a walk cycle, it's sometimes a good idea to start off by animating the character literally walking across the screen – one image positioned after another like the thumbnails along the top and bottom of these pages. This might help you fine-tune the overall mechanics and the rhythm of your walk cycle.

10 To prevent your character's feet from slipping along the surface as it walks across the stage, set the symbol to graphic and playback to loop. Turn on the Onionskin tool and make sure that the feet overlap fully when they're placed on the ground. The advantage of having the walk cycle nested in a single symbol is the ability to scale the walk cycle quickly and easily. You can also flip the walk cycle horizontally to make the character walk in either direction.

SHORTCUTS
MAC WIN BOTH

141

Anticipation

1 Here the character is in its initial position. Not much going on in terms of action but we can assume he might do something due to the slight tension in his stance and his hands being in close proximity to both holstered guns.

BY DEFINITION, anticipation is the preparation for a particular action or movement. It can also be used in animation to attract the viewer's attention to a specific event that is about to occur. An example of this would be an archer pulling an arrow back along its bow or a baseball player raising his arm to throw a ball. Anticipation can also be used to build suspense in a scene. It tells the viewer something is about to happen, and the longer the anticipation is, the more suspenseful it can be.

Anticipation is critical to making believable animation. Without anticipation, your animation may appear too abrupt and unnatural. It is important as an animator to study from life and notice how we move and react anatomically.

4 The first step shows the character still on one foot but also leaning back a little further and crouching lower with all his weight on this one leg. This is obviously not a comfortable gesture and could not be held for very long. Hence the anticipation that something is about to happen.

2 To anticipate the action, animate the cowboy in the opposite direction he will be moving. Make a new keyframe across all layers where the next position change will occur and use the Free Transform tool **Q** to rotate and position your character. Apply a motion tween and some easing out to imply physical tension within our character.

3 Sometimes an animation requires more than one keyframe position to achieve the right movement and gesture. For this particular animation I used four different gestures for the anticipation animation, each with a motion tween and some easing applied.

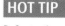

HOT TIP

Refer to the topic in this chapter on "Hinging body parts" to help you rotate symbols based on a customized center point.

5 Here I am pushing the envelope by adding even more tension in the character's overall gesture. There's no doubt he is about to react in a very physical way.

6 Sir Isaac Newton showed us for every action there is an opposite but equal reaction. In keeping with this law of motion, animate the character moving in the opposite direction and ultimately performing the anticipatory action.

SHORTCUTS
MAC WIN BOTH

5
Drawing upon oneself

Contributed by Laith Bahrani
www.monkeehub.com
www.lowmorale.co.uk
www.jcbsong.co.uk

THE MOST COMMON technique I use to make a character or an object appear as if it's drawing itself into the scene is purely frame-by-frame animation anyone can achieve. Although the effect can be quite labor intensive, it can also be visually effective if you want to achieve a very organic hand-drawn effect. The basic principle involves starting with a finished drawing, and then over a series of keyframes, cutting away bits of the drawing with the Lasso tool. You will work backwards starting on what will eventually be the end keyframe of the animation. When you play back the animation from frame 1, the drawing will appear to draw itself. The same effect can be achieved by using a mask to reveal the character or object. I find this works best on areas of color as opposed to lines. Let's look at how you can incorporate both techniques to animate a chicken character to appear to draw itself.

1 The first step to animating the chicken character is to spend decades studying and sketching this wonderful species of bird. As you can see I skipped this part and just scanned in the first chicken I drew. Resize the scanned sketch into a workable and desirable size in Photoshop and then import it into Flash.

2 With the scanned sketch imported and on the stage, convert it to a movie clip. This will be the drawing guide and this is how I do a lot of my characters. Adjust the alpha of this "guide" to about 50% so the contrast of the lines you draw over it will be clearer.

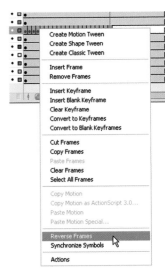

6 Now lock all the layers, then unlock just the body outline layer; doing this helps ensure you only work on the appropriate area. Insert a keyframe in frame 2. Select the Lasso tool **L** and cut away a small portion of the line.

7 Repeat this procedure of adding keyframes and removing small portions of your line work until they are completely removed. Select the entire range of keyframes, right-click over them and select "Reverse Frames" from the context menu. Repeat this process for all other outline layers.

3 Build the chicken character up in layers, keeping individual parts on separate layers. The techniques of splitting a character up are fairly universal and logical – head/body/arms/legs/eyes/mouth (or in this case beak). Create a new layer (above the guide) and, using the Paintbrush tool, draw the outline of the chicken's body.

4 When you've drawn the body outline, fill it with a color. Next click on the filled color area to select it, cut it using ⌘X ctrl X, create a new layer underneath the outline, and paste the fill using ⌘Shift V ctrl Shift V. Create one more layer, above the others, and draw the wing as an outline only. This gives you three layers for the body: one for the outline and one for the fill and wing.

5 Create the head and other parts in the same manner. Add a new layer for each new body – errr – chicken part, keeping them all separate. Remember to cut and paste each color fill to individual layers as well. If you are familiar with character animation, then you are already used to working with multiple layers and layer folders.

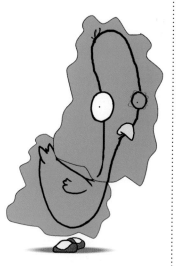

8 To create the effect of each color fill being "drawn" in, add a new layer above the body layer and convert it to a mask layer. In this layer create an irregular shape and convert it to a symbol.

9 Insert a keyframe in the mask layer in a frame at the end of your timeline. Position the symbol containing your shape so it completely covers your fill color for the chicken's body. Apply a motion tween to animate the mask so it "reveals" this color fill.

10 Add a mask layer and create new mask shapes for each color fill. Motion tween each one into position to reveal each chicken part. Lock all layers or publish your movie to see your animation effect.

SHORTCUTS
MAC WIN BOTH

5 Character animation
Looping backgrounds

Contributed by Kirk Millett
www.kirkmillett.com

1 The key to a seamless looping background is creating graphics that can be joined together seamlessly. The rock formation art is only slightly wider than the stage. By duplicating it and aligning its left edge with the right edge of the original, you can double its width.

BACKGROUNDS ARE CHARACTERS too. They can often take on personalities all their own and be brought to life just as much as a character (with eyes, a mouth, arms, legs, etc...) can. Backgrounds are also a classic way of complementing a character's actions within its environment. Remember Fred Flintstone's marathon runs through his own living room? Even though we'd see the same lamp and hanging picture pass by over and over, we remained focused on the action and story. An effective background loop will allow your viewers to do the same. The illusion is created by repeatedly tweening background art across the stage. The art has matching left and right edges so multiple copies can be seamlessly stitched together. A greater sense of depth can be achieved when individual background elements are placed on separate layers and moved at different speeds.

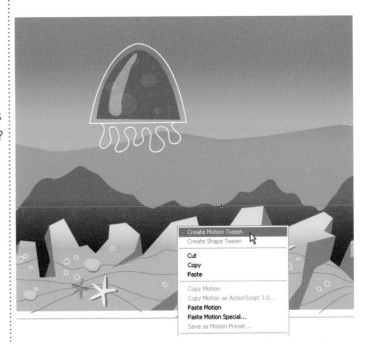

3 Position your objects on stage so they are aligned along the left edge of the stage. Right-click over them and select Create Motion Tween. Flash will create motion spans for you in each object's respective layers. The duration of each tween needs to be consistent, ending on the same frame number to allow the animation to loop seamlessly. Drag the right edge of each span to the right to accommodate the overall length of the timeline. This particular animation is 162 frames long. The trick here is the ability to "tile" your background graphics so they seamlessly align with each other when positioned horizontally.

2 Join and group multiple art copies on each layer. The back layer should have shorter art and use more duplication than the foreground layer. This will allow the back layer to move more slowly than the foreground layer, even though their tweens will use the same amount of frames. This is commonly referred to as a "2.5D" effect since

it creates the illusion of a third dimension (Z-axis), but you never leave Flash's two-dimensional environment. That third dimension simply doesn't exist except in the viewer's mind as they watch the foreground and background elements move across the screen at different rates.

4 Place the frame indicator in the last frame of your timeline. Position the background graphic so that it aligns perfectly with the instance in the first keyframe. It's good practise to check the alignment of these graphics by testing your movie several times.

5 Adding a foreground element can add a convincing sense of depth to the overall scene. Because the plant is closer to us in relation to the other elements, it moves at a higher speed.

6 The central character or object can also have movement. The squash and stretch motion of the jellyfish clip completes the illusion of motion across a seemingly never-ending underwater terrain. Here I have taken this illusion even further by duplicating the jellyfish and animating them in the opposite direction of the scrolling background. This suggests even faster movement and suggests the jellyfish may be racing each other.

Tradigital animation

THE FUSION OF TRADITIONAL and digital animation has given us "tradigital" animation. I don't know who invented the term but the effect was first shown to me by Ibis Fernandez (www.2dcgi.com), a well known and talented animator who blew me away when he sent me a sample of this technique a few years ago. Up until that point in my career, I had been using Flash for four years and thought I knew every trick in the book. It was clear to me I had more to learn.

Tradigital animation is the result of traditional animation techniques translated by the use of digital tools. The end result may look traditional, but the process is very different and less time-consuming. When a client deadline is looming, traditional animation goes out the window. A common argument among traditionalists is that tweens are too easy to use and often become relied upon for every aspect of an animation. This may result in your animation looking very mechanical and stiff. So where do you draw the line (sorry, bad pun)? What technique should you use? Motion tweens? Shape tweens? Frame by frame?

Answer: All of the above. Don't limit yourself to just one technique if you don't have to. Use the technique that the action calls for, even if it means combining two or more techniques. What is so impressive about this particular technique is the fluidity of the movement you can achieve. Draw image "A" and then image "B" with the Line (or Pencil) tool, and then with each line segment on its own layer, apply the shape tween from "A" to "B". Merge all your layers, clean up your lines, add some fills and shading - *voila*! You're a "tradigitalist".

1 For this technique to be a success, you need two different drawings of your character or object. Object Drawing mode is highly recommended here as each stroke will remain as a separate object that can still be edited. It is also critical because you will later distribute each stroke to its own layer.

2 Insert a blank keyframe (F7) in a new frame (frame 30 will do), and draw the new angle of your character or object. The trick here is to use the same number of strokes as you did in the first drawing. You could also choose to insert a keyframe (F6) and edit the same strokes to reflect your new angle.

6 Make sure you have the Merge Layers extension installed (see Chapter 12 and the source CD). Make sure all layers and keyframes are selected and go to Commands > Merge Layers. This will run the JSFL command, which will compress all keyframes and layers to one single layer for you. The time you just saved will allow you to grab another cup of coffee.

7 You can delete all the old layers as they will all be empty after the merge. Go to File > Save As and save this file with a new name. This is important because you may decide to make some changes to your image at some point in the future. After all layers are merged, this becomes very difficult.

3 For both drawings, select all of your strokes, right-click over them and select Distribute to Layers from the context menu. Since this will create a whole new set of layers for each drawing, you will need to select all the keyframes for one drawing and drag them to the other drawing's layers.

4 Drag across all layers, right-click and select Create Shape Tween from the context menu. Previous versions of Flash didn't offer this option in the context menu. If you are using an older version of Flash, apply the shape tween using the Properties panel or drop-down menus. Now is the time to add easing if preferred.

5 Next you need to prepare your layers for merging. Drag across all layers and frames, selecting them all in black. Hit the F6 key to convert all the shape tweens to keyframes. While selected, remove the shape tween using the Tween drop-down menu in the Properties panel. Go to File > Save and save your work at this point.

Flash doesn't have a built-in "Merge Layers" feature. Not sure why this feature was never considered but with JSFL (JavaScript Flash), we can make our own features. David Wolfe has created a "Merge Layers" extension for Flash that is available on the source CD in this book. Techniques like those used for the "tradigital" topic would take at least five times longer to complete without the use of a Merge Layers extension. So make sure you check out how to use this handy extension in Chapter 12 and install it before attempting the technique on these pages.

8 Next, you need to break apart strokes from the Object Drawing mode. Why? Because if you have overlapping strokes and want to add color fills to your image, it needs to be flattened one step further for editing. Turn on the Edit Multiple Frames feature and adjust the frame indicator brackets to span all keyframes. Break apart (Ctrl + B) to merge all strokes.

9 Use the Selection tool while holding down the Shift key to select all unwanted strokes and delete them. In this situation it is simply a fact of life that, as an animator, eventually you will have to perform the tedious chore of cleaning up after yourself or, even worse, someone else's work.

10 As tedious as the last step was, here's your reward – a very slick looking animation that looks like it was made using three dimensions. But it gets even better when you add color and shading.

Continued...

Tradigital animation (cont.)

11 Once all your strokes are connected and cleaned up, mix your colors and start filling. You will need to apply all color fills across all keyframes by hand. Flash has no automatic way of doing this for you.

12 Occasionally you may find an area of your image will not accept the fill color. Usually the cause for this is a gap between strokes that is hard to see. Make sure Snap is turned on and use the Selection tool to drag their end points until they "snap" together.

13 Let's take this effect to the next level by adding shading. Add two new layers above your animation and draw two shapes in each new layer. Use the color black mixed with about 30% alpha. Make sure the brush has Smoothing set to 100. The fewer vector points the better.

  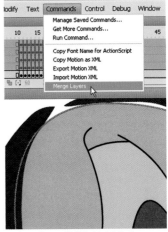

17 Turn on the Edit Multiple Frames feature and make sure the Frame Indicator brackets span all keyframes. Select all (Ctrl + A) and break apart (Ctrl + B) all Drawing Model objects to merge all the strokes together.

18 Copy all frames of your outline from the previous step and paste them into a new layer above your shading layers. Make sure all other layers are locked, turn on Edit Multiple Frames, and select all strokes and change their color to bright red or something in contrast to the character itself.

19 Turn off Edit Multiple Frames, and unlock the two layers containing the shading animations. Select all frames across all three of these layers and go to Commands > Merge Layers to compress them down to one layer. Delete the remaining empty layers.

14 Insert a keyframe in both layers in the last frame of your animation. Move the left shape about 20 pixels to the left and the right shape the same distance to the right. Use the Selection tool to bend their outlines to reflect the new contour of your character and apply shape tweens.

15 Remember the previously saved version of this animation? Open it and find the layers containing the outline strokes of your character. Select them and Copy/Paste Frames, into a new document. You will use these strokes to "cut" away the shading you will not need.

16 Select all frames and layers and convert them to keyframes (F6). While they are still selected, remove the tween from the Tween drop-down menu (Properties) and merge all layers using the Merge Layers JSFL extension (Commands > Merge Layers).

20 Use the Selection tool to click anywhere outside the shapes to deselect them. Select the shaded area outside of your character's outline and delete it. Repeat this procedure for every keyframe.

21 The final step is to double-click the red stroke (double-clicking selects all segments in the stroke), and delete it. Repeat this for every keyframe until you are left with just the shading shapes inside the contours of the original character.

22 Next, test your movie and sit back to enjoy the fruits of your labor. This technique is great when you want to add some realism and drama to your shot. But remember to plan ahead carefully to avoid having to spend more time making revisions.

How did I get here?

I SPEAK AT MANY CONFERENCES, schools and user groups throughout the country. It's a very fun thing to be able to do as it allows me to not only share tips and tricks; it also connects me with other designers and animators on a personal level. Don't get me wrong; email, chat and phone are great ways to communicate, but they are no substitute for sharing the same physical space with other developers, designers and animators who all share the same interest.

Being able to travel to conferences in various cities and connect with users from all over the world has given me the ability to tap into the pulse of the culture that surrounds Flash. I hear first hand the thoughts, opinions, gripes and questions users have about this industry. There is always one particular question I am asked by students, teachers and fellow users: "How did you get to where you are now?" Now, I am very well known for dragging out even the shortest of stories and the answer to this question is lengthy to begin with. With limited space on these pages I will give it my best shot to provide you with the abridged version.

The road that led me to where I am now was, to say the least, full of twists, turns, roundabouts and in some areas, U-turns the led to dead ends. It was hardly eight lanes of traffic-free straight-aways with clear signs with arrows pointing me away from hazards and obstacles. But somehow, throughout the journey, I still managed to make all the correct turns, even when I didn't know where each one would eventually take me. I was somehow able to remain on course, towards the direction that led to me to where I am now. Ten years ago if you told me I was going to be a successful freelance animator, I would have laughed. Even the realization of it now makes me chuckle to myself.

I first started using Flash in 1999 and had never seen anything like it. At that time I was a Creative Director for a small animation studio in the Boston area and we turned to Flash as our main animation program. Most of the content we created was for broadcast television and my understanding of how to deliver engaging content for the Web was minimal at best. That was all about to change. Shockwave contracted us to create an animated series for their site **www.shockwave.com**. I was already a fan of Shockwave, which made this project particularly exciting. It became a crash course on how to use

Flash to create animation optimized for the Web that also had a fully functional game incorporated into a preloader for dial-up users. As a company we had no experience developing for the Web. As an individual, this was a brave new frontier. To make it even more interesting, I had strict deadlines to meet, which all but eliminated the research and development portion of the process. I was smack in the middle of all this unfamiliar technology, directly between the Shockwave producers and my own bosses. All eyes were on me to figure out the artistic and technical issues involved with delivering engaging and interactive content. Funny thing was, I was very new to vector-based animation and my skill level with ActionScript was not too much beyond a gotoAndPlay command. Despite my technical shortcomings, I embraced the challenge. Ask me if I was under-qualified and I would answer "yes", but not without the confidence to deliver the project complete and on time. It just meant I needed to roll up my sleeves a little further.

The series was a success. I managed to fulfill every technical and artistic requirement and delivered it on time. None of which would have been possible for me without the help of the Flash community. I frequented the Macromedia Flash forums and various online resources such as **www.moock.org**, **www.were-here. com** and **www.ultrashock.com**, where I found an endless community of users willing to provide a helping hand. The most important aspect of this experience wasn't about the amount of learning I achieved, but rather the community and its selflessness to help others. My community involvement became a daily ritual, and over time, I found myself providing more answers than questions. Not only did I advance quickly, but I made many friends and networked myself into a few high-profile freelance gigs. I started to specialize in animation and motion graphics for the Web. I was hooked.

It was an exciting time to be a Flash user as the Internet was literally bursting with dynamic and engaging content. It was the beginning of the "dot-com" boom and little did I know just how much of an effect it would have on my career.

(...cont.)

A couple of years later, Macromedia announced the creation of the "Team Macromedia" program and soon after a Macromedia employee suggested that I personally submit my application. I wasn't sure exactly why but I decided to fill out the application anyway. To my surprise, I was accepted into the TMM program. I was now officially recognized as a member of the Flash community by the company that makes Flash. This was so cool! I was now one of "those" guys. Since the Adobe/Macromedia acquisition, this program continues under the name Adobe Certified Experts, which I guess makes me not only a "team" member but also an "expert". But as far as I'm concerned, I am just a user of Adobe's products, still working in the trenches just like everybody else, exactly where I want to be.

My community affiliation has provided many opportunities to be a featured speaker at various conferences and user groups. These experiences have given me an up-close and personal way to network with peers from around the world, not to mention how much fun it is to be among hundreds and, sometimes, thousands of users who have the same excitement and passion as I do.

Aside from populating the online Flash forum with technical answers, I found myself delivering live Flash technical presentations via Adobe Connect and what is commonly referred to as "Tech Wednesdays". One such presentation has been overwhelmingly popular (**http://adobe. breezecentral.com/p46515568/**). This was my very first recorded Breeze presentation and it has been one of the most popular resources for Flash character design and animation on the Web. The surprising aspect of this presentation was that I was merely filling in for the original presenter, who had to cancel last minute. With no time to prepare anything, I simply demonstrated what I do on a daily basis for clients and sometimes for self-amusement. It was just another day at work for me, but this time I had the world looking over my shoulder. Luckily it was a topic that many users were very interested in. Due to its popularity I was asked to host more online presentations, all of which were recorded and featured on Adobe's website. This is one of my most rewarding community experiences due to the number of users who continue to benefit from these recordings.

Ask me how I ended up here and I will tell you it was the result of hard work, a little luck and the generosity of the Flash community. Ask me why I volunteer so much of my time helping others, and I will tell you, because I remember how precious the help was from others when I needed it most. I am proud of my accomplishments as a Flash user and when there's an opportunity to pass along this knowledge to others, we can all benefit. It's what makes the community vibrant and alive for the benefit of all who wish to get involved. Flash is just a tool, but it is the community that surrounds this tool that transforms it into a culture.

http://my.adobe.acrobat.com/p46515568/
http://www.adobe.com/devnet/flash/articles/design_character.html
http://www.adobe.com/devnet/flash/articles/adv_char_anima.html
http://www.adobe.com/devnet/flash/articles/tween_macrochat.html

■ One day your client may request that their online content be re-purposed for video. They may look to you for answers as to how possible this process is. Rest assured, Flash to video is widely produced for a variety of broadcast content. The line between online and off-line Flash content is officially blurred.

6

Flash to video

FLASH IS EVERYWHERE. Not only is Flash developed
for online and offline movies, websites, games and
applications, but also for DVD and broadcast television. In
fact, my first years as a Flash user were spent authoring
Flash content for several broadcast animated series.
Exporting from Flash to video formats (QuickTime and
AVI) to be imported and edited in an Avid workstation
was my only authoring requirement of Flash. I had no
knowledge of Flash for the Web, including ActionScript,
optimizing, preloaders and even buttons of any kind. It
was analog Flash at its purest and that was the Flash
world I lived in.

Document setup

SOME OF THE most popular Flash to video questions I am asked are: What Flash content can be and cannot be exported to video? Why do some animations play in video format while others do not? What frame rate do I use? What is NTSC? What is PAL? What is the resolution for a 16:9 screen? What is the correct stage size? Should I be concerned about color correction? What video format should I export to? Do you export the audio from Flash? Are you getting enough sleep?

(OK, that last one was from my mother, but you get the idea.) This entire chapter is devoted to the topic of getting your Flash project to video format. Sounds simple enough but there's a lot to know, so let's boogie.

1 Let's start with the basics and open a new Flash document. Open the Document Properties panel using ⌘ ctrl J or click the "Size" button in the Properties panel. Here you can determine the width and height of the movie and its frame rate. But before we change anything we need to decide what aspect ratio we are authoring to.

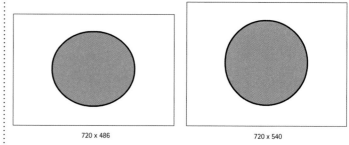

720 x 486   720 x 540

3 NTSC doesn't use square pixels; they are rectangular. A problem arises when you develop content for video on your computer because you are creating square pixels to be displayed as rectangular pixels. That means your video will look slightly stretched. To compensate for this, adjust the width of the movie so that the aspect ratio is 720 x 540.

720x576

5 PAL (Phase Alternating Line), the predominant video standard outside the Americas, also uses the 4:3 aspect ratio but uses a 720 x 576 pixel aspect ratio. The frame rate is 25 fps. PAL has a greater resolution than NTSC and therefore has a better picture quality. Its higher color gamut level produces higher contrast levels as well. But the lower frame rate, compared to NTSC's frame rate, will not be as smooth.

6 Film uses 24 fps, which is also a popular frame rate among animators. Although you can use 24 fps in your Flash project, when you export it to video, you will need to convert the frame rate as well. This is easily done during the export process by specifying the appropriate frame.

Standard Television
4:3

Widescreen Television
16:9

2 NTSC (National Television Standards Commission), the video standard used in North America and most of South America, uses a 4:3 aspect ratio, which essentially means the width and height of a standard television set. To break it down in even simpler terms, 4:3 means that for

every four units wide, the picture is three units high. Apply this formula to a 16:9 screen and you'll get 16 units of width for every nine units of height. Simple arithmetic so far but it's about to get tricky.

4 NTSC uses a frame rate of 29.97 fps. You can export Flash movies that have different frame rates such as 12, 15, or 24 fps and convert them to 30 with video editing software, although a movie converted from 12 to 30 fps will not look as smooth as a movie originally authored at 30 fps.

You can save your NTSC Flash document as a Template if you plan to create multiple files (File > Save as Template...). You can also create your own template categories by creating new folders in the "Templates" folder on your local hard drive where Flash CS4 is installed.

7 Exporting your movie as a PNG image sequence is often the best and most popular method. Go to File > Export Movie and select PNG Sequence as your format. I highly recommend creating a new folder to save your image sequence to since the number of images Flash creates is directly related to the number of frames in your animation

(which can easily be hundreds or even thousands). A PNG sequence insures your animation is frame accurate with lossless compression. If you are using After Effects to further refine or add effects to your animation, a PNG sequence import is not only supported, but is also treated as a single object, making it easy to manage.

159

Ape Escape

APE ESCAPE IS BEST known as a platform game for Sony's Playstation gaming console. But it is also an animated series for television. Recently I was asked to help animate a few scenes and thought it would make for a great example of how a professional production creates animation with Flash as its primary tool for television broadcast. Many of the animators worked virtually, including myself. We shared files via FTP (File Transfer Protocol) and we were initially given storyboards in Quicktime format to work from. The main characters were already set up for us in Flash and each episode was broken down into several small chunks of time – specifically from 5 to 10 seconds in length. This created more files but they were very small in size and easily shared via the Web. All we had to do was upload the Flash source file so that the post-production crew could then export a PNG image sequence or Quicktime movie and edit all the scenes together using a video editing tool.

As you can see here the duration of this scene is 2.3 seco The entire duration of this shot is only about 5 seconds. Each episode is a total 2 minutes in duration, made up of several 5–10 second shots. Each 2-minute episode could take anywhere from 10 to 20 different scenes.

Ape Escape 2 © 2003 Sony Computer Entertainment, Inc.
Ape Escape animated series © 2008 Bellport Cartoon Company, Inc. and HFP Productions 3, LLC.

All animation is either on the main timeline or nested in graphic symbols, keeping it in sync with the main timeline. The rule is, if it plays inside of the Flash authoring tool when you scrub the playhead or play your animation, it will export to video format successfully. This is true for all versions of Flash.

The safety zone contains guides for action and text as well as a 4:3 aspect ratio.

The Flash stage is set to 1920 × 1080 HDTV widescreen aspect ratio and the frame rate is set to 24 fps.

161

Title and action safety

TELEVISIONS DO NOT generally display the entire width and height of your movie. In almost all cases, televisons will show a smaller portion of the true display size. Using a visual guide that represents the potential stage area in danger of being cropped will help guarantee that what you create in Flash shows up in its entirety on a variety of television sets.

1 There's nothing worse than finding out too late that the title sequence you labored over for ten hours appears on most televisions with several characters cropped, or is even completely invisible. To prevent this, you need to define which area is considered the safe zone within the dimensions of your movie. There are two safe zones to consider: the action-safe zone and the title-safe zone.

2 The title-safe zone is smaller than the action-safe zone because it is much more important to ensure that all titles are clearly legible without any chance of a single letter being cropped. For this reason, the title-safe zone lies 20% in from the absolute edge of the video. When you add titles to your movie, make sure they are positioned entirely within this safer title-safe zone to avoid being cropped.

3 The action-safe zone lies 10% in from the absolute edge of the video. You can assume that everything falling within this zone will appear on a television screen. Anything outside this zone can potentially be cropped and not visible. Compose your scenes based on the area within the action safety zone, assuming this will be the only area not cropped by the majority of televisions.

4 Place the title-safe zone in your Flash project on its own layer above all other content. When you are ready to export to video, delete this layer to prevent it from being included in the video file. If you don't want to delete it from your document, just convert the layer to a guide layer. Guide layers will not be included in your final export.

Convert the layer containing the title-safe graphic to Outline mode to reduce its visual impact and make it less noticeable. You can easily change the color of Outline mode by clicking on the color swatch in the layer and selecting a different color in the swatch panel.

5 View > Pasteboard will allow you to see the work area beyond the stage dimensions. This is useful for working with graphics that extend beyond the width and height of the stage. Having the title-safe graphic visible will indicate where the stage is in relation to your artwork. This is particularly useful for simulating camera moves such as panning and zooming.

Safe colors

IN PREVIOUS VERSIONS of Flash, support for video export was lacking in several areas. Dynamic content such as ActionScript, button symbols and movie clips could not be exported to a fixed-frame video format. These types of Flash object could only be supported in the Flash player during runtime. Any animations nested inside a movie clip would not render beyond their first frame and any ActionScript in the movie would cause the export to video to fail and generate errors. Dynamic content and rendered video have always been two different animals never meant to play well together.

Welcome the Flash CS4 QuickTime Exporter. You now have the ability to export dynamically created Flash content including effects generated with ActionScript.

1 Your computer monitor is designed to display the full range of RGB color values (0–255). Television can only display a limited range of color values. There's a good chance you may be using colors in your Flash movie that fall outside the television value range, resulting in very noticeable color bleeding.

3 To add your new color as a swatch, use the drop-down menu in the upper right corner of the Color Mixer panel. An alternative method for adding colors to your Swatch panel is to hover over the empty area below the existing swatches. Your cursor will automatically become a paint bucket and when you click anywhere in this area, the current color will be added.

2 You will need to limit this range to between 16 and 235. The RGB color value of the darkest color (black) is 0-0-0. For television this must be limited to 16-16-16. This should be your new black color for any project exported to video. The RGB value of the lightest color (white) is 255-255-255. This must be limited to 235-235-235 for export to

video format. Since this will be the brightest color in your palette, it will appear to be stark white in comparison to all other colors. The color red has a tendency to bleed more than any other color so it may be a good idea to compensate more than you need to by lowering the value to around 200-16-16.

HOT TIP

Remember, Flash is resolution-free; as long as you are working in the correct aspect ratio, you can always resize when exporting without a loss in quality. If you have imported bitmaps in your Flash movie, you will want to use a width and height that is 100% of your final output to avoid having them scaled in Flash.

NTSC.clr

4 Sometimes the default color palette is not needed and simply gets in the way of your workflow. This is a good time to remove or replace the current swatches. You can start all over by mixing and adding new colors one at a time or by importing an existing color set, color table or even a

GIF file. From the drop-down menu choose Replace Colors and navigate to the *.clr, *.act or *.gif file containing the colors you want to use. Here I have imported an NTSC safety color palette provided by Warren Fuller (**www.animonger. com**). This palette is included on the source CD (NTSC.clr).

SHORTCUTS

MAC WIN BOTH

Safe colors (Kuler)

THE ADOBE KULER PANEL is new to Flash CS4. Access it by going to Windows > Extensions > Kuler. Kuler (pronounced *cooler*) began as a Web-based application (http://kuler.adobe.com/) for creating color themes that can be saved and shared with other Kuler users all over the world. The success of Kuler has spawned a vast community of designers from around the world as well as thousands of themes on the Kuler website that you

can browse and download to use in your own projects. Kuler is now integrated into Adobe Illustrator® CS4, Photoshop® CS4, InDesign® CS4, Fireworks® CS4, and Flash® CS4 Professional software. As a stand-alone color mixer, it provides several options the standard Flash color mixer lacks. Here I will show you how to use Kuler to mix NTSC safe colors to add to the Flash Swatch panel.

1 Open the Kuler panel and then click on the Create button to begin mixing your colors. The default theme shows a set of colors that follow the Analogous color rule. The Base Color is the color that determines the other colors in your theme using your selected color rule.

2 Select a different rule using the rule drop-down menu. Choice of rules include Analogous, Monochromatic, Triad, Complementary, Compound, Shades and Custom. For this example "Custom" will do. The Custom rule will unlink your colors so you can move the color markers around the wheel individually.

3 The first step to limiting the brightness of a color is simply to adjust the vertical brightness control. Slide the handle down until the brightest value is 235 or less to insure the color is not too bright for NTSC standards.

For a video on the Kuler panel, see www.adobe.com/go/lrvid4088_xp

For an article on Kuler and color inspiration, see Veerle Pieters' blog at http://veerle.duoh.com/blog/comments/adobe_kuler_update_and_color_tips/

Browse, search, and save themes directly from your desktop with the Adobe AIR™ application. Drag individual themes to your desktop, where they can be scaled to any size (requires Adobe AIR). http://www.adobe.com/go/kuler_air

HOT TIP

Double-click any of the swatches in the color group to set the color of the stroke or fill in Flash depending on which one is currently active.

4 Select the Shades rule to create different shades of the base color. If mixing NTSC safe colors, just pay attention to the RGB values and change them if necessary.

5 I like to add the theme to Flash's Swatches panel by clicking the Add To Swatches Panel button at the bottom of the panel.

6 You can also share your themes online by clicking the Save Theme button. Provide a descriptive name and click save. Then click on the Upload to Kuler button to share your theme with the Kuler community.

167

Keeping it all in sync

1 If your timeline contains movie clips, you must convert them to Graphic behavior. To convert a movie clip to a Graphic symbol, select the movie clip instance on the stage and change its behavior from Movie Clip to Graphic using the Properties panel. Then change its property from Single Frame to Loop or Play Once depending on your needs.

WE HAVE TWO OPTIONS for authoring Flash for video output. The old school method requires everything to be on the main timeline. Movie Clip symbols have to be avoided altogether since their timelines are independent of the main timeline and only render during runtime in the Flash Player.

Flash 8 introduced filters and the ability to add drop shadows, blurs and other cool effects to Movie Clip symbols. But due to the dynamic nature of movie clips, they had to be avoided as well. Flash CS3 introduced the Quicktime Exporter, which solves this problem and is a feature in Flash CS4 as well. We will take a look at that later in this chapter.

For now, let's take a look at the old school method of creating Flash animation for export to video. This is analog Flash in its purest form, straight-ahead timeline animation, streaming sound and nested Graphic symbols.

3 One of the disadvantages of using scenes is confusion during the editing process as it can be difficult to find assets within multiple scenes. Another disadvantage with multiple scenes is having more content in your FLA, which can result in a very large file size. This increases the chances of corruption and loss of work. It's usually better to work with several smaller files, then edit the individual exported video files together in your video editor.

5 Layer folders are a great way to organize your timeline, especially if your animation involves a great number of layers, which is often the case with animation. Layer folders combined with nesting animations can go a long way in making efficient timelines. You can place all your character animations inside a Graphic symbol. This makes it much easier to edit and control your entire scene from the main timeline if you need to position, scale, pan, and zoom as if playing the role of a Director. Since the nested animations are inside Graphic symbols, you can still scrub the timeline with the playhead to see the animations play.

2 Scenes are a great way to manage long timelines. For example, you could have your title sequence in scene 1, your story in scene 2 and ending credits in scene 3. Using scenes is similar to multiple files chained together since each scene has its own timeline. The timeline of each scene combines into a single timeline in the exported file. The advantage here is having the entire project in one FLA.

4 The Flash timeline has its own limitations. 16,000 is the number that represents the maximum number of layers in a single Flash movie as well as the maximum number of symbol instances and number of frames. It is rare to see this number reached in any situation, but it is good to understand the limitations in order to avoid them. A Flash document that is 16,000 frames long at 30 fps is nearly 9 minutes long. A file that large will cause problems even in the best situations. The file will take longer to open as well as to save. It will exhaust your system's resources

and make it harder to work with multiple Flash documents open at the same time. It will also take a very long time to export to video and will create an enormous file. If you export to AVI, you will very likely exceed the 2 GB limit that is placed on AVI files on most operating systems. Best practise is to break up your project into several smaller FLA files, typically between 30 and 60 seconds each. I often work with FLA files less than 20 seconds in length. It makes the entire process more manageable when animating, exporting and editing.

6 You can quickly expand all layer folders by right-clicking over any one of your folders and selecting "Expand All Folders" from the context menu. Collapsing all folders is done the same way.

7 To sync your animations to a soundtrack, import your Sound file and place it on the timeline in its own layer. You can drag it from the Library to the stage or use the Sound drop-down menu in the Properties panel to select the file. By default, the Sync setting will be Event and must be changed to Stream. The Stream behavior embeds the sound into the timeline and will be in sync with any timeline animation. You can adjust the height of a layer by right-clicking over the layer name and selecting Properties. In the Layer Properties panel you can set the layer height to as much as 300%. This can be useful if you want to see the waveform in as much detail as possible.

QuickTime Exporter

EXPORTING FLASH MOVIES to video format used to require that all animation be on the main timeline. Dynamic content such as ActionScript, button symbols and movie clips could not be exported to a fixed-frame video format. This included movie clip animations, filters, ActionScript and just about anything dynamically loaded into your SWF file.

Welcome the Flash CS4 QuickTime Exporter. You now have the ability to export dynamically created Flash content including effects generated with ActionScript as well as effects created with movie clips and filters.

Proceed with caution when using the Flash CS4 QuickTime exporter. If the dimensions

of your document are particularly large (for example, 720 x 540 pixels), it may be necessary to change the frame rate of the Flash movie to avoid dropping frames during the export process. Why does this happen? The QuickTime Exporter, during the export process, is actually capturing the playback of your movie as an SWF movie in the background. Various aspects of your animation can cause frames to be dropped and the exported QuickTime file to not be frame-specific as intended in the Flash timeline. A large stage size, a high frame rate, multiple filters and animated effects can all contribute to frames being dropped during the export process.

1 You have more than one option when you export your video, and there are slight differences depending on whether you are authoring in Mac OS or Windows. Basically it comes down to three different options: AVI (Audio Video Interleave), Apple QuickTime, or an image sequence. Formerly your choice of platform dictated your format. Macintosh users exported to QuickTime and Windows users exported to AVI. Now both formats are compatible across platforms.

2 When you export from Flash to QuickTime, you will have several options to choose from. Typically it is good practise to keep your movie as uncompressed as possible and at the highest color bit available. You can change the width and height of your movie based on a maintained aspect ratio, or you can choose to change the aspect ratio by deselecting this option. Select "Ignore stage color" to add a transparent alpha track to your video. You must select a video Compression Type that supports 32-bit encoding with an alpha channel such as Animation, PNG, Planar RGB, JPEG 2000, TIFF, or TGA. You must also select Millions of Color+ from the Compressor/Depth setting.

3 The Movie Settings panel allows you to adjust the video and sound settings. If you are exporting sound, you can set the amount of compression, sample rate, sample size and number of channels.
You can also prepare your movie for the Internet if it is intended for online viewing. Select "Fast Start" to allow the movie to start playing from a Web server before the movie has completely downloaded.
If you plan on importing your Flash animation to After Effects or Premiere, export as a PNG sequence. After Effects CS4 supports SWF format as well. So you can simply publish your Flash movie to SWF and import that into After Effects.

4 If you choose to click "Settings", the Standard Video Compression Settings will open, allowing you to refine how your movie will be exported. This is where you can select the compression type and frame rate, and click the QuickTime Settings button to select the type of compression desired. Typically no compression is best but I have had great results using the Animation codec. In this panel you can also adjust the color depth, change the frame rate (useful if your Flash movie isn't using a standard frame rate for video), as well as set the amount of keyframing and, once again, the size.

SHORTCUTS
MAC WIN BOTH

171

SWF2Video

THE FLASH QUICKTIME EXPORTER allows you to export dynamic content to the QuickTime video format. But dynamic content that pushes the limits of the Flash player may have undesirable results upon export. The process of the QuickTime Exporter is to capture each frame of your movie as it plays in the Flash player. This all happens behind the scenes during the export process. If the frame rate is relatively high and your movie contains animated movie clips with filters applied to them, the results may be dropped frames or a slow frame rate after exporting. The width and height of your movie may be a factor in how well the exporter performs. A larger stage translates to more data that have to be captured on the fly, with results dependent on the amount of RAM and your processor speed. A large stage, high frame rate, long timeline and multiple animations with some filter effects will most likely choke the Flash QuickTime Exporter.

You do have an alternative solution, however. Welcome SWF2Video, a powerful utility that uniquely supports the conversion of Flash SWF format to AVI. This conversion supports movie clips, ActionScript, user interactions and audio. SWF2Video can output an alpha channel to be used for compositing effects in video post-production. There is also an SWF2Video Plug-in for Adobe Premiere Pro to enable the import of SWF files directly into Premiere projects for editing.

SWF2Video can be found at **www.flashants.com** and is a valuable tool to have if your project contains dynamic content and requires output to video.

1 The SWF2Video IDE is amazingly simple. Upon launch there's little more than a window with the familiar File, Control, Options and Help menus. Select File > Open and navigate to your SWF. Open the File menu again and select Create AVI or Create Image Sequence. SWF2Video even supports batch processing of files. Using SWF2Video is super simple. Go to File > Open and locate the published SWF file on your hard drive. The first frame of your SWF movie will be displayed in the SWF2Video interface.

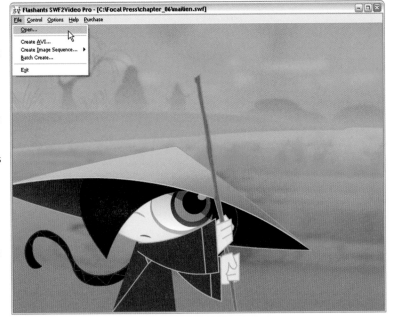

2 When you select Create AVI, the AVI Export Setting dialog box opens, allowing you to refine your movie considerably further.

The Sequence settings are as follows:

Skip "goto backward frame" in main timeline: If the Flash movie contains a loop in the main timeline by using the gotoAndPlay(0); command, select this option to break the loop by ignoring the ActionScript code.

Frame by frame in main timeline: Convert the main timeline animation into a keyframe sequence.

Normal: Convert with the movie's normal playback sequence, including movie clips and ActionScript events. For the Duration setting, specify the start and end points during export by entering the exact frame numbers.

Color depth: Select 24 bits RGB or 32 bits RGB with Alpha format. The 24-bit color setting represents eight bits for every RGB color value. The 32-bit color setting is the same as 24 bits with the addition of eight more bits representing the transparency of the color value.

Record from current SWF file: Record audio from the current SWF file and then merge it with the video.

Recording volume: Adjust the volume level of the waveform recording device.

From WAVE file: Use an external WAVE file to create your audio by clicking Browse to choose the WAVE file. The audio data of this WAVE file are merged with the video data; the audio in the original SWF file is ignored.

3 Clicking Select in the Video section opens the Video Compression dialog box. Here you can choose the appropriate compressor to apply to your video. Leave this set to Full Frames (Uncompressed) because this is always best when working with high-quality video.

4 The Seek Controller helps to browse into Flash movie's frames easily by dragging the slider bar or entering the frame number in the Current Frame field. It is a very handy tool to help you quickly and easily locate the frame number range in the Flash movie to convert.

SHORTCUTS
MAC WIN BOTH

173

Graphics tablets

THERE ARE SOME THINGS I JUST CAN'T WORK WITHOUT, and one of them is my Wacom tablets. They are indespensible when it comes to my workflow and actually save valuable production time on a daily basis.

My first experience with a Graphics tablet of any kind was during my employment at a small production company creating animated television shows. Early on we had very small budgets and therefore relatively cheap equipment to work with. We used Summasketch Graphics tablets (Summagraphics) and even though they got the job done, they were pretty clumsy to work with. The main reason was the lack of wireless technology – the stylus was not cordless. It constantly got in the way of my arm as I moved across the tablet's surface and would get pretty twisted and tangled. If you weren't careful you could easily get the cord on the wrong side of a full cup of coffee and with one artistic stroke of the stylus, end up with a huge mess. The learning curve was not so bad, however. It took me about three full days to get used to not looking where I was actually drawing. There's a slightly uncomfortable feeling of not looking at the actual surface where your pen meets the paper. Once I got used to looking at the computer display and not my own drawing hand, the next learning hurdle was the relationship of the tablet angle and the display angle. If my tablet was rotated as little as an inch or less, any vertical or horizontal lines became exponentially difficult to draw. Alignment between the tablet and monitor became important and soon I had a specific setup that worked for me, which was having the tablet to the right side of the computer and at a slight angle towards me. Some of the other animators had their tablet directly in front of them, center to their body. Of course left-handed people had their tablets to the left of the computer or centered. There was one particular illustrator who, being left-handed, used his tablet with his left hand and trained his right hand to use the mouse. Truly an ambidextrous advantage.

Eventually, as the company became more successful, the budgets grew. Better equipment was being purchased and soon we graduated to Wacom tablets. My appreciation for the quality of Wacom tablets is directly related to having used tablets of lesser quality. The look and feel of the Wacom tablet was truly awesome. Not only is the stylus cordless, but it requires no battery either. The tablet surface is super-smooth and a joy to work on. Some people find it to be too smooth and one nice trick is to tape a regular piece of copy paper to the tablet. The stylus will work fine and the extra friction lends to a more realistic drawing feel.

Wacom has recently introduced a new budget-friendly line of Graphics tablets called "Bamboo". There are two different kinds: the Bamboo and the Bamboo Fun. The Bamboo is 7.8 × 7.3" in size while the Bamboo Fun offers two different sizes: 8.4 × 7.3" or 11.0 × 9.3". Both share similar technical specs but when compared to the Intuos 3 line, they offer about half the features. But if you are on a budget, or you are more of a casual user, the Bamboo is very capable.

I have used tablets in various sizes: 4 × 6, 6 × 8, 9 × 12 and 12 × 12. My personal preference is the 6 × 8 and the 9 × 12 sizes. As Goldilocks found out while visiting the home of the three bears, these sizes are "just right". I don't have to physically move my hand and arm as much as I do with the 12 × 12 version and the 4 × 6 is simply too small for any serious graphics work. My 17" laptop display is in perfect harmony with the 6 × 8" tablet and they both fit perfectly in my laptop bag.

Then there's the ultimate in Graphics tablet technology and what I consider the best piece of hardware around, the Wacom Cintiq 21UX. I can honestly say I fell in love within the first 5 seconds of using it. With the Cintiq you work directly on the screen, allowing you to take advantage of your natural hand-eye coordination since you are looking directly where you are working. There is little or no learning curve because of this natural "pen-on-paper" approach. The Cintiq works with any Graphics application and is especially useful with Flash and Photoshop. It feels as close to natural as any paperless production process could.

■ Surprisingly, the most impressive of Flash effects are often the simplest to create. The above characters are animated running in place as a looped sequence. It looks cool as it is but if you copy and paste an instance of it, flip it vertically and lower its opacity, you can achieve the sense that the surface they are running on is reflective and maybe even a bit slippery.

7 Animation examples

I HAVE SPENT MY FAIR SHARE of time on various Flash online forums, reading, learning and providing my own perspective when needed. As a result, I have seen what animation techniques and examples Flash users are always requesting. I will often create a sample FLA and make it available for everyone to download and dissect for themselves. It's very difficult to teach design and animation in text format and, often, a simple FLA can make all the difference.

This chapter contains some of the most popular "How do I..." animation requests from Flash users as far back as Flash version 4. If this chapter teaches you one thing, I hope that it teaches you how to think differently about how you approach Flash as a tool.

Super text effect

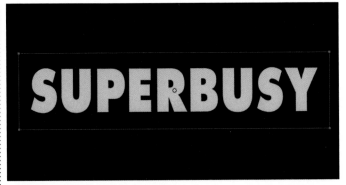

1 Start off with a text field set to Static and type in your text. Nothing fancy here, just some basic text to get you started.

S O OFTEN THE simplest of animation techniques is the most effective visually. Take this simple website introduction for Superbusy Records as an example of simplicity at its finest and how to get the most bang for your buck with the basics of Flash animation. The text animation is comprised of basic motion tweens and scaling, and the bee animation takes advantage of some old school blurring with a linear gradient. Timing is everything and the fast-paced editing of this animation makes it look more complicated than it truly is.

4 Select all layers on a frame somewhere down the timeline (frame 30 will do) and insert a keyframe for every layer by hitting the F6 key. Go back to frame 1 and select your first letter. Use the Scale and Rotate (Ctrl + Alt + S) to scale it to 400% or greater.

7 The bee graphic is introduced using a simple linear gradient first, then the bee "pops" into position. This technique is identical to the "Flying text" topic in Chapter 4.

2 Break apart the text field once using ⌘ B ctrl B and each letter will be broken apart but still editable. Break apart twice to convert your text to raw vector shapes. Your text will no longer be editable once broken down this far. You can choose to break apart only once if you think you might want to edit the text at a later time.

3 Select each letter individually and convert each to a Graphic symbol. Once all letters are converted, select them all, right-click over them and select Distribute to Layers from the context menu.

HOT TIP

You may want to break apart your text into raw vector shapes if you plan on sharing this FLA with someone else on a different computer. If the font you use is not installed on the other machine, then Flash will substitute that font for the default font or a font of your choice. If this project is for a client and they request the FLA, you should make sure they have the same font you are using or break apart the text into shapes.

5 Apply a motion tween to animate this letter scale from 400% to 100%. Select the keyframe in frame 30 and move it to around frame 5. Play back to test the speed based on your frame rate. Adjust the tempo as necessary by adding or removing frames in the motion tween.

6 Repeat this procedure for each letter. Then stagger each letter's animation by sliding the motion tween down the timeline so each letter animates into place one after the other. Your timeline tweens should resemble a staircase.

8 The bee is a movie clip containing a very simple, two-framed animation of the wings. The original wing is replaced with a radial to provide the illusion that it is blurred because it is moving faster than our eye can see.

9 The blur animation is comprised of only two frames with the radial gradient slightly rotated between them. The looping of these two frames at 30 frames per second is enough to convince us that they are oscillating at a very high speed. Adding the appropriate sound effect makes it even more convincing.

SHORTCUTS
MAC WIN BOTH

Page turn

PAGES THAT CURL up and away to reveal more pages are always an appealing effect for introducing content on your website or as buttons to other Web pages. There are variations created entirely with ActionScript, but my AS skills are not anywhere near the level required to generate this effect dynamically. But that doesn't mean you can't add some interactivity by placing this animation in a movie clip and controlling its playback when the mouse rolls over it. I leave that part up to you (see Chapter 10 for a detailed explanation about adding interactivity to your Flash project).

For more robust and dynamically controlled page flip effects, check out:
http://page-flip.com/
http://www.flashpageflip.com/
http://www.pixelwit.com/blog/page-flip/

1 Start with a simple rectangle with a linear gradient fill or your own color fill preference. Convert it to a Movie Clip symbol and apply a drop shadow filter to add a little depth.

2 Duplicate the cover symbol, and place it on a new layer above the original. Edit the graphic inside by filling it with a different color. Add some text or an image of your choice.

6 Insert a new layer and create a triangular shape that resembles a page curl similar to the example above. The easiest way to make this shape is to start with a rectangle. Turn on the Snap tool and drag one corner until it snaps to another corner. Now that you have made a triangle, move the remaining three corners into the positions as seen in the above example.

7 Mix a linear gradient using three colors. The first and last color swatches should be the brightest and similar in value. The middle swatch should be the same color but darker in value. Fill the curl shape and use the Gradient Transform tool **F** to rotate and position the gradient so its bottom edge shows a slight amount of the lightest value.

3 Insert a new layer again above your existing layers. Convert it to a mask layer and draw a shape that spans the lower right corner. Insert a keyframe in frame 30 so that a duplicate of this shape is created.

4 Select the shape in frame 1. With the Free Transform tool **Q**, position the center point at the bottom corner. Hold down **⌥** **alt** and scale the shape until it is very small.

5 Holding down **⌥** **alt** will constrain the shape based on its center point. Apply a shape tween so the shape grows from small to large. This animation will reveal the content page.

HOT TIP

You can duplicate this effect to create additional page curls, allowing the user to turn more pages to reveal more content. Nest the page curl animation into a Movie Clip symbol and drag multiple instances of it to individual layers. With some basic ActionScript, you can control the page turns during runtime in the Flash player.

8 Convert the shape from step 7 to a Graphic symbol and double-click it and add a new layer inside this new symbol. Create another shape in this new layer using the Rectangle tool for the shadow created by the page curl. This shadow will be cast onto the page below, so draw the shape to span only the area necessary inside the content page.

9 Fill this shape with a linear gradient consisting of two colors. Mix about 50% alpha into the first color and 0% alpha into the second color. Use the Gradient Transform tool **F** to rotate the shadow so that it fades away from the curl. Convert both shapes to a Graphic symbol.

10 Animate the curl just as you animated the mask in steps 4 and 5. Insert a second keyframe in frame 30 and select the curl graphic in frame 1. With the Free Transform tool, move the center point to the lower corner, hold down **⌥** **alt** and scale it until it is the same size as the mask shape in this frame. Apply a motion tween.

SHORTCUTS
MAC WIN BOTH

181

Smoke with gradients

THERE ARE SEVERAL ways to animate smoke and each technique is based on the style of the smoke itself. Do you need your smoke to be a cartoon style smoke cloud? Maybe you want a more realistic billowing of soft puffy clouds? How about a very stylized smoke effect with curling hard-edged shapes simulating the basic movement of smoke? There are many different ways to achieve the same results in Flash – whether it's with ActionScript or animation. Flash has always been a blank canvas for us to express ourselves on. Let's take a look at a few ways to approach the dynamics of the elusive smoke cloud.

1 Create a radial gradient with a dark gray center and the outer color mixed with 0% alpha. Create a circle with the Oval tool ⊘ with this gradient as your fill color (no stroke). Convert this shape to a Graphic symbol.

4 Select the entire motion tween, copy all frames and keyframes, insert a new layer and paste all frames into it. Select the graphic in the first frame and move it a few pixels in any direction. Do the same for the Graphic symbol in the last keyframe. Select the entire motion tween and drag it down the timeline a few frames. Repeat this procedure until you have several layers of slightly different animations of your gradient starting small and rising while fading out completely.

2 Select the Graphic symbol and convert it to a Movie Clip symbol. Double-click this movie clip to enter edit mode. This is where the animation will take place.

3 Insert a second keyframe several frames down the timeline. Scale the Graphic symbol to about 200% and move it up about 75 pixels. Apply a motion tween.

5 On the main timeline, copy and paste the movie clip containing your "smoke" animations to a new layer. Drag the keyframe to a frame later in the timeline; frame 25 will work fine. Select the instance and flip it horizontally to help change its appearance from the original.

6 Since the animation is inside a movie clip, it is best to stop the timeline once the second instance is introduced on the timeline by adding a stop action. The Movie Clip instances will continue to play and loop. Since they start on different frames, they will overlap to produce a constant flow of smoke.

Smoke stylized

S TYLE WILL ALMOST ALWAYS DICTATE the
animation technique. Often the client
will request a specific artistic style based on
a pre-existing logo or company identity. The
challenge here is to be consistent, not only with
the artwork but also with the animation style.
A realistic smoke animation would look nice but
not match the client's style preference. It's time
to be inventive and to create a smoke animation
that is stylized, yet simple and effective. Oh,
and the client needs it yesterday.

1 The easiest way to start is with the
final shape you will want as your
stylized smoke shape. This shape can
be drawn with any of Flash's drawing
tools. I recommend no outlines stroke.

2 Insert a keyframe (F6) in frame 2
and, with the Lasso tool, select
a small section at the top end of the
smoke shape and delete it.

6 Copy and paste all frames into a
Graphic symbol so it can be reused later. Create a second keyframe
down the timeline and, with the Free
Transform tool, skew it and move it up
about 30 pixels.

7 Create a third keyframe further
down the timeline and adjust
the alpha to 0% so it fades out. Apply
another motion tween and maybe a
little more skewing.

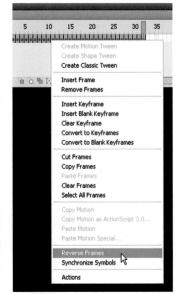

3 Repeat the process of inserting a keyframe and selecting a small section of your shape and deleting it. Use your keyboard shortcuts to make this task faster and easier.

4 Toggle between F6 and the Delete key while selecting sections of your shape until it has been completely removed from your stage.

5 Select the entire range of keyframes and then right-click over them to bring up the context menu. Select Reverse Frames. This will reveal your shape when you play back your animation.

8 Add another layer and drag an instance of the same symbol (containing your animated shape) to the stage. Flip it horizontally and repeat steps 6 and 7.

9 Add a third layer and repeat steps 6 and 7 again. Play back your animation frequently and adjust the amount of skewing, tweening and the overall timing as necessary.

10 You may want to apply a bit of easing out to the symbols as they fade away. Although it may not be necessary, it might just add that final touch to your overall effect.

185

Full steam ahead

FILTERS ARE ANOTHER great way to create realistic smoke or, in this example, steam. Since the image we are working with is an actual photograph, the animation needs to be just as convincing. Without the presence of steam, this cup of tea looks cold and somewhat unappealing. Not only can you use filters to blur objects in Flash, but you can also animate these filters.

1 Start off by drawing some simple shapes with the Brush tool. They should be random and abstract.

2 Select this shape (or shapes) and convert it to a Movie Clip symbol. With this symbol still selected, convert it to a movie clip once again so you end up with two movie clips, one nested inside the other.

6 Select the Movie Clip instance in the second keyframe and apply another Blur filter. Increase the amount of blurring so it is slightly more than the blurring in the first keyframe.

7 Select the Movie Clip instance in the third keyframe and apply another Blur filter. Increase the amount of blurring even more than you applied in the second keyframe.

3 Double-click the Movie Clip symbol on the main timeline to edit it. Insert a second keyframe a few frames down the timeline and scale the original Movie Clip symbol as shown above.

4 Insert a third keyframe down the timeline and scale the movie clip even wider and position it a little higher.

5 Go back to the first keyframe and apply a Blur filter using the Filters panel (Window > Properties > Filters).

HOT TIP

Filters can only be applied to Movie Clip symbols and you must publish Flash Player version 8 or 9. Animated effects involving filters can be very processor intensive. Use them sparingly and test often to make sure playback performance remains acceptable.

8 Apply motion tweens to all keyframes. Play back your animation and make adjustments as necessary. You may want to adjust the amount of blurring, alpha or transforming to your animation. You can also create a second steam animation by creating a new layer and drawing more shapes, convert them to a Movie Clip symbol and repeat steps 1–7. Then select and drag the entire range of keyframes and frames down the timeline so they start after the original animation. This will help eliminate the repetition of one single looping steam effect.

SHORTCUTS
MAC **WIN** **BOTH**

187

Fireworks

1 Start with a radial gradient with at least four colors. The middle and outer colors should be mixed with 0% alpha. The second and third colors are based on your own fireworks color scheme. Convert the gradient to a Graphic symbol.

EVERYBODY LOVES FIREWORKS. There's nothing like a warm summer night under the stars watching the skies light up with the brilliance of pyrotechnics. You can make every day the fourth of July by animating your own fireworks display, and there's no danger of getting hurt either. With some simple gradients, a little masking and some tweens, you'll be hearing "Oohs!" and "Ahhhs!" in no time.

5 Insert keyframes for both layers somewhere down your timeline and scale them both up about 300%. The gradient should be at least as big as the mask.

6 Insert two more keyframes much farther down the timeline and scale both the mask and gradient about 125% more. Fade out the gradient to 0% alpha.

10 Since this stroke and its shape tweened animation simulate the ascending explosive, you will need to slide the actual fireworks animation down the timeline to make room for it. At this point, it comes down to artistic license and how you want the entire animation to play out. Here I have the ascent disappear just before the burst effect appears. The speed of the ascent can be adjusted by adding or removing frames during the shape tween.

2 You need to create a mask that resembles the shape of exploding fireworks such as in this example. Convert it to a Graphic symbol.

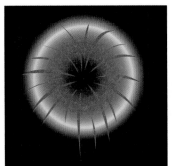

3 Place the radial gradient in the masked layer so when the layers are locked, the gradient shows through the mask only.

4 Scale both the mask and gradient in frame 1 so they are very small. Scale the gradient even smaller than the mask.

7 Lock both layers and play back or test your movie. You should have a pretty convincing fireworks explosion.

8 Draw a stroke and fill it with a linear gradient that contains two swatches mixed with 0% alpha at both ends.

9 Shape tween the gradient so it starts at the bottom of the stroke and ascends until it reaches the top and beyond so it disappears.

11 If you nest this animation in a symbol, you can duplicate it in the Library to create additional fireworks with different colors.

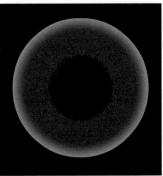

12 Edit the duplicate symbol(s) with a new radial gradient symbol. The darker the background the more vivid the fireworks will be.

13 Drag multiple instances of your fireworks to the stage and start them on different frames to vary their timing.

189

Soft reveal

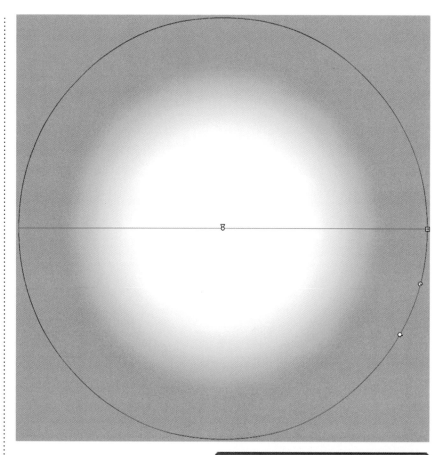

F LASH LACKS THE ABILITY to create masks with soft edges. When you use masks in Flash, you are limited to a hard edge, even if the mask contains a gradient with one color mixed with 0% alpha. Perhaps someday a future version of Flash will support masks with feathered edges. Until then, we need a work-around. So far the only solution I have been able to come up with is not even a mask at all. It's a simple gradient with at least one color mixed with 0% alpha. In the end, the effect is successful because it is what the viewer doesn't see that convinces them visually.

1 Start with a radial gradient (shown here with orange for clarity) with two colors. The outer color should match the solid color background which you will need for this effect to work. The middle color should be mixed with 0% alpha to make it completely transparent.
Use the Rectangle tool **R** to make a very large shape with this radial gradient as your fill color.

2 Convert this rectangle to a symbol and place it on a layer above the image you want to reveal. Scale the rectangle large enough so you can see the entire image through the middle color that you made transparent.

In frame 1, position the rectangle so that the image below it is completely obscured from view. This is if you want to start your animation by revealing the image over time.

HOT TIP

This effect can be achieved not only with a radial gradient, but also a linear gradient. It depends on your needs of course, but a feathered edge can always be achieved if your animation contains a solid color background.

3 Create a second keyframe somewhere down the timeline and position the gradient so that the image below it is clearly seen through its transparent center. Apply a motion tween and play back your animation.

Star Wars text

TEXT EFFECTS ARE ALWAYS a popular request among Flash users – specifically the "Star Wars" effect made famous during the opening scene in the original 1977 film. The effect is relatively simple to create but comes with a price: playback performance can suffer. Proceed with caution and test your animation often to make sure playback doesn't suffer. Remember, the text must be legible without giving the reader a headache.

> This is how to make a "Star Wars" style opening text effect. It ain't too hard once you know how. This is how to make a "Star Wars" style opening text effect. It ain't too hard once you know how. This is how to make a "Star Wars" style opening text effect. It ain't too hard once you know how. This is how to make a "Star Wars" style opening text effect. It ain't too hard once you know how. This is how to make a "Star Wars" style opening text effect. It ain't too hard once you know how. This is how to make a "Star Wars" style opening text effect. It ain't too hard once you know how. This is how to make a "Star Wars" style opening text effect. It ain't too hard once you know how. This is how to make a "Star Wars" style opening text effect. It ain't too hard once you know how. This is how to make a "Star Wars" style opening text effect. It ain't too hard once you know how. This is how to make a "Star Wars" style opening text effect. It ain't too hard once you know how. This is how to make a "Star Wars" style opening text effect. It ain't too hard once you know how. This is how to make a "Star Wars" style opening text effect. It ain't too hard once you know how.

1 Start by typing your block of text. Try to use a simple and bold font that is easy to read. You will be transforming this text and animating it. Since it will be constantly moving, priority should be making sure it is legible and easy to read for the viewer. Select your text field and break it apart until the text becomes raw vector shapes. The amount of vector information will be substantial and will most likely cause some performance issues during playback. This is another reason to choose a font that is as simple and clean as possible as it will produce fewer vector points.

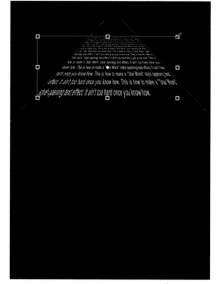

3 Insert a new layer and convert it to a guide layer. Make sure the layer containing your text is not "guided" or linked to it. You can drag the guide layer below your text layer to prevent them from being linked together. Anything on a guide layer will not be included in the exported SWF. Flash CS4 offers a nice feature that provides the option to export or not export hidden layers. This option is accessible by going to File > Publish Settings > Flash tab. On this layer use the line tool to draw a stroke at the same angle as your text field. Copy and paste it in place, flip it horizontally and position it on the opposite side of your block of text.

4 Add a second keyframe and scale your text until it fits inside your guides at their smallest point. You will need to insert several frames between these two keyframes and apply a motion tween.

2 The next step is to simulate the perspective needed to provide the illusion that the text is receding. Select the Free Transform tool **Q** and then the Distort (subselection) tool. While holding down the **Shift** key, drag one of the upper corners horizontally towards the middle of the

text. Holding down the **Shift** key constrains the proportions of the transformation by distorting the adjacent corner in the opposite direction. Convert this block of text to a Graphic symbol. If you have several blocks of text, it might be best to keep them as smaller individual symbols.

HOT TIP

You could try this effect with a block of text made in Photoshop that is distorted in the same perspective. Import the text as a bitmap with the same solid color background as your Flash movie. It may result in a more processor-friendly animation sequence but will suffer from loss of quality when scaled. Flash doesn't scale imported bitmaps very well and the results may not be visually appealing. The trade-off is using crisp vector text with some possible performance issues during playback. Test often is your best defense.

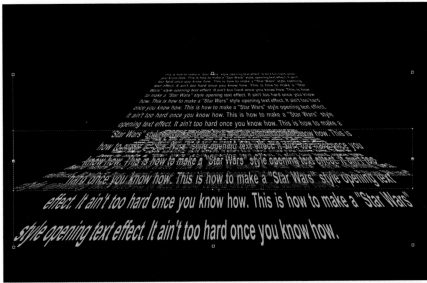

5 The final step actually breaks the one and only perspective rule this animation relies on. I also think it is the most important step since it really helps provide the illusion of the text disappearing into infinity yet it is so simple. In the very last frame of the tween, select the symbol containing the text field and using the Free Transform tool scale it vertically using one of the 2 middle handles along the top or bottom edge. In essence you will be squashing the symbol to make it flatter (do not widen it).

For smooth playback, you will need a combination of hundreds of frames and a high frame rate. The exact amount depends on the amount of text, the font style and how large (width and height) your movie is. The larger the movie, the more processor intensive it will be. Any animated effect that uses a combination of these factors can cause poor playback performance. Test often and know your target audience.

SHORTCUTS
MAC **WIN** **BOTH**

Color adjustments

BEFORE FLASH 8 introduced filter effects, advanced bitmap effects meant having to spend time outside of Flash editing several duplicates of the original image. Depending on the desired effect(s), several different versions of the same image would have to be created and imported into Flash. With Flash CS3 and now CS4, this process became much easier. Using only one single bitmap image and the Adjust Color filter, you can create some striking color effects with minimal time and effort. The advantages of using this filter technique include smaller file sizes and faster results that can be mixed with any of the other filters.

1 To convert a full color image to gray scale, slide the Saturation slider all the way to the left.

2 Click the Reset button in the Filters panel to return each color setting to "0".

3 To adjust the overall color hue of your image, use the Hue slider. Here the Contrast and Saturation have been slightly adjusted as well.

1 The imported image here has been blurred and adjusted using the Blur and Adjust Color filters.

2 Here the Saturation and Hue have been increased as well as the Contrast.

3 Here's the original image without any filtered effects.

4 Each of these color adjustments can be keyframed and motion tweened to create smooth color transitions.

5 Any of these color effects can be visually effective when introducing images for a variety of uses.

6 You can also add some basic ActionScript to control color changes when the user rolls over various menu buttons.

▽ FILTERS	
Property	Value
▼ Adjust Color	
Brightness	-38
Contrast	100
Saturation	100
Hue	52

▽ FILTERS	
Property	Value
▼ Adjust Color	
Brightness	-34.6
Contrast	91.2
Saturation	91.2
Hue	-164.1

▽ FILTERS	
Property	Value
▼ Adjust Color	
Brightness	-38
Contrast	56
Saturation	-75
Hue	-71

SHORTCUTS
MAC WIN BOTH

Vertigo

CAUTION: THIS EFFECT MAY CAUSE temporary headaches and possibly some minor nausea if stared at too long.

Well, perhaps it won't cause sickness but it is a great effect for representing vertigo: a balance disorder that causes a spinning sensation. If you are familiar with Alfred Hitchcock's film "Vertigo", you will already be familiar with how this visual effect can be used to induce the image of something or someone spinning out of control. With animation, it can also represent time travel or a worm hole or even the beginning of a dream sequence or hallucination.

1 The success of this effect is in the one single graphic: the spiral. It was created in Adobe Illustrator using, you guessed it, the Spiral tool. Flash does not have a tool like this so Illustrator proved to be a huge time saver. Of course you can always draw this spiral graphic by hand using the support of a pressure-sensitive stylus, but that would certainly require a very skilled hand.

3 This is a great effect to place a character or an object on top of. Place the object in a Movie Clip symbol and rotate it in the opposite direction as your swirl. This will enhance the effect by providing the illusion of the object traveling through time or space and may even induce some minor headaches and nausea.

2 Convert your spiral graphic to a symbol. Insert a second keyframe about 100 frames from the first keyframe. Apply a motion tween. Of course nothing will happen on playback because no change has been made to either instance of the spiral. Select a frame anywhere along the motion tween and in the Rotate drop-down menu, select CW (clockwise) or CCW (counter-clockwise). Type in the number of rotations desired.

HOT TIP

You can get a lot of mileage from this spiral effect by adding objects that do more than just spin in the center of the spiral. You could add a rocket that is motion tweened from outside the stage into the center of the spiral. You'd want to scale it very small as it reaches the center point of the spiral.

4 It's time to have some fun! Change the colors of your spiral and then select the character or object (make sure it is in a movie clip) and experiment with some of the Blend modes available from the Properties panel. There are some interesting effects to play around with here that may provide some cool results.

SHORTCUTS
MAC WIN BOTH

197

Let it rain

1 Use the Brush tool to draw your rain drop. Gravity suggests that the shape of the drop is thicker and rounder at its bottom. Fill your rain-drop with a solid color or a radial gradient for some extra realism. This is a style choice for you to decide.

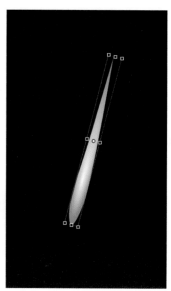

2 Convert your drop to a Graphic symbol and rotate it slightly. The amount of rotation is up to you based on how strong a rain storm you want to have. The more angle your rain has, the more wind is suggested.

THERE ARE SEVERAL WAYS to approach animating rain, probably because rain falls in several ways depending on wind conditions. I chose an average style of falling rain that can easily be expanded upon based on your own needs.

Rain, to our advantage as animators, is repetitive. Reusing assets is one of the strengths of Flash. You only need to animate one raindrop and then populate your scene with multiple instances of it. You can then control how your rain acts by adjusting the angle at which it falls, its speed and how many instances of it appear at any given time.

6 Copy all frames of your circle animation. Insert a new layer and paste the frames into it. Select all the frames in this new layer and drag them about five frames further down the timeline.

7 Navigate back to the main timeline and transform your water drop symbol (containing its animation) by dragging the middle handle along the top or bottom edge (Free Transform tool).

3 Insert a keyframe further down the timeline. In frame 1, position the drop outside of the stage. In your second keyframe, position it near the bottom of your stage area. Apply a motion tween.

4 Let's create a ripple effect for the rain drop after it reaches its destination. Using the Oval tool **O**, draw a circle with a stroke color only. Hold down **Shift** to constrain its proportions. Convert it to a Graphic symbol.

5 Convert it to a Graphic symbol again and double-click it to edit it. Insert a second keyframe and motion tween it from small to large over approximately 10 frames. Select the instance in the last frame and apply 0% alpha so it fades out completely.

8 Place the symbol containing your ripple animation in a blank keyframe (F7), in the frame after your rain-drop animation. Position the ripple just below the rain drop in its last frame. Copy all frames in this layer.

9 Paste these frames into a new symbol. Add several layers and continue to paste your animation into each one. Select and drag each layer's animation so that they start each on their own unique frame number.

10 Now that you have a rain sequence nested in a symbol, drag as many instances of this symbol as you need to the stage. Scale them and even tint some darker to suggest more depth to your scene.

Playing with fire

NO FLASH ANIMATION BOOK is complete without a topic involving fire. How many times have you ever wanted to animate fire and had no idea how to even approach it?

The first technique that comes to mind for animating flames is shape tweening. It just seems like the appropriate choice because of the nature of fire and how flames dance and flicker. But in my experience, shape tweening doesn't seem to ever produce realistic results. Often, the shapes "implode" or simply morph in all the wrong ways. The effect of fire is simply not achievable using tweens.

Motion tweens are not an option for the obvious reason that they can only be applied to instances of symbols.

ActionScript might be a solution, but if you are like me, your scripting skills are not up to the challenge of producing fire from within the Actions panel.

Don't be frightened by what I am about to say, but frame by frame is the best option for animating fire. Don't be fooled, it's not that hard or time-consuming.

1 Start by making several overlapping rectangles (with no stroke outline). Don't concern yourself with color at this stage of the process; any color will do.

5 Ultimately your flames in frame 1 should look something like this. Try to alternate the direction of each flame. Fire is random and travels in unpredictable ways.

9 Create a Linear gradient using bright red and bright yellow as the two colors.

10 In each keyframe, select all and drag the Bucket tool vertically inside your flames to fill them. The gradient will follow the direction you drag in.

2 Use the Selection tool **V** to pull edges to create peaks.

3 Fire is naturally unpredictable. Avoid repetition with your shapes.

4 Try to incorporate some shapes with "S"-shaped curves for some added realism.

6 Insert a keyframe (F6) on frame 2, turn on Onionskin and begin editing the next frame by pulling each point higher and lower.

7 "Punch" holes in the flames by drawing different colored shapes and deleting them. Fire is not solid; it will break up as it rises into the air.

8 Continue to create keyframes and edit the shape of your flames in each one by pulling and pushing with the Selection tool.

11 Copy all frames of your animation and paste them into a new Graphic symbol. Add three new layers to the main timeline and drag instances of this symbol to each of them. Delete your original layer. Select one of the instances and flip it horizontally. Scale two of the instances so they are much wider than the stage. Position them off-center from the stage while leaving one of the instances at its original size and position. Create a background shape with the same linear gradient to make it look like the entire scene is ablaze.

Winter wonderland

L ET IT SNOW, LET IT SNOW, LET IT SNOW. Creating constantly falling snow is fun. Like the rain example, snow can be animated several different ways. The easiest way is to motion tween a snowflake symbol along a Motion Guide path. Other methods include using ActionScript-generated snow but don't ask me to show how that is done because I admittedly do not know how to write scripts on that level. Let's stick with my "analog" method of animating in Flash shall we?

The more snow you create, the more processor intensive your animation becomes. Proceed with caution and test your animation frequently to make sure the constant looping snowfall doesn't cause unexpected playback issues. There's nothing worse than creating a cool animation only to find it skips and chugs during playback.

I highly recommend Chris Jackson's book *Flash + After Effects* (Focal Press) because he teaches you how to create snow in Adobe After Effects that is easily imported into Flash. His book contains a ton of other cool examples that you will find very useful on a day-to-day basis.

1 Start with a snowflake design using the Line tool. It's hard to make a mistake here since there's no real way to create an incorrect snowflake pattern. Make one "arm" of the snowflake; convert it to a symbol or as an Object Drawing. Copy it using ⌘C ctrl C and paste it in place using ⌘Shift V ctrl Shift V, then rotate it 45 degrees. Repeat until you have pasted enough to complete the pattern.

4 Here's what your Movie Clip's timeline should look like (give or take some frames or layers). Notice the *stop();* action in the last frame of the top layer. This prevents this Movie Clip from looping. Since all instances of the snowflake Movie Clip are present, they will loop by default.

2 Convert your snowflake to a Graphic symbol and then convert the Graphic symbol to a Movie Clip symbol. Double-click the Movie Clip and edit it by inserting a Motion Guide layer. Draw a curvy stroke for the guide and motion tween your snowflake along the path (traveling downwards of course).

3 You now have a Movie Clip containing an animation of a snowflake tweened along a motion guide. Next, in your Library panel, create a new Movie Clip and insert several new layers. Drag an instance of your snowflake Movie Clip into each layer. Position each snowflake Movie Clip randomly throughout your scene. For each layer, select and drag the keyframe in frame 1 to a different frame number so they each start playing at different times. Make sure each snowflake animation begins outside of the viewable area of the stage.

5 On the main timeline, place an instance of your Movie Clip containing your snowflake Movie Clips onto the stage in its own layer. You can place multiple instances of this Movie Clip around your stage as many times as you like. But be aware that the more instances of the snowflake animations you have present on the stage, the more processor intensive your movie will be. If maintaining a high frame rate is your priority, you may want to experiment by using a simple oval shape for your snowflake graphic. Remember, fewer vector points means better playback.

3D perspective

1 Start with a simple background graphic that shows a clear horizon line. Here the sky and ocean are convincingly represented using 2 simple radial gradients. This simple illusion is created due to the alignment of the gradients vertically, thereby making our eye translate the bottom gradient as a reflection.

ADAM PHILLIPS IS BEST KNOWN for his award winning Brackenwood series:

http://www.biteycastle.com/content/animation_brk.html

The rest of his animation is equally as brilliant and I highly recommend treating yourself to his entire website:

http://www.biteycastle.com/

Adam has generously provided a couple of killer Flash examples that showcase the new 3D capabilities in Flash CS4. Flash CS4 allows you to create 3D effects by moving and rotating movie clips in 3D space on the stage. Flash represents 3D space by including a *Z-axis* in the properties of each Movie Clip instance. You can add 3D perspective effects to Movie Clip instances by moving or rotating them along their *Z-axis* using the 3D Translation and 3D Rotation tools. Moving an object in 3D space is called a *translation* and rotating an object in 3D space is called a *transformation*. You can take advantage of this powerful new 3D feature for scenes like this one where the perspective of a landscape fly-over animation needs to look realistic.

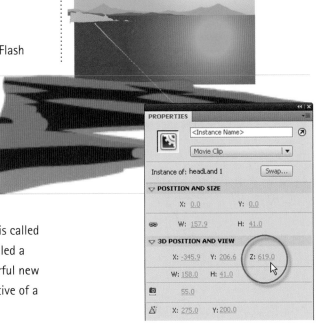

4 Verify the playhead is in the last frame of your tween span in the timeline. Open the Properties panel and select the first Movie Clip symbol. Use the Z-axis hot text slider in combination with the X- and Y-axis sliders to position your object off the bottom edge of the stage.

2 Next some background elements are added to provide depth to the scene. A mountain range divides the sky and ocean while some shoreline elements are positioned in the distance. The plan for this scene is to provide the illusion that we are flying towards the horizon along the shoreline. To set this up from the start, begin with your shoreline objects at their starting point, scaled down at their furthest point away from the "camera". Convert them to Movie Clip symbols.

3 Distribute each of these Movie Clip objects to layers, then right click over each of them and select Create Motion Tween. Do not use Classic tweens since they are not supported by the 3D Translation and Transformation tools. I recommend going to View > Pasteboard and making sure you can see beyond the stage area of your document. This will help you when positioning your objects beyond the viewable stage area.

5 Repeat this procedure for all the remaining objects on the stage. You will also want to increase or decrease each tween span to adjust the timing of each object to prevent them from all moving simultaneously.

6 Adding the Gull animation to the foreground adds 2 important elements to the scene: it enforces the illusion of depth as well as something interesting to look at. Even though there's no "camera", upon playback, the human eye will perceive us as literally flying through the scene.

HOT TIP

It is worth noting that these 3D tools will not work with objects on mask layers. You can not convert a layer containing 3D objects to a mask layer either.

SHORTCUTS

205

Bone and Spray

HERE'S ANOTHER COOL example from Adam Phillips that combines two new CS4 tools in Flash: the Bone tool and the Spray Brush tool.

What's a little different about the Bone tool here is that it is being applied to a shape instead of a symbol object. This blade of grass is then animated by manipulating the armature inside a Movie Clip symbol.

The advantage of using the Spray Brush tool is having the ability to assign this custom grass Movie Clip as the object to be sprayed.

1 Start with a blade of grass drawn with the Brush tool **B** or a shape tool. It doesn't really matter as long as it remains as raw vectors. Select it and convert it to a Movie Clip symbol. Then double click this symbol to enter *edit in place* mode.

4 Select the Spray Brush tool and in the Properties panel click the Edit button. The Swap Symbols panel will open allowing you to select a Movie Clip symbol from the document's Library. Select the grass symbol containing the animation. Click "OK". The hard part is over.

2 Using the Bone tool **X**, click and drag to create a chain of bones inside your shape. Flash will automatically place this shape in a container. Animate the shape by inserting frames in this layer and manipulating the armature by dragging the last bone in the chain.

3 Flash will insert keyframes automatically wherever the playhead is in the timeline when you manipulate the armature.

5 All that's left to do now is use the Spray tool to "paint" the animated grass across the stage. With each spray, the objects are automatically grouped. You can select a group and convert it to a symbol in order to apply a color effect. Adjust the brightness or apply a tint color to suggest some depth between groups of grass.

6 Add in some additional background elements to complete your scene. Hours of production time were saved here by nesting an animation made with the Bone tool and taking advantage of the Spray Brush tool. Locate the SWF file in the "Chapter 7" folder on the CD to see the final animation.

207

From the inside out

I AM A DIGITAL ANIMATOR. A "digimator" if you will. I learned how to animate on a computer, which is inherently different than the traditional animation process. Sure, it shares some similarities when it comes to animation techniques, but ultimately any animation program can have a mechanical feel to it since we work by selecting options from menus much of the time. The trick I have learned is how to make a software program like Flash feel more organic, as if it were a ball of clay, starting with a basic shape and pushing and pulling it into something unique. If this book teaches anything, I hope it teaches you to think differently as to how you approach Flash. Just because the help docs, online resources or even other books tell you how something can or should be done, don't take that as carved in stone. Take it as carved in clay, meaning you can continue to expand on the ways the tools are used, even beyond what you may have elsewhere. If 100 people were given their own ball of clay, they would all create something unique. No two clay creations would be the same because of the organic nature of the medium. Clay can be pushed and pulled in any direction, and this is how I will teach you to approach Flash.

Many years before Flash even existed, I studied everything from art history to sculpture, color theory to lithography and, above all, how to draw. This combination made the progression to the world of computer graphics and animation tremendously helpful. I feel just as comfortable with a mouse or stylus in my hand as I do with pencil, paintbrush, airbrush or printing press. They are all just tools, nothing more. Each tool is just as powerful as the other. A quick and loosely sketched pencil drawing can have just as much impact visually as a full-blown animated action sequence that took three months to complete. It's the subject matter that counts and this applies to Flash as well. Several people have asked me why I am so forthcoming with my home-grown tips and techniques and why I'm not afraid that many will use them to emulate my own personal style. As with the ball of clay metaphor, everyone is different, and therefore everyone will express themselves in a unique fashion whether it's through a ball of clay or an animation program like Flash. These are just tools, and in different hands come unique results. I'm here to show you how I use these tools for my own self-expression. Your own results may, and probably will, vary.

I have spent several years adopting and inventing Flash drawing and animation techniques. This book will show you different ways of approaching Flash and how to make it work for you. Whenever possible, I will try to avoid explaining what is readily available in the help docs and the multitude of online resources. You bought this book for a reason, to learn what isn't found anywhere else. You will get a first-hand look at how I create characters and motion graphics from scratch, and learn how Flash, as a tool, can be pushed and pulled, limited only by your imagination.

My philosophy, with tools like Flash, is to learn as much as I can, then go back to the first 10% of what I learned, and take a left turn.

Having the ability to record your own high quality sound effects, vocals and musical soundtracks opens up a world of artistic possibilities. Many of my daughter's candid recording sessions have inspired several popular original animations, one of which was chosen as a Flash Forward Film Festival finalist.

Working with sound

FOR ME, ANIMATION IS about timing and rhythm. I've always been visually sensitive to the moving image and as a drummer for three decades, my senses are also very fixed on musical patterns. The combination of animation and the right soundtrack can be a wonderful experience for both senses. When the right sound complements the perfect animation, it can produce a most memorable experience for the viewer.

In this chapter we'll look at how you can incorporate sounds into your animations, where to find them, and how to record, edit and load them dynamically.

Recording sounds

SOUNDS CAN ENHANCE your animation in wonderful ways. Recording and designing sounds is an art form all its own and a job typically left to dedicated sound editors who have an innate ability to edit, mix and craft sounds into works of audible art. But chances are you don't have a dedicated sound designer at your disposal 24 hours a day. Since Flash does not record or create sound files, you need to find or record your own and import them into Flash. So what is the best way to find, edit and incorporate sounds into your Flash projects? The easiest way is to purchase sound effects from your local music store or online. A quick search on Amazon.com for "sound effects" will return a few dozen audio CDs available for purchase. These are handy to have around, but may include some legal restrictions as to how you can use the sounds. Some publishers may retain the royalty rights to the contents of CDs, limiting you to non-commercial usage. This may pose some legal

Get yourself a good microphone. I'll be honest, you will get what you pay for when it comes to the quality of recording. There are several different microphones designed to record sounds for almost every situation you can think of. The cheapest solution would be something like the Logitech USB microphone that can be found at your local computer supply store for around $20 US. A microphone like that is great for transferring your voice during an Internet phone conversation, but I wouldn't rely on it for high quality recordings.

On the other hand, you don't need to spend your next five paychecks on the most professional studio microphone either. The microphone pictured on the right is an AKG Perception 400 and retails for around $300 US. It produces great sound whether you are recording voice, sound effects or musical instruments. It is a condenser microphone, which tends to be more sensitive and responsive, making it well-suited to capturing subtle nuances in sounds. The best feature of all is the three different recording settings you can switch between depending on the recording situation. You can set it to record only what is directly in front of the microphone, which is great for voice, sound effects and intruments. If you have two voices or instruments next to each other, there's a setting to record bidirectionally. The third is an omnidirectional setting that will record sounds in a 360 degree pattern around the mic. This is great for picking up general room or ambient sounds.

issues for you and most importantly your client, who would rather avoid paying legal fees for a few *thumps*, *swooshes* and *pop* sound effects in the project you delivered to them six months prior. Another potential issue with published sound effects CDs is their sound quality. Depending on the equipment used to record and edit the sounds, there is no guarantee they are of high enough quality to justify using them. It's always a good idea to try to find out the technical information regarding the actual

sound files before you purchase the CD. You will want sounds that are high quality, usually 44 kHz, 16-bit stereo. You may also want to edit your sounds by applying effects or editing loops, or even compose original soundtracks. For this you'll need to choose a decent audio editing program. Some of you may already be using an audio editing application, but for those of you who are unfamiliar in the area, we'll take a look at what's available a bit later in this chapter.

Next, you need a way to get your shiny new microphone to connect with your computer. Once again you have a variety to choose from. Assuming you don't need every bell and whistle available, a good choice is something like M-Audio's FireWire Solo mobile audio interface. It has a standard XLR microphone input and a 1/2" guitar input, allowing you to record guitar and vocals simultaneously. There are also dual line inputs for effects, drum machines and other outboard gear. The biggest decision to make when purchasing an interface like this is whether you want to use USB or FireWire connectivity. FireWire may provide faster data transfer over USB, but double check that your computer's hardware supports FireWire. If not, you can purchase a FireWire card separately.

So now how much can you expect to spend? An audio interface is between $200 and $400 US depending on how many features it offers. The M-Audio FireWire Solo mentioned here will

set you back about $250 US but I found one on sale for $200 at my local music vendor. Throw in a microphone stand and cable and you could be looking at spending around $600. Yeah, I know what some of you are thinking: "I just spent that much to get Flash! Are you kidding me?" I can understand this being an expensive decision but I'm providing information based on equipment I feel provides the best bang for your buck. There are many less expensive microphones to choose from, some with USB connectivity that avoid the need to purchase a FireWire interface. It's a balance between the level of quality you prefer and the size of your budget.

PHOTO: M-AUDIO FIREWIRE SOLO

Audacity®

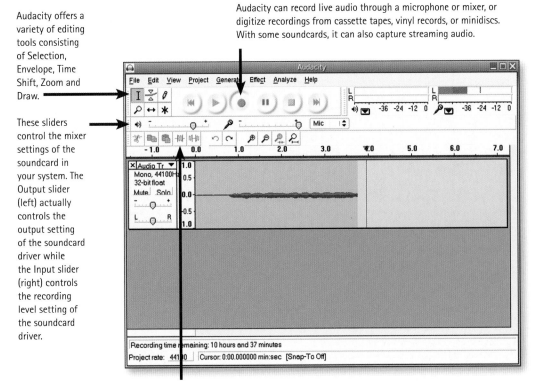

A UDACITY IS A FREE downloadable audio editing application that boasts a surprisingly robust feature set. Audacity can record live audio through a microphone or mixer, or digitize recordings from cassette tapes, vinyl records, or minidiscs. With some sound-cards, it can also capture streaming audio. Audacity supports several popular audio file formats allowing you to cut, copy, splice and mix various files together as well as change their pitch and speed. If you have a limited budget, look no further and even if you can afford software that offers more, Audacity still might be enough to satisfy your needs. Go to **http://audacity.sourceforge.net/** to learn more and download the installer. I've also included the installer file on the CD included with this book (look in the "Chapter 8" folder).

Audacity offers a variety of editing tools consisting of Selection, Envelope, Time Shift, Zoom and Draw.

These sliders control the mixer settings of the soundcard in your system. The Output slider (left) actually controls the output setting of the soundcard driver while the Input slider (right) controls the recording level setting of the soundcard driver.

Audacity can record live audio through a microphone or mixer, or digitize recordings from cassette tapes, vinyl records, or minidiscs. With some soundcards, it can also capture streaming audio.

Audacity's handy Edit Toolbar allows you to cut, copy, paste, trim, and silence your audio, and more.

Audacity certainly doesn't make its most basic of controls hard to find. Cursor to Start, Play, Record, Pause and Stop and Cursor to End are all over-sized and easy to find.

You can mute and solo (isolate) when working with multiple tracks.

Audio tracks contain digitally sampled sounds. In Audacity, a channel of sound is represented by one mono audio track and a two channel sound by one stereo audio track. You can specify a different sample rate for each track. You can import audio of any sample rate or bit depth and Audacity will resample and convert it to the project rate and bit depth on the fly.

Adobe® Soundbooth® CS4

![Sb]

SOUNDBOOTH IS AN audio editing program from Adobe that is designed for the casual Flash user and video editor while offering professional-level features. Soundbooth is streamlined in a way that doesn't require you to be an audio expert. You will not be overwhelmed with a plethora of knobs, buttons and sliders, or effects that require hours of reading through pages of help docs, but don't underestimate its capabilities either. From real-time effects processing to composing your own custom music bed, Soundbooth is the perfect complement to Flash. You can even add Markers to your audio wave form in Soundbooth, and export them as XML data that can then be used with a Flash FLV component and ActionScript. Soundbooth fills a much-needed niche for the casual audio editor who doesn't mind getting professional results.

The Tools panel offers Time Selection, Frequency Selection, Rectangle Marquee, Lasso, Hand and Zoom tools.

The scrollable Files panel lists all currently opened audio and video files.

Soundbooth offers several real-time effects such as Channel Volume, Invert, Parametric EQ, Swap Channels, Phaser, Vocal Enhancement and more. Effects are applied in real-time and therefore are non-destructive to the original source file. You always have the option to turn on or off selected effects until you wish to apply them permanently.

The Video panel plays back video files for referencing while editing an audio waveform.

The workspace in Soundbooth is completely customizable. Not unlike Adobe Audition and Premiere, you can scale and drag panels to new locations and in configurations that suit your working needs. As you rearrange panels, other panels will resize themselves automatically to fit the workspace.

The Editor panel is the main area where audio waveform editing takes place.

Use the Navigation Bar to zoom in or out and navigate throughout a waveform.

Manage your customizable workspace with the Workspace drop-down menu. You can add or remove workspace layouts similar to how you can in Flash.

An integrated search input field for finding help-related topics fast.

HOT TIP

If you require more advanced audio editing features, you might consider Adobe Audition (see the following page), a more advanced, full-featured audio editing program for those who need just about every bell and whistle available to them.

Quick Editing controls.

The Remove a Sound feature works in conjunction with the Frequency Spectrum panel. This panel can also be resized by dragging the divider bar vertically.

Adobe® Audition® 3.0

Au

AUDITION IS A VERY robust audio editing program from Adobe that offers a fully integrated set of audio-editing and restoration tools. This is a complete audio-editing program from recording to editing to mixing and exporting. It is packed full of features too long to list here. If you are a sound editor and composer, Audition will satisfy most if not all of your needs. I use it for recording voice over, sound effects and also sounds from my digital keyboard. I can then switch over to Multitrack View and mix all my sounds together using an unlimited number of stereo mixing tracks. Audition offers over 50 real-time audio effects including echo, flange, reverb, and more. You can even record and edit MIDI.

Simply put, if you need a complete audio studio out of the box, Audition delivers.

Switch between Edit, Multitrack and CD views easily. ➡

Record, edit, and mix any number of stereo tracks in Multitrack View.

Work with more than 50 real-time audio effects including echo, flange, reverb, and more. Manipulate recordings with digital signal processing (DSP) tools, mastering and analysis tools, and audio restoration features.

The workspace in Audition is completely customizable. You can scale and drag panels to new locations and in configurations that suit your working needs. As you rearrange panels, other panels will resize themselves automatically to fit the workspace.

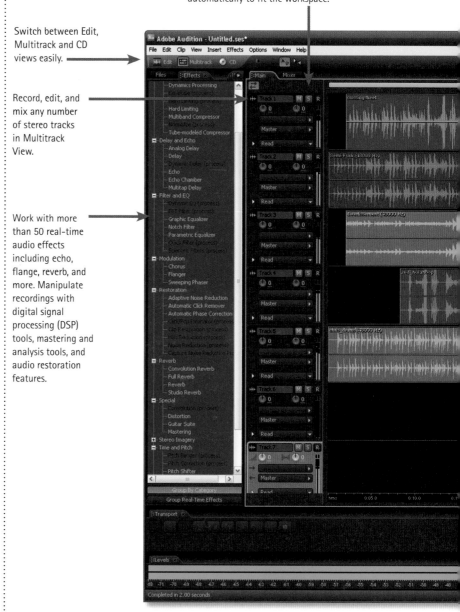

Apply various colors to your
tracks for easy identification.

Manage your customizable workspace
with the Workspace drop-down menu.
You can add or remove workspace
layouts similar to how you can in Flash.

Workspace: Multitrack View (Default)

HOT TIP

Also included
with Audition is
the "Loopology"
collection, a
CD containing
hundreds of
drums loops,
percussion, and
guitar, bass
and many more
instruments for
you to use in
your projects.

0:46.569

View and zoom controls provide a
helpful way to isolate and focus
on specific portion(s) of your audio
track(s).

The Session Properties panel provides a
quick and easy way to make adjustments
to your project.

SHORTCUTS
MAC WIN BOTH

Sound in Flash

THE EDIT ENVELOPE WINDOW offers some limited sound editing features without having to leave the Flash environment. There's enough features here to control the starting and ending points of your sound file, as well as some basic fading effects. But don't expect much more beyond that.

As much as Flash could use a few more bells and whistles in this area, it was never meant to be a sound editing program in the first place. Let's leave that for the dedicated sound editing applications and use Flash for what it is. We can't expect Flash to do everything can we?

1 Select frame 1 in your Flash document and then go to File > Import > Import to Stage and select your WAV or AIF file. Your sound will be in frame 1 but you will need to insert enough frames to accommodate its length. By default, the sound will be set to Event. Use the drop-down to change the sound's behavior.

Event: This is used to play a sound at a particular point in time, but independently of other sounds. An Event sound will play in its entirety even if the movie stops. An Event sound must be fully downloaded before it will play.

Start: The same as Event, except that if the sound is already playing, no new instance of the sound plays.

Stop: This stops the selected sound.

Stream: This is used to synchronize a sound with the timeline and, subsequently, the animation. Streaming sounds will start and stop with the playhead.

4 To change the start and end points of a sound, drag the Time In and Time Out controls in the Edit Envelope. The tricky thing about this is, without the ability to scrub the waveform in the envelope window, it's a game of hit or miss (mostly miss). If you need to continue a long sound file across multiple Scenes, you will have to add a new instance of the sound to each Scene. Next, determine where the sound ended in the previous Scene and manually adjust the Time In controller for the current Scene so that the sound starts where the previous Scene ended. It's not an exact science and not an ideal solution if your audio file is one continuous sound (such as a musical score).

5 In some situations, having the ability to view the waveform is helpful. For example, having a clear visual indicator of when sounds start and stop can help speed up this tedious process. Right-click over the layer name containing your sound and select Properties from the context menu. In the Layer Properties panel, locate the Layer Height drop-down menu and select 300% to increase the height of the layer to its maximum.

2 Click the Edit button in the Properties panel to open the Edit Envelope window. Here you will see the waveform of your sound file and a few basic control features. The Effect drop-down menu offers some convenient effects to add to your sound.

Left Channel/Right Channel: Plays sound in the left or right channel only.

Fade Left to Right/Fade Right to Left: Shifts the sound from one channel to the other.

Fade In/Fade Out: Gradually increases/decreases the volume of a sound over its duration.

Custom: Lets you create custom in and out points of sound using the Edit Envelope.

3 You can add up to eight envelope handles by clicking anywhere within the sound window. Each handle can be dragged around to control the volume of the sound at that point in the sound file. The higher the handle is positioned, the louder the sound. To remove a handle, drag it out of the window. To change the sound envelope, drag the envelope handles to change levels at different points in the sound. Envelope lines show the volume of the sound as it plays.

HOT TIP

Once the sound has been set to Stream behavior, you can then drag the play-head across the timeline to hear your soundtrack. The default Event setting sends the sound to your system's sound card and forgets about it. It is no longer part of the timeline and will not maintain sync with any animation. The only way to stop an Event sound from playing while in the Flash authoring environment is to hit the Esc key. Event sounds are typically used with shorter sounds and attached to buttons.

6 Many people have experienced a serious issue with sounds, even when set to "stream", falling out of sync with the animation in the Flash player. The only solution I have found for this is to change the default MP3 compression in the document's Publish Settings panel. Go to File > Publish Settings and click on the Flash tab. The default MP3 compression is 16 kbps, Mono. Click the "Set..." button next to the "Audio stream..." and change the bit rate to 20 kbps or higher. I personally recommend 24 kbps as the minimum compression setting. Click "OK" and test your movie. Your sync issue should now be resolved.

221

Dynamic sounds (AS3)

I'S ALWAYS FUN when sound and graphics come together to create an engaging and dynamic experience. This example uses ActionScript 3.0 to assign sounds to invisible buttons. The sounds are triggered when you roll over individual drums and cymbals. Each sound file in the Library is exported for ActionScript, allowing you to assign each sound to a different keyboard command as well. As a result, the Flash movie converts your keyboard to a musical instrument.

This is just one of an infinite number of ways sound and ActionScript can be combined to create a fun, interactive experience.

1 The first step is to create an invisible button for the area you want to assign a mouse command to. On a new layer above your image, draw a solid color in the same shape as your image. Convert the shape to a Button symbol and then double-click it to enter Edit Mode. Drag the Up keyframe to the Hit frame. The Hit state dictates the active area of the button and will not be visible in the compiled movie. Back on the main timeline the button is semi-transparent for editing purposes. With the instance of the button selected, type in a descriptive instance name in the Properties panel so you can assign some commands to it.

4 The first line creates a suitably named variable and sets it to an instance of *Tom1.* You'll do this for each sound clip class, which preps each sound for play. The other lines here show how to trigger the sound with a keystroke. Set the focus to the stage, then add a "key down" event that checks for the event's charCode. In case it's 68 or 100, play the *sndTom1* sound. What are 68 and 100? These happen to be ASCII codes for the letter *D.* See asciitable.com for a chart (you'll want the Dec column).

```
var sndTom1:Tom1 = new Tom1();
stage.focus = this;
addEventListener(
    KeyboardEvent.KEY_DOWN,
    function(evt:KeyboardEvent):void {
        switch(evt.charCode) {
            case 68:
            case 100:
                sndTom1.play();
                break;
        }
    }
);
```

6 Now that you have created a hit area and assigned a mouse and key command to trigger a sound dynamically, repeat steps 1–5 for each additional sound you want to add to your project. In the dynamic_sounds_AS3.fla provided on the source CD, I have created an additional 12 invisible buttons "mapped" to specific areas of the image of the drum set. Each Button was given a unique instance name.

2 Import your sound file into your Flash document. In the Library panel, right-click over the sound and select Linkage from the context menu.

3 In the Linkage Properties panel, click the Export for ActionScript checkbox. That will automatically check the Export in the first frame for you. If you're using AS3, provide a unique Class name (AS2 uses Identifier instead). Here, I've named it "*Tom1*". The Base class must be "*flash.media. Sound*" but Flash is smart enough to fill that in for you. When you click OK, Flash may give you a warning about a missing class in the classpath. That's the *Tom1* class you just named, so let Flash generate its automatic fix. If you like, check "Don't warn me again" to avoid a repeat warning. Click "OK".

5 If you want to trigger the sound with a mouse movement, add the desired mouse event handler to your *btnTom1* button and have the function play the corresponding Sound instance. Check out the sample file to see how easy it is to repeat this small block of code as often as necessary.

7 Open the library and you'll find a total of 13 sounds, each exported to ActionScript and given a unique Class name. Open the Actions panel and you'll see all the ActionScript has been provided as well.

This example was written by David Stiller (quip.net) in AS3. He has also written a version in AS2 which has also been provided on the source CD. We hope that these samples will provide a springboard for your own dynamic sound projects and experiments. Have fun!

Flash wasn't always this good

DURING THE PROCESS OF UPDATING THIS BOOK, specifically this interlude, I realized that many of the imperfections I wrote about in the first edition are now obsolete. What Flash CS3 lacked, Flash CS4 has made up for. Adobe has truly listened to its users, especially the designers and animators, by providing several new design and animation-centric tools. The previous title of this interlude was actually called "Flash isn't perfect", and with all the fun new features Flash CS4 has to offer, I had to make a slight change to it.

I have been on several of the Flash beta teams and it's always an honor to be invited to test and provide critical feedback on the toolset I rely on every day. Therefore I spend a lot of time putting the software through its paces in as many real world situations as possible. Being granted a direct line of communication to the Flash team is a privilege and an experience I always enjoy. I have seen how the beta process works externally as well as internally, and I can say first hand that Adobe listens to our feedback. In the first Flash CS4 beta build we discovered that the classic way of tweening was completely replaced by the new Motion model. After testing it thoroughly we discovered that it broke too much of our previous workflow as animators. We liked the benefits and improvements the new tweening method offered, but it also meant giving up full control of nested animations in Graphic symbols. We asked the Adobe Flash team if we could have both tween models in CS4 and in the very next beta build we saw Motion and Classic tweens as options. Now we have the best of both worlds. Thanks Adobe. So what else has Flash CS4 improved upon since CS3? Let's take a quick look at how these two versions stack up against each other.

In CS3 the frame number indicator in the Properties panel was only wide enough to display a total of two digits. This was frustrating when Graphic symbols contained more than 99 frames. Let's say the nested animation was 1000 frames long; in the CS3 Properties panel it looks like there were only "10" frames. CS4's new vertical Properties panel finally solves this issue with a much wider frame number field.

Flash CS3 had no native Inverse Kinematics (IK). We had to simulate this by editing the center point of symbols. It was crude and, let's be honest, it barely resembled a true inverse kinematics method. On one particular day at the Macromedia MAX conference in New Orleans, I was demonstrating how to fake IK by editing the center point of a symbol instance. Immediately after my session, a man with laptop in-hand rushed the stage to show me a Flash plugin prototype of an Inverse Kinematics tool running in Flash MX! This man turned out to be Eric Mueller, a Flash engineer for Macromedia (now with Adobe), who was one of the first advocates for IK in Flash I had ever met. He sent me the IK protoype for testing, and although it was buggy and crashed a lot, I was excited knowing that someone on the "inside" was thinking the same way as I was. Although it took 4 more years for this tool to see the light of day, I'm glad it is here. Flash CS4 now offers this highly anticipated feature and named it the Bone tool.

Flash CS3 provided the classic tweening method that was essentially unchanged since it was first introduced when Flash was called FutureSplash Animator (version 1). The classic method of tweening is frame-based and somewhat limiting. Flash CS4 makes up for many of the Classic tween limitations we have learned to live with but while Motion tweens offer more control over individual properties of a tween, Classic tweens provide certain specific capabilities that have been proven useful in certain applications. You will likely not choose one method of tweening over the other but rather select which tween works best for the task at hand.

Flash CS4 introduces the Motion Editor, a powerful new timeline panel that provides a way to view and edit all tween properties and property keyframes with precision. Previous versions of Flash never had a tool remotely close to this.

There is still no camera or three-dimensional stage to set up scenes and animate the camera within. But we do have the 3D Transformation and 3D Rotation tools in CS4, so it seems we may be heading in that direction for a future release.

There's still no option in CS4 to place the Grid on top of our content and we can't add custom eases to shape tweens like we can to Motion tweens. Flash doesn't offer artistic brush styles like Illustrator and, so far, no option to bend gradients. When copying symbols from one Library to another, it would be nice if any offending symbol names provided more options than what currently exists (like the ability to itemize the conflicting symbols and rename them). There are no keyboard shortcuts for resizing the Brush tool like we can in Photoshop.

There will always be features we will want to see added to or improved in future versions of Flash, which is why Adobe offers us our own wishing well: http://www.adobe.com/cfusion/mmform/index.cfm?name=wishform Feel free to drop in a coin or two and make your voice heard. The best part is, Adobe is listening.

■ The above image shows a video sequence composited with Flash animation for a popular children's television program. The bottom image shows an animation in the FLV format, seamlessly integrated into a website.

9 Working with video

FLASH VIDEO HAS REVOLUTIONIZED online video. Since its inception, the FLV format has grown exponentially as the favored medium for delivering video content. Google Video, You Tube, AOL, Yahoo! Video and MySpace are just some of the websites that have adopted Flash as their method of video deployment. Not to say other media players such as QuickTime, Windows Media and Real Player are "dead" by any means. But in comparison, it's as if they stood silently by as Flash boarded the Internet video bus and drove away.

This chapter features two separate client projects that show how video was used with Flash in different ways to achieve two very different goals.

Importing video

BETWEEN THE LIONS is a popular children's education television series designed to foster the literacy skills of its viewers, while playfully demonstrating the joys of reading. Teaching is done through the use of catchy songs and often animated shorts. This particular segment combines live action puppet characters, music and animation.

The main characters were videotaped against a blue screen. The idea is to replace the blue screen with animation. It was our job to create the animated sequences while maintaining sync with the provided video and ultimately deliver the final product suitable for high quality broadcast television.

Between the Lions is produced by WGBH Boston, Sirius Thinking, Ltd. and Mississippi Public Broadcasting. BTL ®, TM and characters WGBH Educational Foundation, © 2007 WGBH & Sirius Thinking. Animation production by Pileated Pictures.

1 The purpose of the blue screen is to provide an evenly lit, monochromatic field of color that can be easily keyed out using a video editor and replaced with a different image or video. Open the video in QuickTime and go to Window > Show Movie Properties and extract the audio track as a WAV file. Import this into Flash on its own layer and set it to Stream to sync with the animation.

3 Once the wizard has finished importing the video, insert enough frames on the main timeline to accommodate its length.

4 Import the audio track you extracted in QuickTime earlier and place it on its own layer. Set its behavior to Stream.

7 The script called for the live action puppet to react to an animated character falling from the sky. Having the video in a Graphic symbol embedded into the main timeline made it easy to sync the animation with the puppet's reaction.

8 Once the animation is complete it's time to export it to video format. But you don't want the embedded video to be included. Convert this layer to a guide layer so it will not be included in the exported file. You could also delete this layer.

2 Import your video file to launch
the Import Video wizard. Since you will need to
sync timeline animation to the video, select the option
to embed the video in SWF and play in the timeline. Select
Graphic as the Symbol type to embed the video and then
finally choose an encoding profile. Since this video track
is for reference only, select a low quality profile. The video

track in Flash
will be deleted
before exporting the animation and added later in After
Effects using the original uncompressed video file.

5 Since the video was converted to a Graphic symbol
during the import process, you can transform it over
time with motion tweens.

6 The video is motion tweened smaller to make room for
the animation sequences. Don't worry about how the
blue screen looks at this stage; it's only used as a reference.

9 The exported animation from Flash is composited with
the high quality video of the live action puppet in Adobe
After Effects. The blue screen is replaced with an alpha
channel so the animation can be seen through it. Syncing
both the video and animation sequences back together is

easy since they both share the same frame rate (29.97 fps)
and start on frame 1. As video files, all you need to do is
place them both on the After Effects timeline on the same
starting frame. A drop shadow was applied to the live action
puppet as a final touch.

SHORTCUTS
MAC WIN BOTH

Flash Video (FLV)

FLASH MAKES IT easy to add video into your project. The best part is that video can be treated like an object in Flash, allowing you to layer it, add ActionScript and even animate it. Depending on your project needs, video can be imported into the Flash timeline or kept external of the SWF and progressively downloaded.

Due to the ubiquity of the Flash Player, the client was confident integrating Flash video into their website while providing their audience with an engaging online experience.

1 Let me explain why Flash video was used for this project in the first place. The client's logo incorporates a photograph of a rubber band. The concept is to animate the rubber band flipping and catching the "Cone" logo in a *rubber band-like* way. It is rare that I ever need to leave the Flash toolset, but in this situation, Flash simply doesn't offer the essential tools to manipulate

a photograph in such a way. I turned to Anime Studio Pro (e-frontier.com) because of it's *Bones* and *Image Warp* features – perfect for this style of animation. I was able to manipulate the rubber band image over time by assigning an IK (Inverse Kinematics) chain to it. Anime Studio also supports native motion blur effects as seen above. The animation was then exported to QuickTime.

4 Click on the Video tab and select either On2 VP6 or Sorenson Spark. If your video includes an alpha channel that you want included in the FLV, you must encode with the On2 VP6 codec.

5 The Video Encoder allows you to adjust Audio (if any), add Cue Points and Crop and Resize the video before exporting. Try cropping the video as much as possible to keep the file size down.

8 With the FLV Component on the stage, you can position it based on any other design elements you wish to include. Here a simple graphic was added on a layer above to hide the top edge of the FLV. Content was also added with simple text fields. When compiled, the FLVPlayback component will load and play the external FLV during runtime in the Flash Player. You can control when the FLV starts by moving the component to a later or earlier frame in the timeline.

The FLV progressively downloads, which simulates streaming. Depending on its size, playback starts within seconds of loading.

2 File size is always a concern when dealing with video files. Since this is only a site introduction, loading the animation quickly is priority. The QuickTime file is over 6 megabytes, an unacceptable size given it's only 7 seconds long. Launch the Flash Video Encoder and add your video file. Then click on Settings to launch the Flash Video Encoding Settings window.

3 In the Encoding Profiles tab, select an encoding profile that best suits your image quality, file size requirements and Flash Player version.

6 Open Flash and go to Window > Components to open the Components panel and drag the FLVPlayback component to the stage. In the Component Inspector you can specify the path to your FLV file.

7 The intro animation is designed to fit in seamlessly with the rest of the page. Therefore the controller skin is removed completely using the Component Inspector.

9 Once your Flash document is published to the Web, visitors to the website are introduced with a Flash Video animation that they, without any inside information, assume is an animation made entirely with Flash. There is no indication that an FLV is being progressively downloaded, especially when combined with actual vector graphics. The resulting file size of the FLV is under 200kb, very acceptable for web animation.

Taking advantage of the FLV fomat can be very useful if you have very long animations that are very processor intensive as when played back in the Flash Player. Export your movie to the FLV format and progressively download it instead.

FLV tools and articles

THE UBIQUITY OF THE FLASH PLAYER is the reason why most of the Web surfing public can view Flash video without downloading additional plug-ins. This is the main reason why Flash video has grown so rapidly in recent years; the player had already penetrated the market as the most downloaded plug-in

in the history of the internet. Now that the FLV format has reached overwhelming popularity, various tools have sprouted that cater to this platform.

Wimpy is a free FLV player available from **wimpyplayer.com**. It is cross platform (Mac and PC) compatible, allowing you to watch your FLV and SWF files on your local drive.

An alternative free FLV player is available from Martijn de Visser and can be downloaded from his wesbite **martijndevisser.com**. Keep in mind, Martijn's player is still in beta and he admits it may have some rough edges. Martijn offers the source files if you have an inkling to improve upon what he has already started.

The Flash

Video Encoder lets you encode video files in either the On2 VP6 or Sorenson Spark video codecs. The Adobe Media Encoder CS4 is a stand-alone product that comes with Flash CS4. You can install it separately from Flash or other Adobe Creative Suite programs. The most useful feature is the ability to batch-process multiple video clips.

You may find that Adobe Bridge fulfills your needs when it comes to previewing and managing your FLV files. With Bridge, you can easily organize FLV files and folders, preview their contents and display their metadata.

There's more to the FLV format than what this chapter offers. I recommend visiting Adobe's Flash Developer Center, where you'll find a number of in-depth articles, tutorials and example files that will broaden your own Flash video horizons.

Flash Developer Center

http://www.adobe.com/devnet/flash/video.html

Encoding Flash Video

http://www.adobe.com/designcenter/dialogbox/encode_video.html

Selecting a Flash 8 video encoder

http://www.adobe.com/devnet/flash/articles/selecting_video_encoder.html

Handling cue points for audio files in ActionScript 2.0 and ActionScript 3.0

http://www.adobe.com/devnet/actionscript/articles/cue_points_audio.html

Controlling Flash video with FLVPlayback programming

http://www.adobe.com/devnet/flash/articles/flvplayback_programming.html

Examining the ActionScript 3.0 Flash video gallery source files

http://www.adobe.com/devnet/flash/articles/video_gallery.html

Using the Adobe Flash CS3 Video Encoder

http://www.adobe.com/devnet/flash/quickstart/video_encoder/

Wimpy FLV Player (free)

http://www.wimpyplayer.com/products/wimpy_standalone_flv_player.html

Martjin de Visser FLV Player (free)

http://www.martijndevisser.com/blog/article/flv-player-updated

■ Flash really comes to life when animation is combined with ActionScript for a truly interactive experience. The possibilities are endless when it comes to what can be achieved when design, animation and code overlap.

Interactivity

ACTIONSCRIPT KEEPS GETTING more powerful with each new release, but don't be afraid to experiment with older versions of the language. In some cases, you may need to! For example, many ad agencies still require that SWFs be published for Flash Player 7, or even 6. In a situation like that, ActionScript 3.0 is out of the question. If you're a die-hard fan of on() and onClipEvent(), you'll find you can't use those any more in AS3, so even if you publish for Flash Player 9 or higher, you'd have to bump back the version of ActionScript in your publish settings.

The choices are yours, and Flash now offers more choices than ever. Although ActionScript 2.0 was introduced in Flash MX 2004 (Flash Player 7), it is supported by Flash Player 6, so for the purposes of the following pages, AS2 refers to Flash Player 6 through 8 and AS3 to Flash Player 9 and up. That said, you'll find tutorials on the Web for ActionScript 1.0 and even earlier, before the language had numbered versions. Flash Player 9 supports all of them but only one at a time, based on publish settings.

Event handling

Contributed by David Stiller (www.quip.net)

WHEN SOMETHING OCCURS in a Flash movie, the occurrence is called an event. Events can be triggered by something in the Flash Player itself (system events) or by interaction from the person enjoying your content (user events). System events include, for example, the completion of an audio file or the incidence of a timeline frame. Let's explore that second one for a moment. Think of the playhead in terms of a car. When the playhead moves along the timeline, like a car driving along the street, it dispatches an "enter frame" event at a rate comparable to the movie's frame rate (by default, 12 frames per second). The event is simply a behind-the-scenes message that states, "Hey, I just entered a frame!" This happens, by the way, even if a *stop()* action tells the timeline to halt.

If a car arrives at a duck crossing and hits the brakes, its engine continues to idle, after all. At any time, you can program other objects to react to this event. We'll build up to this ourselves in just a bit. First, let's respond to some user events.

When a user clicks one of your buttons, a number of mouse-related events are dispatched in much the same way as above. One event happens when the mouse is pressed, another when the mouse is released and, depending on the version of ActionScript you're using, yet another when the mouse is pressed inside a button symbol but released outside of it. In all of these cases, the event happens whether you respond to it or not. If you do respond – this is called event handling – you need to write a function for it.

1 Let's say you've paused the timeline at frame 20 with a *stop()* action. From that point forward, you're halting the timeline every ten frames, because you want to give the user a chance to read something important on each of those keyframes. You have the *stop()* part down, but how do you get the timeline moving again?

2 Since you're planning to use a button, you'll need to put a button symbol on the stage. Use the Property inspector to give your button an instance name – that's what allows ActionScript to call out this particular object from all the others and use that instance name to tell the button what to do. In this example the instance name is *myButton*.

ActionScript 3.0

myButton.addEventListener(event, function);

3 In ActionScript 3.0, the main way to associate an event handler function with an event is the *addEventListener()* method. In this case, we're "wiring up" the myButton instance by way of two parameters. The first parameter specifies what event to listen for and the second defines the function to perform.

4 These parameters can be simple, such as the event part *MouseEvent. MOUSE_UP* or fairly complex, such as the complete definition of a function, which might otherwise stand on its own.

5 Putting the pieces into place, these parameters would fit as shown. Use the Actions panel to type the following code into a keyframe at frame 1.

6 You could optionally use a named function, like this. See the difference? In this second approach, you're defining the function as an entity of its own, a custom function arbitrarily named *startTimeline()*, then using that function's name as the second parameter. Notice that it doesn't matter how many lines it takes to code up the *addEventListener()* method. As long as you provide the two parameters it's looking for, you're good.

HOT TIP

The version of ActionScript you're using determines how this function is associated with the event at hand. Every object has its own selection of events, and these are listed in the relevant ActionScript Language Reference entry for the object in question.

(Continued...)

Event handling (cont.)

7 This ActionScript appears in frame 1 in a layer named "scripts," while the myButton symbol appears in its own layer, but also in frame 1. That's the important part, that they line up vertically; that is, they both appear in frame 1, so that they can "see" each other, otherwise the code and the button can't be associated. They might both appear in frame 2 or frame 10, it doesn't matter – as long as they line up.

....

ActionScript 2.0

ActionScript 2.0 handles things a bit differently. If you're publishing for Flash Player 8 or earlier, you can't use ActionScript 3.0 (only Flash Player 9 contains AVM2, the virtual machine that understands AS3). If your project specs require Flash Player 8 or back to Flash Player 6, here's a more "old-fashioned" approach to the previous scenario.

8 This time, the pattern is *myButton.onRelease =* function; and here, too, the function can be dictated right in the event handler or defined elsewhere as a named function.

```
1   myButton.onRelease = function():Void {
2       play();
3   };
```

Or...

```
1   function startTimeline():Void {
2       play();
3   }
4   myButton.onRelease = startTimeline;
```

9 Let's make sure we're caught up on the nitty-gritty details. In the AS3 version, the event handler function receives a parameter that the AS2 version's function does not, captured here under the arbitrary name *evt*.

```
1  function(evt:MouseEvent):Void {
2      play();
3  }
```

What's going on here? In this version of the language, every event carries with it an event object. In this sample, that incoming object isn't actually being used – we're just having the function execute a native *play()* action – but AS3 is pretty strict, so the function needs to at least let that object "in the door" even if it just sits there. The type of object matters, and this is a MouseEvent, so that explains the *:MouseEvent* suffix after evt. Finally, there's that :void business at the end. In AS3, type matters not only for incoming objects, but also for outgoing objects. This is a function, and functions either return a value or they

don't. This function does not – it just performs an action, then quits – so the *:void* suffix lets AS3 know not to look for a return value. In the AS2 version, you'll notice the *:void* suffix starts with an upper case letter. It's just one of those things. In AS2, all datatype suffixes start that way. In AS3, most do, but a handful don't, and those are all lower case. Yes, it's like learning state capitals back in grade school, but there are only three all-lower case examples: *int* (integers), *uint* (unsigned integers) and *void*.

10 In both AS3 and AS2, neither of these named function approaches (above) uses parentheses after the *startTimeline()* function. What gives? The reason for this omission is that the parentheses actually carry out whatever the function does. By leaving them off in these lines, you're telling ActionScript to carry them out when the event occurs, rather than when the playhead encounters them.

```
1  myButton.addEventListener(MouseEvent.MOUSE_UP, startTimeline);
2
```

```
1  myButton.onRelease = startTimeline;
2
```

11 In the Help files, which open in a browser, look up "on handler" and "onClipEvent handler," then use the "Refine results" area to filter your search for ActionScript 2.0, which covers both AS1 and AS2. To look up the AS2 events for buttons, search "Button class"; for movie clips, search "MovieClip class". You'll find even more events to pick from! For ActionScript 3.0, filter the Help books appropriately and look up button events under "SimpleButton" and movie clip events under "MovieClip". When you see a hyperlink under the Events heading (Show Inherited Events), click it. Believe it or not, buttons support around 30 events in AS3 – the exact number depends on the version of Flash Player you choose – so bear in mind that each new version of the language gives you greater control. In addition, the AS2 and AS3 approaches allow you to reassign and even cancel event handlers after the movie is compiled. The full list for each of these can be found in the built-in documentation and in the live docs:
http://help.adobe.com/en_US/AS3LCR/Flash_10.0/flash/display/MovieClip.html

239

What a drag

T HE *StartDrag()* METHOD accepts a number of optional parameters that allow you to constrain the drag, that is to box it in to specified dimensions and it's really easy to do.

ActionScript 3.0

ACTIONS - FRAME

Script Assist

```
1   smileyFace.buttonMode = true;
2   smileyFace.addEventListener(
3       MouseEvent.MOUSE_DOWN,
4       function(evt:MouseEvent):void {
5           smileyFace.startDrag();
6       }
7   );
8   smileyFace.addEventListener(
9       MouseEvent.MOUSE_UP,
10      function(evt:MouseEvent):void {
11          smileyFace.stopDrag();
12      }
13  );
```

1 In this example, we're using a Movie Clip symbol, because the MovieClip class supports *startDrag()* and *stopDrag()* methods. The movie clip has the instance name *smileyFace*. This code goes in a keyframe where that movie clip starts. Two event handlers, this time. The *MouseEvent.MOUSE_DOWN* event occurs when the user clicks the mouse over the movie clip and triggers a function that initiates the *startDrag()* method. The *MouseEvent.MOUSE_UP* event occurs when the

user lets go of the mouse over the movie clip. It triggers a function that initiates *stopDrag()*. The very first line makes the finger cursor show when the mouse moves over the movie clip. Unlike buttons, movie clips in AS3 don't show the finger cursor by default, even if you're handling mouse-related events. Note that the functions mention the *smileyFace* instance by name. This is a difference from how things worked in AS2.

ActionScript 2.0

ACTIONS - FRAME

Script Assist

```
1   smileyFace.onPress = function():Void {
2       this.startDrag();
3   };
4   smileyFace.onRelease = function():Void {
5       this.stopDrag();
6   };
```

2 Here's the AS2 version. This code goes in a keyframe where the movie clip starts. Note the absence of any sort of *buttonMode* reference. In AS2, buttons and movie clips alike display the finger cursor when mouse-related events are being handled. If you want to turn the finger cursor off, precede the code below with a single line:

smileyFace.useHandCursor = false;.
Even more important is the presence of the global *this* property. In AS2, the lines of code inside the function actually see that function as their "point of view". Because the function is associated with the *smileyFace* instance, the term *this* ultimately refers to *smileyFace* in this context.

Constrained drag and drop

ActionScript 3.0

1 Because AS3 has no "release outside" event, you can use a "mouse up" event for the stage itself. If the movie itself is listening for the mouse to lift, it doesn't matter where the event occurs, even if the mouse lifts outside the button or movie clip it started in. The trick is to only handle this event when you need it. You might, after all, want to listen for stage-wide "mouse up" events for other reasons, so we'll only commandeer this event while the mouse is pressed for the drag. We'll give the event back after the release. To do this, use the named function approach.

```
1  function startDragHandler(evt:MouseEvent):void {
2      smileyFace.startDrag(false, new Rectangle(50, 50, 250, 100));
3      stage.addEventListener(MouseEvent.MOUSE_UP, stopDragHandler);
4  }
5  function stopDragHandler(evt:MouseEvent):void {
6      smileyFace.stopDrag();
7      stage.removeEventListener(MouseEvent.MOUSE_UP, stopDragHandler);
8  }
9  smileyFace.buttonMode = true;
10 smileyFace.addEventListener(MouseEvent.MOUSE_DOWN, startDragHandler);
```

ActionScript 2.0

2 Thanks to the *onReleaseOutside* event, things are much easier in AS2. Notice that AS2's version of the *startDrag()* method accepts five parameters instead of two. The last four correspond more or less to the Rectangle object in AS3's version, except these are actual coordinates rather than a starting point plus a width and height.

In the last line, the *onReleaseOutside* event is set to the same thing as the onRelease event, so the mouse will stop dragging whether or not it's inside the movie clip when the user lets go.

```
1  smileyFace.onPress = function():Void {
2      this.startDrag(false, 50, 50, 300, 150);
3  };
4  smileyFace.onRelease = function():Void {
5      this.stopDrag();
6  };
7  smileyFace.onReleaseOutside = smileyFace.onRelease;
8
```

// ActionScript 1.0 and 2.0
someMovieClipInstance.startDrag
(lockCenter, left, top, right, bottom);
// ActionScript 3.0
someMovieClipInstance.startDrag
(lockCenter, {x, y, width, height});
The first parameter isn't so much about constraint as it is where the mouse stays during the drag. By default, the lockCenter parameter is false, which means dragging occurs from wherever the mouse first clicked the movie clip. If you set this parameter to true, dragging occurs from the movie clip's registration point.

The rest of the parameters are numbers, based on the parent timeline of the movie clip. The way these numbers are provided depends on the version of ActionScript.
An interesting thing happens with constrained dragging: if the mouse goes outside the bounds of the constraint, it might actually end up outside the movie clip when the user lets go. When that happens, the "release" event doesn't apply, because a bona fide release hasn't occurred. Instead, a "release outside" has. In AS1 and AS2, there is an event tailor-made for this circumstance. In AS3, it takes a bit more effort.

HOT TIP

In AS3, drag methods originate with the Sprite class, and movie clips inherit some of their functionality from Sprite. Buttons do not inherit from Sprite, which means they don't have access to these drag-related methods. That explains why we're using a movie clip in this example.

SHORTCUTS
MAC WIN BOTH

Pausing the timeline

ActionScript 3.0

```
1   function pauseTimeline(howLong:Number):void {
2       stop();
3       var t:Timer = new Timer(howLong, 1);
4       t.addEventListener(
5           TimerEvent.TIMER,
6           function(evt:TimerEvent):void {
7               play();
8           }
9       );
10      t.start();
11  );
    pauseTimeline(2000);
```

scripts : 1
Line 11 of 11, Col 3

SOONER OR LATER you're going to want to pause the timeline for a few seconds or even a few minutes, then resume the action after the viewer has had the chance to read something important or cast a lengthy gaze at your artwork. Flash banner advertisements are commonplace throughout the Web and the ability to pause the playhead to help emphasize a specific advertisement message can be critical to the success of the ad itself.

The obvious way to handle this is to add extra frames where you want the pausing to occur. Depending on the length of the pause, though, that can make for an unwieldy timeline, especially if you have a high frame rate (five seconds at 30 fps is a 150 frames of "dead space"). What if you could pull that off with a single frame?

1 This pause mechanism comes in two parts. If you only need to pause once, put both parts in the same frame; otherwise, put the function in frame 1, then call that function in later frames as needed. This is like an "everything" burrito. Everything you need is stuffed into this custom function. The first thing it does is stop the timeline. Next, it declares a variable, *t*, and sets it to an instance of the *Timer* class. The two parameters, *howLong* and *1*, tell Flash how long to wait before the timer completes and how often to run the timer, respectively. Once the Timer variable is in place, things start looking familiar again: a *TimerEvent.TIMER* event is added to the *t* instance and told to perform a function that causes the timeline to play again. Finally, the timer is started.

Once the function is in place, call it by name from the same frame or any subsequent frame. The value 2000 refers to 2000 milliseconds (that is, two seconds).

ActionScript 2.0

```
1   function pauseTimeline(howLong:Number):Void {
2       stop();
3       var id:Number = setInterval(
4           function():Void {
5               play();
6               clearInterval(id);
7           },
8           howLong
9       );
10  };
11
```

2 The AS2 version relies on the *setInterval()* function, which repeatedly triggers whatever other function you tell it to, as provided in its first parameter. The second parameter here, *howLong*, defines when the triggering should occur, in milliseconds. A companion function, *clearInterval()*, stops the repeated triggering after a single run. How? Earlier, *setInterval()* returns a Number value that gets stored in the id variable, then *clearInterval()* references that number by way of id as its own parameter. Here, again, you've got two parts. Put the first in frame 1. Then call it in that same frame or any later frame(s). Calling the function is the same as the AS3 version.

```
1   pauseTimeline(3000);
```

Loading images (AS3)

1 The simplest way to load an image is to use the Loader class. Three short lines will do it. The variable photo is set to an instance of Loader. The *Loader.load()* method is invoked on the photo instance, with a *URLRequest* instance provided as the parameter. If you wanted to, you could certainly create a separate variable just for the *URLRequest* instance and pass in that instead, but it's shorter to drop the new *URLRequest()* expression inside the parentheses

```
1   var photo:Loader = new Loader();
2   photo.load(new URLRequest("dolphin.jpg"));
3   holder.addChild(photo);
```

of the *load()* method. The quoted string is the name (and path, if needed) of a JPG file. Finally, invoke the *addChild()* method and pass it the photo instance in order to actually display the loaded image. Without that third line, the image will load, but you'd never see it.

FLASH IS CAPABLE OF loading quite a few file formats at runtime, including audio (MP3), motion graphics (FLV and SWF), and images (JPG, GIF and PNG). When you load such files with ActionScript, you're doing your visitors a favor: not only does this practise reduce the file size of the main SWF, but it also gives users the chance to decide which files they want to see. Why make them download it if they're not interested, right? With dynamic loading, everyone wins. Let's look at a JPG example using ActionScript 3.0.

3 If you want to change the scale of the imported image, or manipulate it in any other way, you'll have to wait until its fully loaded before you do. An event handler makes this easy.
Handling Loader class event handlers is a bit different from previous examples in this chapter. Instead of applying *addEventListener()* directly to the Loader instance, you have to apply it, instead, to the *contentLoaderInfo* property of that instance. After that, it's business as usual. Here we're listening for an *Event.COMPLETE* event and adjusting the *scaleX* and *scaleY* properties

```
1   var photo:Loader = new Loader();
2   photo.load(new URLRequest("dolphin.jpg"));
3   holder.addChild(photo);
4
5   photo.contentLoaderInfo.addEventListener(
6       Event.COMPLETE,
7       function(evt:Event):void {
8           holder.scaleX = 0.45;
9           holder.scaleY = 0.45;
10      }
11  );
```

of the holder movie clip to 45%. Again, this only works because the adjustment occurs after the image has loaded.

5 Create a third layer, name it scripts, and type the following ActionScript (top, right). Pretty familiar, huh? This line is identical to the corresponding line from the Loader example. The UILoader Component makes things a bit easier for you in that it turns the earlier three lines into one line of code.
At this point, you're set, but you'll probably want the progress bar to disappear after its work is done. You can take care of this with an event handler (bottom, right).

```
1   photo.load(new URLRequest("dolphin.jpg"));
```

```
1   photo.load(new URLRequest("dolphin.jpg"));
2
3   progressBar.addEventListener(
4       Event.COMPLETE,
5       function(evt:Event):void {
6           progressBar.visible = false;
7       }
8   );
```

2 The *addChild()* line happens to give you some leeway. For example, create an empty movie clip and drag an instance of it to the stage. Position it at 50 pixels in and 50 pixels down from the upper-left corner of the movie. Give this movie clip the instance name *holder*, and change that last line to *holder. addChild(photo)*. This time, the image loads into the empty movie clip, which means you can easily position it where you like.

```
1   var photo:Loader = new Loader();
2   photo.load(new URLRequest("dolphin.jpg"));
3   holder.addChild(photo);
```

4 If you want to display load progress while an image loads, it's easy to do with the ProgressBar Component. Instead of the Loader class, we'll let the UILoader Component take over loading duties, which means you can also drop the holder movie clip. Starting with a new document, drag an instance of the UILoader Component to the stage and give it the instance name *photo*. Create a new layer and drag an instance of the ProgressBar Component to the new layer. Give it the instance name *progressBar*. Select the progressBar instance and flip to the Parameters tab of the Property Inspector. Set the source parameter to photo. This associates the loading mechanism of the UILoader Component instance, photo, with the visual display of the progress bar.

HOT TIP

The Parameters tab makes it easy to configure Components without having to use ActionScript, but if you prefer to code, you can program parameters by referencing the Component's instance name, then a dot, then the parameter in question. For example, step 4 would look like this: progressBar. source = photo.

6 You can test and simulate your movie by going to Control > Test Movie or using Ctrl + Enter on your keyboard. A new window containing your compiled SWF will open. Go to View > Bandwith Profiler to show a graph of the downloading performance. Go to View > Download Settings to select the bandwidth profile you wish to test with. Once you've made your selection, go to View > Simulate Download to emulate how fast your image will most likely load under these conditions. Keep in mind Flash can only estimate typical Internet performance and not exact modem speeds.

SHORTCUTS
MAC WIN BOTH

Interactivity

Loading images (AS2)

1 AS2 differs significantly in how it loads images. In fact, there's more than one way to do it. The approach that comes closest to the ease of AS3 involves the MovieClipLoader class. In this case, you'll want an empty movie clip. Again we'll call it holder, as before, to act as the container for your image which lets you position the JPG as desired. Loading the image isn't especially complicated, but responding when the load is complete ... that's a little more convoluted. Here's the easy part, first.

3 To recognize when the image has loaded, we'll need to program an event listener using an instance of the Object class. This generic object will act as a liaison between the MovieClipLoader instance and its event handler function. In this case, the association is not as direct as it is in the AS3 examples. The name of the listener variable isn't important, but it's listening for events, so "listener" makes sense enough. This variable points to an object, and the object is given an onLoadInit property, which is set to a function (the event handler). Why onLoadInit? The MovieClipLoader class provides quite a few events, listed in the ActionScript 2.0 Language Reference, and this is the one that not only states when content is loaded, but allows access to the properties and methods of the loaded content. The function references the holder movie clip and sets its _xscale and _yscale properties to 45%. Finally, the MovieClipLoader instance, photo, is associated with the listener object. Note, in AS2, under these circumstances, that method is addListener(), not addEventListener().

```
1   var photo:MovieClipLoader = new MovieClipLoader();
2   photo.loadClip("dolphin.jpg", holder);
3
4   var listener:Object = new Object();
5   listener.onLoadInit = function():Void {
6       holder._xscale = 45;
7       holder._yscale = 45;
8   }
9   photo.addListener(listener);
```

2 In this case, photo is an instance of the MovieClipLoader class. The name is a bit misleading, because this class also loads JPGs, GIFs and PNGs, depending on what version of the Flash Player you publish to (see the Help docs for specifics). The MovieClipLoader.loadClip() method is invoked on the photo instance, specifying the file to load and the movie clip to load it into.

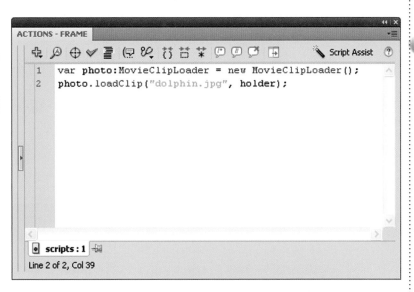

```
ACTIONS - FRAME

1  var photo:MovieClipLoader = new MovieClipLoader();
2  photo.loadClip("dolphin.jpg", holder);

scripts : 1
Line 2 of 2, Col 39
```

HOT TIP

Properties like alpha and scale belong to different camps, between AS3 and AS2. In ActionScript 3.0, these sorts of property generally range between 0 and 1, which makes 22% look like 0.22. In ActionScript 2.0, these usually range between 0 and 100.

4 Now that you know about event handling, dragging and dropping, pausing timelines and loading images, try testing yourself by developing a cool little Flash application that incorporates buttons that, when clicked, load external images to create a fun photo gallery. Then try extending this functionality to allow each image to be dragged and dropped around the Flash stage.

SHORTCUTS
MAC   WIN   BOTH

247

Toggling sound (AS3)

WE TOOK A quick look at ActionScripted audio in Chapter 8, but that was only an hors d'oeuvre. In that exercise, you loaded sounds from the Library. By loading your audio from external files instead, you can reduce the overall size of your SWF and still have all the programmatic control described earlier. 10 to 1, you'll find that sound is a common part of your day-to-day Flash workflow, so let's explore a bit more.

1 One of the most commonly requested audio features in a Flash movie is a mute button, something that gives the user the option to temporarily pause the audio, or silence it while it keeps playing. We'll build up to that in just a moment but, first, you need some ActionScript that summons an MP3 file. In AS3, that means an instance of the Sound class and the URLRequest class. The first two lines create respective instances of the Sound and URLRequest

```
1  var audio:Sound = new Sound();
2  var req:URLRequest = new URLRequest("Tasty Jazz.mp3");
3  audio.load(req);
4  audio.play();
```

classes and store those objects in variables. As the URLRequest instance is created, note that it receives the name of an MP3 file outside the FLA file. After that, the *Sound.load()* method is invoked on the *audio* variable, which loads the file, and finally, the *Sound.play()* method plays the music.

3 Now that the playing sound is associated with a channel, you can invoke the *SoundChannel.stop()* method on the *channel* variable, like this:
In this code, a button symbol has been given the instance name *btnMute*, and its *MouseEvent.CLICK* handler halts the playing sound.

```
1   var audio:Sound = new Sound();
2   var channel:SoundChannel;
3   var req:URLRequest = new URLRequest("Tasty Jazz.mp3");
4   audio.load(req);
5   channel = audio.play();
6
7   btnMute.addEventListener(
8       MouseEvent.CLICK,
9       function(evt:MouseEvent):void {
10          channel.stop();
11      }
12  );
```
scripts : 1
Line 12 of 12, Col 3

5 If you want to resume the audio, rather than restart it from the beginning, use the *SoundChannel.position* property to find out how far the audio has played when you halt it, and add an optional parameter to the *Sound.play()* method. Create a new variable to hold this information, such as *offset*.

```
1   var audio:Sound = new Sound();
2   var channel:SoundChannel;
3   var offset:Number = 0;
4   var req:URLRequest = new URLRequest("Tasty Jazz.mp3");
5   audio.load(req);
6   channel = audio.play();
7
8   btnMute.addEventListener(
9       MouseEvent.CLICK,
10      function(evt:MouseEvent):void {
11          offset = channel.position;
12          channel.stop();
13      }
14  );
15  btnRestart.addEventListener(
16      MouseEvent.CLICK,
17      function(evt:MouseEvent):void {
18          channel.stop();
19          channel = audio.play(offset);
20      }
21  );
```

2 That gets the sound rolling, but it doesn't give you the control to make it stop again. For that, you need an additional object – an instance of the *SoundChannel* class. Note how the instance is created and stored in a variable, just like the other two, but its value (a particular playing sound) is added in the last line of code.

```
ACTIONS - FRAME                                              Script Assist

1   var audio:Sound = new Sound();
2   var channel:SoundChannel;
3   var req:URLRequest = new URLRequest("Tasty Jazz.mp3");
4   audio.load(req);
5   channel = audio.play();
6
```

4 But that's only half the story, isn't it? To do this right, you'll want the user to be able to turn the sound off, and then back on, at will. You can do that with two buttons or a single button. Let's start with two, because it's easier. To restart halted audio, just re-associate the Sound instance with its *SoundChannel* instance, as before (this assumes a second button with the instance name *btnRestart*). Note that the restart button stops the audio, just like the mute button, before it restarts the audio. That extra line is there in case the user clicks the restart button first.

```
ACTIONS - FRAME                                              Script Assist

1    var audio:Sound = new Sound();
2    var channel:SoundChannel;
3    var req:URLRequest = new URLRequest("Tasty Jazz.mp3");
4    audio.load(req);
5    channel = audio.play();
6
7    btnMute.addEventListener(
8        MouseEvent.CLICK,
9        function(evt:MouseEvent):void {
10           channel.stop();
11       }
12   );
13   btnRestart.addEventListener(
14       MouseEvent.CLICK,
15       function(evt:MouseEvent):void {
16           channel.stop();
17           channel = audio.play();
18       }
19   );

scripts : 1
Line 19 of 19, Col 3
```

249

Toggling sound (cont.)

6 Let's face it, two separate buttons are fine, but a single toggle button is definitely more cool. You can combine the previous MouseEvent.CLICK handlers into a single function when you reduce your pair of buttons to a single symbol. Because button symbols don't have programmable timelines, you'll have to make this combined symbol a movie clip. Frame 1 of this movie clip should display whatever graphic makes sense in your case. If audio plays by default, as we've been doing, you'll want the symbol's first frame to show a "mute this audio" graphic, to indicate to the user that clicking the button will stop the audio. If that's your route, then put a "resume this audio" graphic in frame 2 of the same movie clip. Make sure to give your movie clip an instance name, such as *btnToggle*, invoke the MovieClip.stop() method on it right from the beginning, and then update your code as shown in the figure.

Note the addition of a buttonMode setting of true, because this symbol isn't a button symbol. Without that line, the mouse cursor wouldn't become a pointer finger. The trick to this approach is pretty simple. An *if* statement checks the current position of the *btnToggle* symbol's timeline. If the playhead is on frame 1, it means the "mute this audio" graphic is showing and the audio is already playing. Under that circumstance, the code you've already seen is repeated, and *btnToggle* itself is instructed to display

```
ACTIONS - FRAME                                    Script Assist
1   var audio:Sound = new Sound();
2   var channel:SoundChannel;
3   var offset:Number = 0;
4   var req:URLRequest = new URLRequest("Tasty Jazz.mp3");
5   audio.load(req);
6   channel = audio.play();
7
8   btnToggle.stop();
9   btnToggle.buttonMode = true;
10  btnToggle.addEventListener(
11      MouseEvent.CLICK,
12      function(evt:MouseEvent):void {
13          if (btnToggle.currentFrame == 1) {
14              offset = channel.position;
15              channel.stop();
16              btnToggle.gotoAndStop(2);
17          } else {
18              channel = audio.play(offset);
19              btnToggle.gotoAndStop(1);
20          }
21      }
22  );
23
scripts:1    scripts:1
Line 25 of 25, Col 41
```

frame 2 of its own timeline. Otherwise, the opposite is true, and the function restarts the audio and repositions the symbol's playhead at frame 1. If your audio does not play by default, you'll reverse the ActionScript inside the *if* statement. This code allows the same symbol to perform double duty, by shuttling it back and forth between two frames.

8 Another way to pause and resume audio is simply to update the volume while the audio keeps playing, in which case you're not really pausing at all, but muting. For this, you'll need one more object, an instance of the SoundTransform class. This gets a tad more complicated, but it paves the way for volume adjustment in general, which is the last thing we'll look at. The basic idea is that every SoundChannel instance is associated with a SoundTransform partner. The SoundTransform class features a volume property that controls the volume of the channel it's coupled with. See if you can connect the dots. This time, a new variable named adjust holds a SoundTransform instance. The MouseEvent.CLICK handler sets the SoundTransform.volume property of the adjust variable, which mutes the audio, and adjust is then associated with the SoundChannel. soundTransform property of the channel variable. The same thing occurs when the button has already been toggled, except the volume property is set to 1 (100%; half volume would be 0.5).

```
ACTIONS - FRAME                                    Script Assist
1   var audio:Sound = new Sound();
2   var channel:SoundChannel;
3   var adjust:SoundTransform = new SoundTransform();
4   var offset:Number = 0;
5   var req:URLRequest = new URLRequest("Tasty Jazz.mp3");
6   audio.load(req);
7   channel = audio.play();
8   channel.addEventListener(Event.SOUND_COMPLETE, reset);
9   function reset(evt:Event):void {
10      channel = audio.play();
11      channel.addEventListener(Event.SOUND_COMPLETE, reset);
12      btnToggle.gotoAndStop(1);
13  );
14
15  btnToggle.stop();
16  btnToggle.buttonMode = true;
17  btnToggle.addEventListener(
18      MouseEvent.CLICK,
19      function(evt:MouseEvent):void {
20          if (btnToggle.currentFrame == 1) {
21              adjust.volume = 0;
22              channel.soundTransform = adjust;
23              btnToggle.gotoAndStop(2);
24          } else {
25              adjust.volume = 1;
26              channel.soundTransform = adjust;
27              btnToggle.gotoAndStop(1);
28          }
29      }
30  );
```

7 When you're using the single button approach, make sure to write an event handler to set the button to its default state when the audio ends! This will be an event handler for a SoundChannel event.

This event handler has to be reassigned every time the SoundChannel instance is re-associated with a playing sound, so you'll find it convenient in this case to use a named function, as discussed on page 237, for the Event.SOUND_COMPLETE event – otherwise, you'd have to write out that particular function twice.

```
ACTIONS - FRAME                                              Script Assist  ⑦
  1   var audio:Sound = new Sound();
  2   var channel:SoundChannel;
  3   var offset:Number = 0;
  4   var req:URLRequest = new URLRequest("Tasty Jazz.mp3");
  5   audio.load(req);
  6   channel = audio.play();
  7   channel.addEventListener(Event.SOUND_COMPLETE, resetButton);
  8   function resetButton(evt:Event):void {
  9       btnToggle.gotoAndStop(2);
 10   );
 11
 12   btnToggle.stop();
 13   btnToggle.buttonMode = true;
 14   btnToggle.addEventListener(
 15       MouseEvent.CLICK,
 16       function(evt:MouseEvent):void {
 17           if (btnToggle.currentFrame == 1) {
 18               offset = channel.position;
 19               channel.stop();
 20               btnToggle.gotoAndStop(2);
 21           } else {
 22               channel = audio.play(offset);
 23               channel.addEventListener(Event.SOUND_COMPLETE, resetButton);
 24               btnToggle.gotoAndStop(1);
 25           }
 26       }
 27   );

 scripts : 1
 Line 27 of 27, Col 3
```

HOT TIP

ActionScript 2.0 versions of these scripted audio examples are available on the CD. The principles are the same; it's really only the syntax that changes.

9 By applying the same principle, you can use the Slider component from the Components panel to throw together a quick volume slider. Get rid of the toggle button and drag out an instance of the Slider component. Give it an instance name, such as *volumeSlider*, and use the Component Inspector panel to configure its parameters like this:

Name	Value
direction	horizontal
enabled	true
liveDragging	false
maximum	1
minimum	0
snapInterval	0.1
tickInterval	0.1
value	1
visible	true

This code assigns an Event. CHANGE handler function to the volumeSlider instance:

```
ACTIONS - FRAME                                              Script Assist  ⑦
  1   var audio:Sound = new Sound();
  2   var channel:SoundChannel;
  3   var adjust:SoundTransform = new SoundTransform();
  4   var offset:Number = 0;
  5   var req:URLRequest = new URLRequest("Tasty Jazz.mp3");
  6   audio.load(req);
  7   channel = audio.play();
  8
  9   volumeSlider.addEventListener(
 10       Event.CHANGE,
 11       function(evt:Event):void {
 12           adjust.volume = evt.target.value;
 13           channel.soundTransform = adjust;
 14       }
 15   );

 scripts : 1
 Line 15 of 15, Col 3
```

251

Objects, objects everywhere

WHEN PROGRAMMING IN FLASH, it's helpful to think in terms of something called objects. In the real world, an object is generally defined as a material thing, something you can hold in your hands, observe and possibly manipulate, like a Rubik's cube. As often as not, you'll find that multiple copies of a particular object can exist at the same time. For example, you might belong to a Rubik's fan club, where each member brings a cube to weekly meetings in order to see who can solve the puzzle the fastest. On one level, everyone's cube is the same; and yet, everyone's cube is also unique. Each cube can be jumbled into millions of configurations, even though all are made in the same way from the same parts. Mr Rubik presumably has a blueprint for those parts in a filing cabinet somewhere.

Before we get too far afield, how does this analogy relate to objects in ActionScript? Let's look at the parallels. Just about everything in ActionScript can be described as an object. This includes such "material things" as movie clips, buttons and text fields, as well as intangibles like dates, arrays (lists of things) and sounds. Each type of object has its own set of characteristics, comprised of distinguishing attributes, things it can do, or things it can react to. It is the particular combination of these characteristics that defines an object's datatype, the thing that makes an object the type it is. In order to create an object, its "blueprint" must be consulted. In ActionScript, this is outlined by something called a class.

Classes determine objects

Classes define an object's properties, methods and events. Properties are the attributes an object has, such as a movie clip's width and height. Methods are things an object can do, such as loading an external JPG or jumping to a certain frame label. Events are things an object can react to, such as a mouse click or the occurrence of a timeline frame. Conveniently, Flash's documentation features two ActionScript Language References (2.0 and 3.0) that are closely structured around these classes. If you're dealing with a movie clip, search the term "MovieClip" and you'll quickly dial in to a handy movie clip Owner's Manual. If you're dealing with a button symbol in ActionScript 2.0, search the term "Button," making sure you're not reading from the separate Components Reference. For buttons in ActionScript 3.0, search the term "SimpleButton," because the Components Reference is combined with the general ActionScript Language Reference. Many classes build off of each other, so don't forget to click any hyperlinks in the documentation that say "Show Inherited Public Properties", "Show Inherited Public Methods" and the like. Doing so will give you the full picture of an object's capabilities.

By convention, class names are capitalized, and multiple words are combined into a single term, so if you're dealing with a text field, search "TextField"; if mouse events, search "MouseEvent," and so on. That makes it pretty easy to look things up. You just have to ask yourself two questions. First, "What object am I dealing with?" This will lead you to the necessary class entry. Then, "Am I trying to tell this object how to be, what to do, or how to react?" This will steer you toward the relevant property, method, or event summary. These tips should help you avoid a sense of "Where do I even begin?" when dealing with the built-in documentation.

Contributing author David Stiller is a career multimedia programmer/designer and co-author of Foundation Flash CS4 for Designers (friends of ED) and The ActionScript 3.0 Quick Reference Guide (O'Reilly). He likes anaglyph 3D photography, finely crafted wooden game boards, Library of Congress field recordings, and Turkish coffee. David is self-taught and gets a kick out of sharing "aha!" moments with others through consultation, mentoring and regular contributions to a variety of Flash forums. He lives in Virginia with his amazing wife, Dawn, and his beguiling daughter, Meridian.
www.quip.net

The default layout for Flash, above, is suitable for most users, but in time it might become limiting. The addition of a few custom extensions and commands can add a whole new toolset to Flash and an enhanced workflow.

11

Extending Flash

FLASH OFFERS A WIDE ARRAY of features for designing
and animating. As great as it is, Flash can sometimes lack
some of the functionality that you might benefit from.
There always seems to be some drudgery that ought to be
automated or some desperately needed tools that simply
don't exist. Other than petition Adobe for these coveted
new features, what's a poor "Flasher" to do? Thankfully,
since Flash MX 2004, the curious and proactive Flash user
has an alternative: Flash JavaScript, or JSFL for short.
JSFL is a scripting language that interfaces directly with
the Flash authoring environment. In a nutshell, it allows
you to create your own Flash extensions.

Introduction to JSFL

Contributed by Dave Logan
www.dave-logan.com

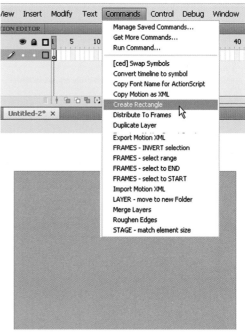

1 Select the Rectangle tool **R** and draw a rectangle. As you can see, the History panel behaves like it does in most Adobe programs, compiling a list of your actions.

AN EXTENSION is basically a plug-in, something that is added to Flash and extends its functionality. JSFL only affects the Flash authoring environment (i.e. Flash CS3) and has no effect on published Flash Player files (i.e. .swf files).

The best part about JSFL is that anyone can use it to speed up and improve their workflow. JSFL is based on the ECMAScript standard, which means it's very similar to other languages based off the standard, such as JavaScript and ActionScript. If you don't know anything about programming, you're still in luck. You can create custom commands without touching a line of code. The best way to dive into JSFL is to play around with the History panel. To open the History panel, go to Window > Other Panels > History.

5 Now go to the Commands menu, and lo and behold, there it is! Your very first Flash command. You can make all kinds of simple commands like this. If you find yourself doing some simple action over and over, create a command for it!

2 Select the Rectangle and delete it. You'll see each action added to the History panel.

3 Select the first event, Rectangle, which popped up when you drew the rectangle. Press the "Replay" button. *Voila!* The original rectangle reappears.

4 Now let's make it into a command. Click the floppy disk icon in the lower right-hand side of the History panel to save this command. Name it something like "Create Rectangle".

6 Afterwards, you can access the command even more easily by assigning it a shortcut by going to Edit > Keyboard Shortcuts.

7 There is a catch, however. Use the Brush tool to draw something on the stage. Look in the History panel. Notice the little red X next to the Brush event? That means that you can't use it in a command. To put it simply, Flash treats some tools a little bit differently than others, and because of that you can't use them in your commands. The important thing to know is that the History panel can be used as the foundation of custom commands. This goes far beyond replicating rectangles.

HOT TIP

To add your own shortcuts, you have to create your own shortcut set. It's easy. In the Keyboard Shortcuts window, click the little Duplicate Set button with two pieces of paper and an arrow at the top right. Name your set (it doesn't matter what) and press OK. Now you can modify and add your own shortcuts.

SHORTCUTS
MAC WIN BOTH

Trace Bitmap and JSFL

ET'S SAY YOU'RE WORKING on a project and decide to give some video an artsy rotoscoped effect. A great way to achieve this in Flash is with the Trace Bitmap command. Trace Bitmap converts bitmap images into vector graphics that can be edited using Flash's drawing tools. Using a video program such as After Effects or QuickTime, you can export the footage as a sequence of images and import them into Flash, ready to be traced.

But the Trace Bitmap command only works for one image at a time. That means to trace a series of images, you must tediously apply the effect to each and every image. Luckily, this is just the type of task JSFL excels at automating.

1 First, you need to apply the Trace Bitmap effect to one image. Import the image sequence from the CD by selecting File > Import > Import to Stage and navigate to *image_sequence001.png*. Select image_sequence001.png and click Open. A menu will pop up asking if you want to import all of the images in the sequence. Click "Yes".

4 The Trace Bitmap panel also allows you to preview your current settings before committing to them. Change any of the setting values and click on "Preview" to see how they will affect your image. When you're happy with the results, click "OK". Depending on the complexity of the image, Flash will pause briefly while it converts the image into a series of vector shapes.

2 Each imported image will be placed in its own keyframe on the main timeline. You can play your movie to see the "video" play as a sequence of frames.

3 Select the image in frame 1. Go to Modify > Bitmap > Trace Bitmap. In the Minimum Area box, type "5". This makes Flash re-evaluate what color to use for every 5 pixels instead of every 8, which produces a more realistic looking trace. Don't click "OK" just yet.

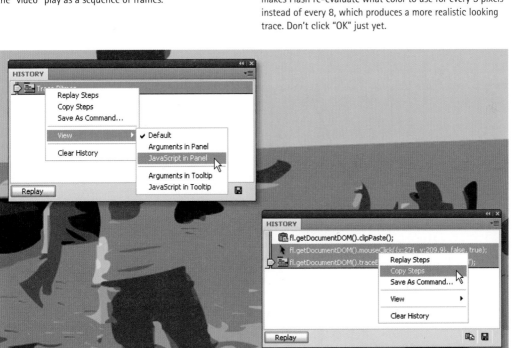

5 Next, right-click on the History panel and select View > JavaScript in Panel. The History panel will update itself, displaying the JavaScript for the commands you just executed.

6 Don't worry if the first set of numbers is a bit different than yours. They correspond to the exact coordinates on the screen that you clicked on to select the image. Copy these steps by selecting them, right-clicking and selecting Copy Steps.

(Continued...)

259

Trace Bitmap and JSFL (cont.)

(Continued...)

HOW DO I KNOW about all this JSFL stuff? Maybe you are thinking I have all of the JSFL methods and arguments meticulously memorized? Not exactly (although that would be convenient and pretty impressive at the next Flash conference I attend).

The secret is, I clicked on the word *mouseClick* and the word *traceBitmap* and hit F1 (Flash Help docs). Flash's Help panel popped up and instantly took me to the entries I selected for these methods. Whenever you get stuck or confused, your first stop should be the Help docs.

7 Go to File > New and select Flash JavaScript File. If you are not running Flash CS3 Professional, you'll notice there is no option to create a new Flash JavaScript File. Don't worry, just open up a text editing program like Notepad and carry on. JSFL in the end is just a text file, so it doesn't matter how you create it. Paste the code that you copied from the History panel.

9 Let's shorten the code we have so far to something a bit more manageable. We'll do this by creating a variable. Add the code to the beginning of the existing code.

```
trace_bitmap.fla*  Script-1*
1  var doc = fl.getDocumentDOM();
2  fl.getDocumentDOM().mouseClick({x:106, y:142}, false, true);
3  fl.getDocumentDOM().traceBitmap(100, 5, 'normal', 'normal');
```

11 While we're at it, let's define a few more variables. The first new variable, *tl*, is another abbreviation. It refers to the document's timeline. The *curLayer* variable refers to the currently selected layer (which it gets from the *currentLayer* method), and the *curFrame* variable refers to the current frame we're on (which, again, it gets from the *currentFrame* method).

```
trace_bitmap.fla*  Script-1*
1  var doc = fl.getDocumentDOM();
2  var tl = doc.getTimeline();
3  var curLayer = tl.currentLayer;
4  var curFrame = tl.currentFrame;
5  doc.mouseClick({x:117, y:160}, false, true);
6  doc.traceBitmap(100, 5, 'normal', 'normal');
```

8 Let me explain a bit of the gibberish that you're looking at. The *fl* at the beginning of both lines refers to, you guessed it, Flash itself. The *getDocumentDOM()* method tells Flash that we wish to work with the currently active Flash document. Both *mouseClick* and *traceBitmap* are pretty self-explanatory; the former is the method that describes a single mouse click, and the latter is the method which actually turns the image into a bunch of vectors.

```
trace_bitmap.fla*  Script-1*
1  fl.getDocumentDOM().mouseClick({x:106, y:142}, false, true);
2  fl.getDocumentDOM().traceBitmap(100, 5, 'normal', 'normal');
```

The stuff inside the parentheses is the arguments that are passed to these methods. So the first line tells Flash to execute a mouse click at x:117 and y:160 within the active document (the false and true after the coordinates have to do with whether the Shift key is down). The second line tells Flash to execute a bitmap trace with the parameters you set when you went to Modify > Bitmap > Trace Bitmap. The threshold, or number of colors in the tracing, is set to 200, the minimum area is set to 5, and the curve fit and the corner thresholds are both set to normal. The ; at the end of both lines tells Flash that the line of code is over. Think of it as a period in a sentence.

10 Now go down to the next two lines of code and replace each *fl.getDocumentDOM();* with the more elegant *doc*. So now you should have something like this.

```
trace_bitmap.fla*  Script-1*
1  var doc = fl.getDocumentDOM();
2  doc.mouseClick({x:117, y:160}, false, true);
3  doc.traceBitmap(100, 5, 'normal', 'normal');
```

12 You now have variables that know what frame the user is on. Now let's find out how many frames are in that layer. In line 5, the frames property at the very end of that line returns an array, which gets stored in the *frameArray* variable. An array is basically a list of items. In this case, it's a list of frame objects. Arrays have a length property that tells you how many items are in the array; that's what's getting stored in the *n* variable from the expression *frameArray.length*; in line 6. (If an array represented a year, it would have a length of 12, for each month.)

```
trace_bitmap.fla*  Script-1*
1  var doc = fl.getDocumentDOM();
2  var tl = doc.getTimeline();
3  var curLayer = tl.currentLayer;
4  var curFrame = tl.currentFrame;
5  var frameArray = tl.layers[curLayer].frames;
6  var n = frameArray.length;
7  doc.mouseClick({x:117, y:160}, false, true);
8  doc.traceBitmap(100, 5, 'normal', 'normal');
```

(Continued...)

HOT TIP

Variables can generally be named whatever you like, but there are a few rules: no spaces in the names, no punctuation except for _ or $, and don't start the name with a number.

SHORTCUTS
MAC WIN BOTH

Trace Bitmap and JSFL (cont.)

(Continued...)

13 Now we have a variable that knows how many frames are in our selected layer. Why is this important? When you imported the image sequence, Flash put each one on its own frame. We want to use the Trace Bitmap command on each one, so the script has to know how many there are so it can tell how many times it should run the command.

```
trace_bitmap.fla*   Script-1*
1   var doc = fl.getDocumentDOM();
2   var tl = doc.getTimeline();
3   var curLayer = tl.currentLayer;
4   var curFrame = tl.currentFrame;
5   var frameArray = tl.layers[curLayer].frames;
6   var n = frameArray.length;
7   tl.setLayerProperty('locked', true, 'others');
8   doc.mouseClick({x:117, y:160}, false, true);
9   doc.traceBitmap(100, 5, 'normal', 'normal');
```

15 All that's left is finding a way to make Flash run the *traceBitmap* method for every frame. Luckily, that's pretty easy to do with a *for loop*.
A *for loop* is a type of control flow statement. A control flow statement is basically a way to change the normal flow of a program, one line after the other. *For loops* are ideal for going through lists of data, or an array of frames. The important parts of a *for loop* are within the parentheses. The first part, *i = 0*, declares that the variable *i* is initially set to *0*. The second part, *i < 10*, is the condition. This means that the code contained within the brackets will only be executed if this condition is met. In this case, the condition is that *i* is less than 10. The third part, *i++*, tells the script what to do after each iteration, or turn. Each time the condition is met, the contained code is executed, and afterwards this statement is executed. Each time the code is executed, the value of *i* will be increased by 1. As complex as it looks, it's pretty simple in function. So the loop starts out

```
trace_bitmap.fla*   Script-1*
1    var doc = fl.getDocumentDOM();
2    var tl = doc.getTimeline();
3    var curLayer = tl.currentLayer;
4    var curFrame = tl.currentFrame;
5    var frameArray = tl.layers[curLayer].frames;
6    var n = frameArray.length;
7    tl.setLayerProperty('locked', true, 'others');
8    for (i=curFrame; i<n; i++) {
9        doc.selectAll();
10       doc.traceBitmap(100, 5, 'normal', 'normal');
11       tl.currentFrame = i + 1;
12   }
```

at the currently selected frame, and as long as the current frame is less than *n* (that is, less than the length of the layer), the code within the brackets will be executed and the image will be traced. Finally, *tl.currentFrame = i + 1;* sets the current frame to the value of *i* (already the current frame) plus 1, which puts us on the next frame.

14 Next, add a command to lock every layer other than the one you're using. Why are you doing this? Because you need a better way of selecting the image we are going to trace. What if you have an image that doesn't end up in the area you clicked when you first ran the Trace Bitmap command? The script will fail. So instead of simulating a mouse click, you're going to lock all the other layers and then perform the *selectAll* method. The *selectAll* method does the same thing as using ⌘ A ctrl A.

```
trace_bitmap.fla*   Script-1*
1   var doc = fl.getDocumentDOM();
2   var tl = doc.getTimeline();
3   var curLayer = tl.currentLayer;
4   var curFrame = tl.currentFrame;
5   var frameArray = tl.layers[curLayer].frames;
6   var n = frameArray.length;
7   tl.setLayerProperty('locked', true, 'others');
8   doc.selectAll();
9   doc.traceBitmap(100, 5, 'normal', 'normal');
```

HOT TIP

Programmers often start *for loops* with 0 rather than 1 because arrays happen to start counting at 0. By matching these starting numbers, the *for loop* easily keeps pace. Frames, however, start at 1, which explains the arithmetic in line 11.

16 You're done! All you have to do is save the command with a descriptive name, such as *Rotoscope.jsfl,* in the Commands folder on your local drive. See the Interlude at the end of this chapter for the folder paths for your operating system. Once you have the command saved, you can import an image sequence into a new document and go to Commands > Rotoscope. Now that all this legwork is done, whenever you want to get this hand-drawn effect, all you have to do is import the images and run the Rotoscope command. And it only took 12 lines of code!

This is just scratching the surface of what is possible with JSFL. As you can see in the following pages, some amazing additions to the program have been created by normal Flash users like yourself. If you're intrigued, I highly recommend the book *Extending Flash MX 2004* by Keith Peters and Todd Yard. While the book is a bit old, JSFL hasn't changed much in the last few incarnations of Flash, and the instruction is still very valid. And, of course, there's always the Internet. Do a search for JSFL, hunker down in your computer chair, and make some kick butt extensions!

Easy Palette

Easy Palette is a color management system developed by Dave Logan that gives you a friendlier and more useful way to manage custom palettes. Easy Palette will allow you to name colors to speed identification (useful for groups that are working on the same project), save and load custom palettes (useful for easily applying color schemes across various documents, or to have specific palettes for each character in your animation), and quickly navigate through saved colors.

This extension is available on the source CD along with several more extensions provided by many kind and generous designers and developers around the world. Check out the Interlude at the end of this chapter for more information.

SHORTCUTS
MAC WIN BOTH

AnimSlider Pro

PIMP MY PROPERTIES panel! Warren Fuller of animonger.com has developed one of the most popular Flash plug-ins for animators. It's called the AnimSlider and it is simply indespensable if you use Flash for animation. In a nutshell, this plug-in literally does everything the Properties panel does, but better and with many more features. Think of it as a one-stop panel for almost all your animation needs. AnimSlider is so useful that it is the first plug-in I install after installing or upgrading Flash. It will save you valuable production time and, as a result, will pay for itself many times over the more you use it. I have included the AnimSlider Limited plug-in package in "Chapter 12/Animonger" folder on the included CD. This is a limited free version to get you started. You can purchase and download the full version at animonger.com.

Warren has developed an NTSC color safe palette that can be imported into the Swatches panel. This is a free *.clr file included on the CD with this book or from Warren's website. To use this palette, open the Swatches panel and click on the upper right corner drop-down arrow. Select Add Colors or Replace Colors and navigate to the NTSC.clr file on the CD provided or if you downloaded it from Warren's website to your local hard drive. You can learn more about color safety and video in Chapter 6.

The AnimTools plug-in is a panel that includes the same editing tools found in the AnimSlider panel but conveniently grouped together for your convenience. The AnimTools panel includes two additional features that the AnimSlider panel does not.

The New Folder Tree feature creates a folder hierarchy in the current document's Library with one simple click. Type in a folder name in the pop-up dialog panel and click OK. Open the Library panel and notice your new folder tree created for you. This will greatly enhance the organization of your Flash file.

The Move to Existing Folder feature allows you to move Library items to existing folders. Select the objects in the Library you want to move, and click the Move to Existing Folder button. In the path dialog box, type in the case-sensitive name and path of your folder. For example, to move the selected items to a folder named "Arms" inside a folder named "Joe", type "Joe/Arms".

The total number of frames in the selected Graphic symbol is displayed here. The AnimSlider supports up to four digits. This is a huge improvement over the Flash Properties panel, which only supports two digits. Being limited to two digits makes it difficult to know how many frames are nested and what frame is actually being displayed.

Button tools are conveniently located and allow you a simple click for many common editing commands: Paste in Place, Flip Horizontal and Flip Vertical, Arrange Forward and Arrange Backward, Convert to Symbol, Reset Transformation Point, New Graphic symbol, Reset Free Transformation, Convert Lines to Fills, New AnimPak Pro symbol, Duplicate Layer, Apply a Motion Tween with or without easing and a Go To Frame Number feature.

You can toggle how AnimSlider reacts when you click on the slider portion of the panel. You can click and drag or click and "float" the cursor along the frames.

Change the Play mode of multi-frame symbols using this handy drop-down menu.

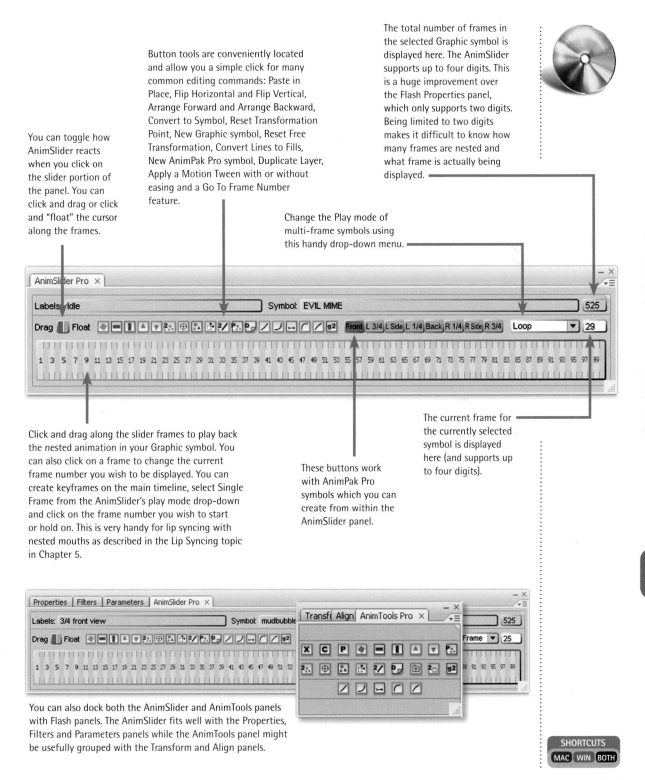

Click and drag along the slider frames to play back the nested animation in your Graphic symbol. You can also click on a frame to change the current frame number you wish to be displayed. You can create keyframes on the main timeline, select Single Frame from the AnimSlider's play mode drop-down and click on the frame number you wish to start or hold on. This is very handy for lip syncing with nested mouths as described in the Lip Syncing topic in Chapter 5.

These buttons work with AnimPak Pro symbols which you can create from within the AnimSlider panel.

The current frame for the currently selected symbol is displayed here (and supports up to four digits).

You can also dock both the AnimSlider and AnimTools panels with Flash panels. The AnimSlider fits well with the Properties, Filters and Parameters panels while the AnimTools panel might be usefully grouped with the Transform and Align panels.

SHORTCUTS
MAC WIN BOTH

Ajar extensions

JUSTIN PUTNEY OF AJAR Productions has written several extensions for Flash, geared towards the designer and animator. Justin is passionate about writing extensions, which is clearly evident in this quote from his website: "*I am officially addicted to making Flash extensions. It seems to tickle some very nerdy part of my brain.*"
I highly recommend visiting and bookmarking his website:
http://ajarproductions.com/blog
http://ajarproductions.com/blog/flash-extensions
http://www.ajarproductions.com

By the time you read this, I am sure he'll have several more extensions available as he seems to post new ones almost daily. Thanks Justin!

FrameSync

This is a handy-dandy animation plug-in similar to Animonger's AnimSlider (previous example), except that it uses frame labels and requires no other setup. Create a new layer in your Graphic symbol containing your mouth shapes and add descriptive Frame Labels for each frame. Select the instance of the mouth symbol and click the "refresh panel" button (or check the "auto refresh" feature) in the FrameSync panel. Create a keyframe and then simply click the desired frame inside the FrameSync panel window to set your mouth shape.

Roughen Edges

Flash is known for its smooth vector looking graphics. This extension adds a command that will remove that typical Flash vector look by roughening the edges of lines, fills, and drawing objects. It can also be re-applied for more dramatic effects. It's an imperfect implementation, so make sure you keep an eye on what you're doing. There can be some unexpected results, especially when applying it to one element repeatedly.

Queasy Tools

This extension creates Classic tweens, applies strong easing (both in & out), automatically adds keyframes, duplicates layers, swaps symbols from the Library, turns on bitmap smoothing, aligns objects, and applies tinting to white and alpha to 50% or 0%, scaling, arranging flipping, and more! It's like an info-mercial where they keep throwing in extra features!

Select Frame Range

Enter a starting frame and an end frame, click "OK" and this clever extension will select all the frames in between.

Motion Preset Preview

Once you've created a custom motion preset, you can use this command to immediately create a live preview from your current document.

Guide Maker

This is a very smart extension that provides a simple and clean way to create guides. You can specify guides based on a percentage of the stage or type in an exact numerical value that represents the number of pixels in between each guide. The integrated color picker is for customizing the color of the guide. Guides can even be saved and reused!

Convert Timeline to Symbol

This extension has been a long time coming. If you've ever needed to copy and paste long complicated animations into a symbol then this is for you. Just run this extension from the Commands menu, provide a name for the symbol and click "OK".

iK'motion

After installing the iK'motion plug-in, go to Window > Other Panels and click on "iK'motion" to launch the iK'motion panel. The interface is clean and easy to navigate.

THE KNEE BONE'S CONNECTED TO the...well, you get the idea. Here's a super cool extension that provides Flash CS3 users with Inverse Kinematics (iK). The iK'motion toolset utilizes Flash's powerful extensibility layer to deliver dynamic inverse kinematics animation capabilities directly to the designer! These tools and commands give you the ability to create parented IK chains, manipulate movements and automatically generate tweens on the timeline, all within the standard flash IDE.

If you haven't upgraded to CS4 and can't take advantage of the new Bones tool, then the iK'motion extension is your answer.

This awesome extension can be found on **www.flashextensions.net,** where you will find a cool collection of extensions, components, tools, vector artwork, sounds and other add-ons for the Flash authoring tool.

The Segment box displays the name of the anchor bone of the current chain (segment) being worked with.

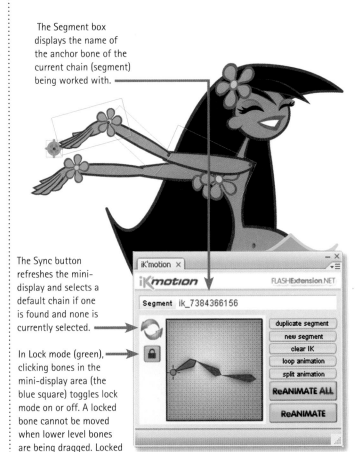

The Sync button refreshes the mini-display and selects a default chain if one is found and none is currently selected.

In Lock mode (green), clicking bones in the mini-display area (the blue square) toggles lock mode on or off. A locked bone cannot be moved when lower level bones are being dragged. Locked bones are marked as red.

Go to Edit > Customize Tools Panel. Here you can add and remove various tools to and from your Tools panel. From the table of tool icons on the left side of the dialog, select the tool that you would like to have the iK'motion picker tool appear underneath. A good choice might be the white arrow (Subselection Tool). After clicking the icon, scroll to the bottom of Available Tools and select the "iK'motion Picker Tool". Click the ">> Add >>" button. You should now see the iK'motion Picker Tool in the list under "Current selection".

Duplicate Segment copies and pastes all movie clips in the currently selected chain. A new layer is created for each copied "bone" and names are changed to avoid duplicates.

All selections made with the iK Picker Tool will attempt to add the selection to the current chain. To create a new chain, use the "new segment" button. To clear iK info from a mistakenly selected object, use the "clear iK" button.

Clear iK removes all iK information from the currently selected movie clips on the stage. Once iK info is cleared on a movie clip instance, the clip is no longer affected by any iK'motion functions. Animations created before iK info was cleared will still run as previously defined, however.

Use the loop function to create precise looping animations where the "ends meet".

(Not available in trial versions.) This is an advanced feature that lets you "split up" a tween into two separate tweens.

Swift 3D Xpress

SWIFT 3D XPRESS is a 3D extension for Adobe Flash that allows users to convert drawings and text on the Flash stage into 3D animations without having to leave the Flash interface. Swift 3D Xpress is a revolutionary 3D extension (plug-in) that allows users to quickly convert 2D text and artwork into 3D animations without leaving the Flash interface. Vector objects on the Flash stage can be brought into the Swift 3D Xpress interface and customized using pre-built animations, lighting schemes and materials. The 3D scenes are rendered and placed into a specialized movie clip in Flash's Library for further use or future editing.

Swift 3D Xpress is a very easy and intuitive tool to use. It provides instant results and real-time 3D feedback when applying materials and animations. It's great for making anything from animated logos to animated buttons and more.

1 Create a shape in a new Flash document and select it. Go to Commands > Swift 3D Xpress to launch the extension. You will find your shape has been automatically extruded and placed in a 3D environment. Now you can modify various aspects of the 3D shape. Start by adding a beveled edge.

3 Click on the Lighting Trackball tab to edit the lighting of your 3D scene. How you adjust the lighting of your scene is directly related to how the materials of your object will look after being rendered. The placement of each light and the number of lights will affect the color contrast of the object. Experimentation here is key. There are several variations of animations that

can be added to your object. Click on each thumbnail in the Animations panel to see a preview of the animation. Once you have decided which animation to use, drag and drop it to your 3D object in the Viewport.

2 Click and drag the Object trackball to rotate the selected object. You can also have the option to lock the rotation based on its horizontal and/or vertical axis.

Click on "Sizing" in the upper left menu and adjust the amount of depth to create a cube.

You can apply different materials by clicking and dragging your preferred material from the Materials panel directly to the surface of your 3D object.

4 When you are satisfied with your work, click on the "Render and Export to Flash" tab. You have two format options to export to: Vector and Raster. Each will generate an image sequence that can then be converted to a movie clip or an SWF file.
The Vector format provides several options such as various Fill and Outline styles. You can also render Specular Highlights, Reflections and Shadows.
The Raster format also provides some options such as Quality level, Color Depth and as Antialias Quality.
Once you have chosen your desired settings, click on Render Frames. Swift 3D Xpress will render each frame of the animation that can also be played within this same panel using the playback controls.
If you choose Create Flash Movie Clip, a movie clip containing your animation will be added to your Flash document's Library.

You can then drag it to the stage and incorporate it into your Flash project. If you choose Export to SWF File, Swift 3D Xpress will provide you with the option to name your SWF file and choose a location on your hard drive to save it to.

Flashjester

THE LIST OF FEATURES that Jugglor and Creator offer are so extensive, it is simply impossible to fit them all on just these two pages. As an animator, you'll be excited about Jugglor's Desktop Pet feature. Extend the interactive capabilities of your Flash animated character by dragging, dropping and bouncing your character around your desktop. This only scratches the surface of Jugglor's full range of features and to really gain an understanding as to how Jugglor can fully extend your Flash projector files, visit their website (www.flashjester.com) for a comprehensive feature list.

Creator is a screensaver creation tool from Flashjester that provides everything you need for converting your Flash movies to screensavers.

1 Jugglor provides the option to specify detailed information about your movie such as a title, a new Juggled name, the path to where you want the Juggled file, the size of the compiled projector file and detailed information regarding the movie's player version, size, width, height, frame rate, etc.

2 Jugglor's ActiveX settings allow you to control how your desktop pet will be rendered, how it will play or loop, how to customize the right-click menu and much more. I have included on the source CD a file named mudbubbleDesktopPet. fla. Open it and locate the layer named "Right-click menu". Select the Movie Clip instance in this layer and open the Actions panel to see the right-click menu code.

3 Jugglor's setup settings offer plenty of options for customizing the level of interactivity, right-click menu visibility, mouse and keyboard interaction, icon tray support and even Joystick support. You can also specify if and when you want your file to expire.

Creator

1 Creator shares a user interface very consistent with Jugglor. After launching Creator, start your screensaver project by populating the available fields in the General Settings section. This information will be available in the screensaver settings menu after it has been installed to the computer's operating system.

2 If your Flash file includes mouse events, or any type of interaction, *Always have Interaction* will allow interaction with the screen saver without closing it. You have the option of including or muting sounds or leaving it for the user to choose. Creator supports right-click menu options and multimonitor support. You can also set your expiration by run times (number of times it is executed), by a certain date, or after a certain by-day period (example, a 30-day trial).

3 This screen is the final step in creating a screensaver. It allows you to build your final project into an .scr screensaver file, and an .exe installer file. Additional files may be created, depending on which options you choose. Creator produces screensavers that are ready for distribution. Simply zip them or copy them to a storage medium, and you're ready to get your product out there. No plug-ins are required to run Creator-compiled screensavers! Creator bundles all required plug-ins so your users don't have to worry about them.

SHORTCUTS
MAC WIN BOTH

Toon Boom Animate

Animates comes with a very intuitive user interface. The wide array of drawing tools include various brush tips to create a unique look. The smart color ID system combined with the color model make it very easy to color characters.

KNOW THIS IS A BOOK focused primarily on the Adobe Flash program, but it seems necessary to mention a wonderful new program called Animate. Animate is a complete animation program from Toon Boom, a company who has been focused on delivering some of the best animation software since 1994. Some of Toon Boom's other popular animation programs include Toon Boom Studio and Digital Pro. Animate is their latest animation tool and it boasts an impressive list of features, many similar to the Flash feature set. But what makes Animate worth mentioning is what separates it from Flash, specifically the features it has that Flash does not and in some cases Animate does better.

Animate's similarities to Flash include vector drawing tools, pressure sensitivity, image vectorization, keyframing, onionskin, inverse kinematics and symbols. But that is where the similarities end and Animate excels with color ID and palette styles, ability to rotate the canvas, an ink and paint tool, X-sheet, 3D multi-plane camera, forward kinematics,

morphing, compositing effects and more. Animate can also export to FLV, SWF, MOV and image sequence formats, allowing content made with Animate to be integrated into a Flash project if desired.

Both share an impressive toolset; these overlap with each other in many areas but Flash remains the choice of platforms when it comes to interactive content such as websites and games due to its native programming language ActionScript.

Both Flash and Animate are powerhouse programs for delivering engaging animation for a multitude of formats. If you come from an animation background then I highly recommend adding Animate to your toolset.

Download the free Personal Learning Edition of Animate here:
http://www.toonboom.com/products/animate/trial.php

The scene planning process is a breeze in Animate. Thanks to the Perspective view you can lay out your scene and plan impressive camera moves. The Function editor conveniently enables you to set your velocity and keyframes. Also the enriched timeline offers direct access to functions.

Add special effects directly in Animate. Effects include blur, shadow, tone, highlight, glow, and transparency, to name a few, and come with customizable parameters to give your animation a more professional and richer look.

HOT TIP

Visit www. toonboom.com to learn more about Animate and the rest of the Toon Boom product family. Aside from offering the best professional level animation software, they provide some very cool animation software for children too!

SHORTCUTS
MAC WIN BOTH

Pimp my Flash

GETTING THE BEST OUT OF FLASH can sometimes mean customizing it to suit your needs. Since Flash MX 2004 and the introduction to JSFL, many commands and extensions have been developed to enhance your Flash workflow. From custom JSFL commands to customizing the panel layout to customizing keyboard shortcuts, Flash can truly be molded into a tool that suits your personal design and animation preferences.

Many of the available extensions for Flash are installed via the Adobe Extension Manager. The AEM is installed along with Flash CS4 and will launch automatically when you double-click a file with the ".mxp" extension. Once installation is complete, Flash will need to be restarted before using the extension. Clicking once on the name of each extension will update the bottom panel with a description of what the extension is designed to do. These descriptions are

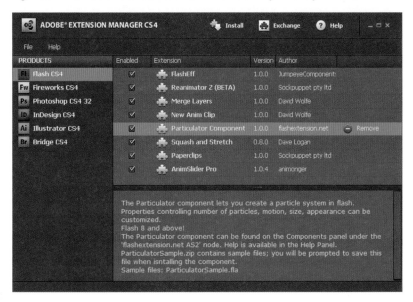

written by the developers of the extensions and often include a URL that explains in more detail how the tools can be used in various workflow environments. In some cases, the developer has links to video tutorials, extension updates and contact information.

Here are some more custom commands and plug-ins included in the "Extensions" folder on the source CD – thanks to your friendly neighborhood Flash users and the community at large. It's all about sharing what we learn and the contributors to this book are testament to that. Warm and fuzzy feelings all around.

David Stiller (*quip.net*):
Apply Motion Tween.jsfl, Apply Shape Tween.jsfl, mudbubble_Pause.mxp, mudbubble_FPSMeter.mxp

Justin Putney (*ajarproductions.com*):

Break text into lines.mxp, Unify Stroke and Fill.mxp, Combine Textfields.mxp, Convert timeline to symbol. mxp, Export as Motion Preset Preview.mxp, FrameSync.mxp, Guide Maker.mxp, Invert Frame Selection.mxp, Move layers to new folder.mxp, Queasy Tools.mxp, Roughen Edges.mxp, Select Empty Layers.mxp, Select Frame Range.mxp, SelectFrames_toStartAndEnd.mxp, Set stage to element size.mxp

Dave Logan (*dave-logan.com*):

AutoColor.mxp, CreateMaskingLayer.mxp, CustomZoom.mxp, DefaultColorsMX2004.mxp, Easy Pallette.mxp, EnterGraphCurFrame.mxp, FrameAllLayers.mxp, KeyAllLayers.mxp, Label Jumper.mxp, Rotoscope.jsfl, SkipAround.mxp, SquashAndStretch.mxp, SwapColorsMX2004.mxp, SymbolizeFrames.mxp, ViewLayer.mxp

Dave Wolfe (*toonmonkey.com*):

drawGuide.mxp, frameEdit.mxp, frameExit.mxp, layercolor.mxp, libAppend.mxp, mergeLayers.mxp, MultiSwap.mxp, NewAnimClip.mxp, TimingChart.mxp, toggleGuide.mxp, toggleOutline.mxp, traceSequence.mxp, tween2keys.mxp

Urami (*njquality.com*):

BitmapSmoothingMultiple.jsfl, BitmapSmoothingSelected.jsfl, Filter Set Selection.jsfl, Filter Set All.jsfl

Patrick Mineault *(5etdemi.com):*

symbolswapper.mxp, pixeltools.mxp

Jarrad Hope:

Camera.mxp, Paperclips.mxp

Senocular *(senocular.com):*

distributetoframes.mxp

....

Some of the JSFL commands on the source CD include a *readme* file to help explain what they do when you run the command. For scripts that will appear as items in the Commands menu, save the JSFL file in the Commands folder in the following location:

Windows XP:

C:\Documents and Settings\user\Local Settings\Application Data\Adobe\ Flash CS3\language\Configuration\Commands

Windows Vista:

C:\Users\user\AppData\Local\Adobe\FlashCS3\language\Configuration\Commands

Mac OS X:

Macintosh HD/Users/userName/Library/Application Support/Adobe/Flash CS3/language/Configuration/Commands

■ CS4 offers two different methods for tweening objects. In the end, both features essentially perform the same tasks but provide very different features. Is one tween method better than the other? Why choose one type of tween over the other and for what purpose? CS4 provokes such questions and this chapter will help answer them.

12 What's new in CS4

ADOBE FLASH CS4 introduces so many new design and animation features, it was hard to determine how best to present them to you in this book. I struggled to decide if these new features should be integrated throughout the various chapters or if it was better to have a single comprehensive chapter dedicated to just the new CS4 features. At this point it is probably obvious to you I decided to do both.

This book will have two audiences: Flash veterans upgrading from Flash CS3 and newcomers learning Flash CS4 from the ground up. For all the Flash veterans coming from CS3, you may want to read this chapter first and then check out the new CS4 examples in the previous chapters. For everyone discovering Flash for the first time, reading this book sequentially from Chapter 1 may be preferred.

Motion presets

OTION PRESETS ARE pre-built motion TWEENS that can be applied to an object on the stage. With the object already selected, choose the desired preset from the default list in the Motion Presets panel and click the Apply button. The preset animation is applied to your new object.

The default presets provide a great starting point but you'll likely want to make your own. Flash CS4 provides the ability to save your custom animations as presets that can be reused over and over. You can build up libraries of animations that not only can be easily applied to any object on the stage, but can also be shared across the entire Flash design community.

1 Go to Window > Motion Presets to open the Motion Presets panel. This panel looks a lot like the Library panel with its preview window on top and list of folders and preset objects below. Just select a preset to preview it.

2 Make sure you have an object selected on the stage before selecting a Motion Preset animation. Once you have a preset selected, just click the "Apply" button. Your object on stage is now animated.

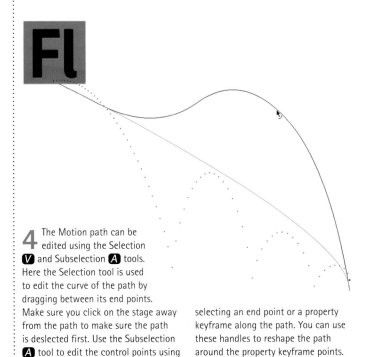

4 The Motion path can be edited using the Selection **V** and Subselection **A** tools. Here the Selection tool is used to edit the curve of the path by dragging between its end points. Make sure you click on the stage away from the path to make sure the path is deselected first. Use the Subselection **A** tool to edit the control points using the Bezier handles that appear when

selecting an end point or a property keyframe along the path. You can use these handles to reshape the path around the property keyframe points.

3 Once the preset is applied, Flash applies a Motion tween to the object containing the property animation data. You can leave the animation as is or use it as a starting point by editing the animation to suit your needs.

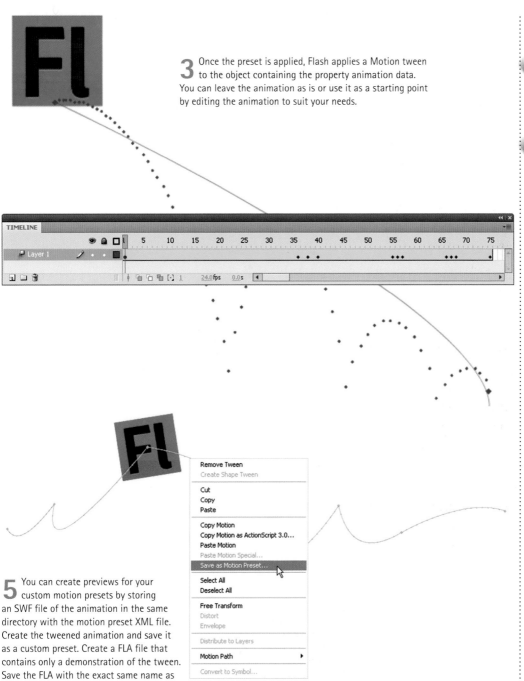

5 You can create previews for your custom motion presets by storing an SWF file of the animation in the same directory with the motion preset XML file. Create the tweened animation and save it as a custom preset. Create a FLA file that contains only a demonstration of the tween. Save the FLA with the exact same name as the custom preset. Create a SWF file from the FLA file with the Publish command. Place the SWF file in the same directory as the saved custom motion preset XML file. These files are stored in the following directories:
Windows: C:\Documents and Settings\<user>\Local Settings\Application Data\Adobe\Flash CS4\<language>\

Configuration\Motion Presets\
Macintosh: <hard disk>/Users/<user>/Library/Application Support/Adobe/Flash CS4/<language>/Configuration/Motion Presets/

SHORTCUTS
MAC WIN BOTH

Motion and Classic tweens

SO MUCH HAS CHANGED in Flash CS4. But so much has remained the same. What does this mean for the veteran Flash animator who already has tried and tested workflows that can't be broken? What features are you more likely to adopt and which ones will help you create new animation techniques that might increase your production?

If you remember one thing about the two tween methods in Flash CS4, remember that the Classic tween is frame-based while the new Motion tween is object-based. There are advantages and disadvantages to using both and the difference depends on what kind of object you are animating and what that object needs to do for you. There are so many different types of object that can be tweened in Flash: movie clips, Graphic and Button style symbols, imported bitmaps and text fields. The 2 different tween methods can complicate matters when trying to understand what tween to use with what kind of object.

Let's start by comparing both tweening methods side by side and find out why Flash CS4 offers both.

Motion tweens have more then 1 type of keyframe. The black circular dot in the first frame of the span indicates the assigned target object. If this dot is hollow (white), it means the object has been removed and a new object can be assigned.

Black diamonds indicate the last frame and any other property keyframes.

Motion tweens provide a tween path that can be edited.

A black dot at the beginning keyframe with a black arrow and blue background indicates a Classic tween.

Use Classic tweens to animate between two different color properties, such as tint and alpha transparency. Motion tweens are limited to 1 color effect per tween.

Motion tweens are indicated by a solid light blue colored layer span. Unlike the Classic tween span, there are no horizontal dashed or solid lines or arrows indicating a broken or completed tween.

Classic tweens can not be saved as Motion Presets. You can only save Motion tweens as preset animations in Flash CS4.

A *tweened frame* is any frame between keyframes within a tween span.

Motion tween spans can be stretched and resized in the timeline and are treated as a single object.

You can animate a 3D object using a Motion tween but 3D is not supported with Classic tweens.

Classic tweens use keyframes. Keyframes are frames in which a new instance of an object appears.

Classic tweens can not be stretched and resized in the timeline like Motion tween spans can. Classic tweens are comprised of frames that have to be selected individually and inserted or removed in order to stretch or shorten the animation.

Creating Motion tweens

THINK OF THE motion tween as a Classic tween on steroids, allowing you to animate each property individually across an entire motion span. This was difficult if not impossible with previous versions of Flash and Classic tweens. The combination of Motion tweens and the new Motion Editor allow for a myriad ways to create motion in Flash. The flexibility of having each property independent of each other is enough to make your head spin. If that wasn't enough, one of the most popular timeline-related enhancement requests is now a reality: the ability to lengthen and shorten the Motion tween and have all keyframes interpolated automatically. With Classic tweens this can only be done manually and the more layers, frames and keyframes, the more of a nightmare this process can be. Let's take a look at more differences between these two tween methods.

1 Motion tweens can be applied to symbols and text fields. A tween span in a layer can contain only 1 object or 1 text field. However, you can have multiple objects nested inside a single object being Motion tweened. To apply a Motion tween, right-click over the object on the stage and select Create Motion Tween from the context menu.

3 The quickest way to create an animation is to simply move the object to a new position on the stage. Flash will automatically create a motion path that can be edited using the Selection **V** and Subselection **A** tools.

2 Flash automatically lengthens the tween span to accommodate a full second's worth of frames based on the document's frame rate. If your frame rate is set to 24 frames per second then your span becomes 24 frames long. The playhead marker is automatically positioned at the end of the tween span.

HOT TIP

The terms "keyframe" and "property keyframe" are different in Flash CS4. The term "keyframe" refers to a frame in the timeline in which a symbol instance appears on the stage for the first time. The separate term "property keyframe", which is new to Flash CS4, refers to a value defined for a property at a specific time or frame in a Motion tween.

4 Use the Position and Size features in the Properties panel to control the exact position and size of the object. These are hot text sliders that allow you to drag across them to change their values as well as select and type in the value manually.

SHORTCUTS
MAC WIN BOTH

Working with Motion spans

S O HOW DOES THIS NEW MOTION tween model work anyway? Not only has Adobe changed how tweens are created and applied, but how we work with frames, keyframes and the tween span itself. The new Motion tween is very different from its predecessor visually, sans any dashed or solid horizontal arrows, or vertical lines indicating the "sync" feature being turned off. The Motion tween span is simple and straightforward, uncluttered and unadulterated, yet provides the ability to create sophisticated animations that go beyond the capabilities of the Classic tween method.

1 It's ironic that Flash CS4's new Motion tween span looks so plain and simple yet offers so much power and flexibility just under its serene facade. You will not find horizontal lines with arrowheads in between keyframes. You will not see dashed lines signifying broken tweens or vertical lines representing non-synced keyframes. This is a brave new world for Flash tweeners and to steal a line from Flash animation legend Laith Bahrani: "All of your tweens have finally come true."

4 To move a span in the timeline, select it by clicking on it and then click and drag it to a new location in the layer.

7 To split a tween span into two separate spans, Ctrl-click (Windows) or Command-click (Macintosh) a single frame in the span and then choose Split Motion from the span context menu.

2 To lengthen the duration of your animation, drag either the left or right edge of the span to the desired frame. Flash will automatically interpolate all the keyframes in the span according to its new length. To add frames to a span without interpolating the existing keyframes, hold down *Shift* *Shift* shift while dragging the edge of the span.

3 You can select a range of frames in a Motion span by holding down *ctrl* ⌘ while dragging across the desired frames.

5 To select a single frame or keyframe in a Motion span, hold down Ctrl and click the frame or keyframe. Once selected you can drag the keyframe to a new frame, or Alt-click to duplicate it.

6 To select a range of frames in a Motion span, hold down the *ctrl* ⌘ key while dragging across the range of frames and layers you want to select.

8 You can duplicate a Motion span by selecting it and then holding down the *alt* ⌥ Alt key while dragging it to a new location. This is a super easy way to duplicate an animation across layers and other Motion spans. If you drag a Motion span and overlap it with an existing span, the frames shared by both spans will be "consumed" by the span being moved into this position.

HOT TIP

When working with Motion spans, keep in mind that controlling nested animations inside a Graphic symbol (see "Lip syncing, nesting method" in Chapter 5, page 114) is very limited. Any settings for Graphic symbols (Loop, Play Once and single frame) are applied once to the entire span. They can not be applied to individual property keyframes in the span. Therefore your ability to control nested animations is lost, which is the main reason why Adobe retained the Classic tween method.

SHORTCUTS

MAC WIN BOTH

Editing Motion paths

IF YOU ARE ALREADY FAMILIAR with Flash and its limited Classic tween method, then you may have, at one time or another, experienced some frustrations trying to work with a frame-based tween model. Throw in the need to animate your object along a path and your workflow just increased even more. Previously, if we needed to animate an object along a path, a guide layer first needed to be created, then linked to the object layer, and then the object needed to be manually *snapped* to both ends of the path with the aid of the Snap tool. The new Motion tween method eliminates the need for all of these extra steps.

1 Right-click over the object and select Create Motion Tween. Flash automatically creates a Motion span in the timeline. With the playhead over the last frame of the span, drag the object to a new location to expose the Motion path on the stage.

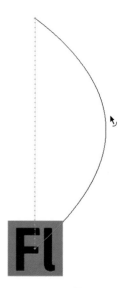

2 Use the Selection **V** tool and click anywhere on the stage away from the Motion path to insure it is deselected. Reshape the path by simply dragging it anywhere along the segment.

6 Use the Free Transform **Q** tool to scale, rotate and skew the Motion path as you would an object.

7 In some cases it may be easier to create a complex path by drawing it on a new layer with the Pencil **Y** or Pen **P** tool.

8 Select the stroke and then copy it *ctrl* **C** ⌘ **C**. Select the Motion span in the Timeline or the object on the stage and paste your stroke *ctrl* **V** ⌘ **V**.

3 With the Subselection tool, you can expose the control points and Bezier handles on the path that correspond to each position property keyframe. You can use these handles to reshape the path around the property keyframe points.

4 Position the play head on a frame where the object resides midpoint along the path. Drag the object to reshape the path automatically.

5 You can reposition the entire Motion path and the animation by selecting it with the Selection **V** tool and then dragging it to a new location.

HOT TIP

With the Subselection tool selected, hold down the *ctrl* ⌘ key to temporarily perform free transforms to the Motion path.

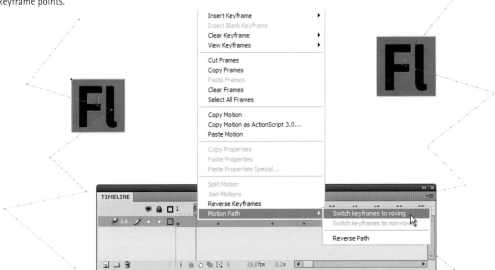

9 If you dig a little deeper into Flash CS4's context menu, you may discover yet another new feature called "Switch keyframes to roving". The dictionary defines *roving* as: "*not assigned or restricted to any particular location, area, topic, etc.*" In keeping with that definition, Flash describes a *roving keyframe* as : "...keyframe that is not linked to a specific frame in the Timeline." What this means in Flash terms is, say

you create an animation like the one pictured above, where an object is following a path with several unequal segments. Each segment spans a different number of frames causing the object to travel at different speeds along each segment. If you want the object's movement to be fixed, then right click over the span and go to Motion Path and select *Switch keyframes to roving*.

289

Motion Editor properties

1 Select a Motion span in the timeline and then open the Motion Editor. If it isn't already open, go to Window > Motion Editor. This panel lets you view all the different properties and property keyframes of the selected tween. Each property is displayed as an individual horizontal row that, when clicked on, expands vertically. Once you have created a tween in the timeline, the Motion Editor allows you to control the tween in several different ways. To add a keyframe, position the playhead on the desired frame and click the "Add or remove keyframe" button (circled). A keyframe is added to the frame in the selected property and you can use the Selection **S** tool to click and drag it. Dragging it vertically increases or decreases the amount and direction of the skew. You can also drag the keyframe to a different frame.

3 Right-clicking over a keyframe along the property curve will provide several curve options: corner point, smooth point, smooth left, smooth right. A corner point is a point that has no curve applied to either side of it. A smooth point is the opposite of a corner point with curves on both sides. Smooth left and right will apply a curve to either side of the point respectively.

2 You can edit the curve by holding down the Alt key while clicking the keyframe. This will expose the Bezier curves and handles, allowing you to fine-tune the shape of the curve. Using these controls is basically the same as how you edit strokes with the Selection **S** tool or the Pen

P tool. Moving a curve segment or control point upward will increase the property value; moving it downward will decrease the value. You can continue to add additional keyframes to create complex curves for complex tweened effects.

4 One of the coolest features of the Motion Editor is the ability to copy and paste curves from one property to another. To copy a curve, simply right-click anywhere in the graph area (away from the curve itself) and select Copy

Curve. Expand a different property and right-click in the graph area and select Paste Curve. You can also copy curves between custom eases and properties.

HOT TIP

The basic motion properties X, Y, and Z are different from other properties. These three properties are linked together. A frame in a tween span that is a property keyframe for one of these properties must be a property keyframe for all three of them. In addition, control points on the X, Y, and Z property curves cannot be edited with Bezier controls.

SHORTCUTS
MAC WIN BOTH

Custom easing

1 Adding easing to your animation using the Motion Editor is very easy and flexible because you can select individual properties to apply the easing to. The Motion Editor also provides several preset easing curves to get you started. In the car example, a very basic ease has been applied to the motion of the car so that it eases in from a still position. This provides a realistic motion to the car.

3 The types of easing that can be created in the Motion Editor are limited only by your imagination. I highly recommend experimenting with various easing curves and the effect they have on your animations. It's the best way to get a feel for how a curve affects various types of motion in a Motion span.

2 One of the most frequently used eases in my workflow is to ease in and ease out within the same span. Click on the "+" symbol in the Eases row and select "Custom". A new row will be added to the Eases category allowing you to edit the curve. Drag the vertex handles to reshape the ease curve similar to what is pictured in the example. I usually try to shape the curve like the letter "S".

4 In this example I animated the car in random positions on the stage, which created several keyframes and several spans of varied lengths. I switched the frames to roving and applied keyframes and easing using the Motion Editor. The resulting effect is an erratic motion as if the object is completely out of control.

293

Motion tweens and 3D

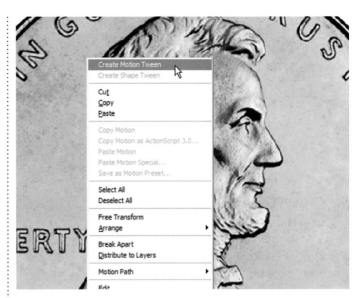

FLASH HAS ALWAYS BEEN a 2-dimensional design and animation program. Making a 2-dimensional object appear to spin in a 3-dimensional space has been a popular effect but very difficult to do due to the lack of that 3rd dimension. Flash CS4 now offers 3D capabilities in the form of a 3D Rotation and Transformation tools.

1 Let's start with the image we want to spin. It can be anything you want but I have chosen a coin because it seems this is the exact object many people want to animate spinning anyway. I am using a bitmap of a 1 cent US penny but you can use a coin of any currency either as an imported bitmap or drawn with Flash's drawing tools. Either way, make sure you convert the artwork to a Movie Clip symbol and then right-click over it and select Create Motion Tween.

4 Next, position the play head marker on the last frame and rotate the object the rest of the way so it is facing us as it was in frame 1. Play back your animation to see the coin spin in 3D space.

5 But wait! Something's not right. Flash spins the coin to the right during the first half of the animation but then reverses direction during the second half. This is easily corrected by placing the playhead on the frame just after the second keyframe and rotating the object slightly more.

2 Select the 3D Rotation tool **W** and with the playhead on a frame other than frame 1, drag the object along its Y-axis (horizontally).

3 Do not try to rotate the coin 360 degrees and expect Flash to know what you want it to do. You will need to divide the animation in half by stopping the coin rotation just short of the half-way point.

HOT TIP

Experiment further by adjusting the Perspective angle and Vanishing point in the "3D Position and View" section of the Properties panel. You can get some very interesting 3D perspectives by applying more depth to your object.

6 With the 3D rotation complete, try experimenting by editing the object's position relative to its center point. Edit the instance of the object by double-clicking on it. Move the object away from the center point (represented by the "+" cross-hairs). The further you move the object from its center point, the more dramatic the effect of the 3D rotation. Here I turned on the Onionskin feature so you can see each frame of the effect when the symbol has been moved horizontally from its own center point.

SHORTCUTS

MAC WIN BOTH

295

3D Position and View

OONE OF THE MOST REQUESTED features from animators over the years has been the addition of a camera in Flash. Having the ability to build scenes involving a background, midground and foreground has always been a part of the production process. With a camera comes the ability to zoom and pan easily through a scene, requiring the movement of only one single object (the camera) instead of simulating a camera by moving all the contents around the stage.

Cameras only work in 3D environments and Flash, up until now, has never supported 3D except for ActionScript-generated 3D engines. But if you are like me, that level of ActionScript prowess is beyond reach.

Flash CS4 doesn't include an actual camera but we do have the next best thing: 3D Position and View, specifically a "Z"-axis that we can now utilize to simulate a virtual 3D stage more effectively than with previous versions of Flash.

1 Setting up your "stage" is the most time consuming part of the process. The more elements in your scene, the more convincing the 3D effect will be. Here I have built a landscape consisting of background and midground elements, all converted to Movie Clip symbols and each residing on its own layer.

4 With the playhead in the last frame of the Motion span and the Properties panel open, select each movie clip individually and use the "Z"-axis hot text slider to scale and position each object outside the stage. You will likely need to edit the X and Y axes to position the object precisely where you want it.

2 To suggest an even more convincing sense of depth I have included several foreground objects by adding several instances of a movie clip containing the flower graphic from Chapter 1.

3 Detirmine what frame you want the "camera" zoom to begin in and insert keyframes for all of the layers containing the objects that will eventually be moved along the Z-axis. Apply Motion tweens to each of the movie clips.

5 For this shot we are simulating a camera zoom, meaning the shot will move us into the scene. Since Flash doesn't have a true Camera, we simulate a zoom by scaling each object from its original size to a larger size. The direction of the zoom is dictated by the final position of each Movie Clip. The key to the success of this effect is how much the objects move in relation to each other. Foreground objects move faster and scale larger than the objects furthest away from us in the background. The sky and largest mountain range do not move at all while the flowers closest to us move and scale the most. This is what gives the viewer a sense of true depth in the scene.

Basic bone armature

THE BONE TOOL is arguably the simplest of tools to use for creating complex animations. But in the real world, many of us do not have the need or desire to create complex designs or animations on a day-to-day basis. Not all Flash users are designers and in many cases their ability to create complex animations is limited. But that does not mean professional level animation is unachievable using Flash. For this example I chose a very simple vector image from iheartvector.com.

1 The first step is to determine and isolate what areas of the image you want to animate individually. Select these areas and convert them to symbols.

4 The bones themselves should not rotate. The Jeeps are suspended by cables at fixed locations. Select each bone and then disable their rotation property in the Properties panel.

5 It is true that you don't even need the Bone tool for this particular example. The same rigging could be done by editing the center point of a symbol to achieve the same rotation.

2 Select the Bone **X** tool and create your armature by dragging from the *parent* symbol to the symbols you will be animating. Here the parent symbol is the helicopter itself while the suspended Jeeps are the *children*.

3 This armature requires only 2 bones, both originating from the same point. This is more like setting up a hinging mechanism than an Inverse Kinematic bone structure.

6 With all of the objects prepared for animation, all that is left to do is right click over the symbols containing the Jeeps and apply Motion tweens. The distance each Jeep sways is a matter of personal preference. The more they sway, the windier the conditions they are in.

7 For some added realism, apply some easing in and easing out by selecting the Motion tween span and then the Stop and Start (Slow) ease. Set the strength to -100.

Complex bone armature

WHEN IT COMES TO character animation, the Bone tool can be quite useful. Applying bones to a character is often referred to as "rigging". The first step is designing the character so that each body part is a separate object that can be articulated with a bone armature. The next step is adjusting the rotation and translation of each bone to limit how much they rotate and move along its X and Y axes. This is the most critical detail of the Bone tool because you don't want the character's limbs and joints to bend past their anatomical limits.

1 Here's the exploded view of the character and all its various body parts. Notice the arms and legs have elbows and knee caps to help eliminate gaps between objects when rotated.

2 The first bone is the root (sometimes referred to as a "parent" bone) in the chain. It seems logical to assign the main torso or chest object to this root bone. Here I have linked the torso and the pelvis objects together.

6 When adding bones to symbols, the stacking order can often change based on the original design. To correct this, right-click over the necessary symbols, go to Arrange and then select the appropriate action.

7 Next, constrain the rotation and translation for each bone. Select a bone and in the Properties panel check the Constrain boxes for each of these properties and use the hot text sliders to set each value.

3 Working downwards, I branch off from the pelvis symbol to both upper leg symbols. The pelvis symbol is important because it increases articulation while hiding any potential gaps between the legs and torso when rotated.

4 The lower portion of the character rigging is complete. Bones were added from the upper leg symbols to each knee cap, then to each lower leg symbol and then ultimately each foot symbol.

5 Continuing from the root bone, connect both upper arms, elbows, forearms and hands. The final step in the armature is adding the last bone from the root to the head symbol.

8 By default, bone translation for the X and Y axes are disabled. When each translation is enabled, a bone can move along the X- or Y-axis to an unlimited degree. Select Enable in the Joint: X Translation or Joint: Y Translation section in the Property panel. A two-headed arrow appears perpendicular to the bone on the joint to indicate that X-axis motion is enabled. Adjusting the minimum and maximum values helps you control the position of the bone, especially when rotation is disabled as well.

9 Another technique I have been playing with is having the root bone start on a "ghost" symbol. A ghost symbol is not part of the character design. Its sole purpose is to separate the root bone from the actual character for even more articulation.

Joint rotation and constrain

THE BONE TOOL IS GREAT FOR creating cool armatures that can be easily animated by articulating them. To create more realistic motion, you can control the movement of your armature by constraining its rotation and translation. For example, two bones that are part of an arm could be constrained so that the elbow cannot bend in the wrong direction. You can enable, disable, and constrain the rotation of a bone and its motion along the X-or Y-axis. When X-or Y-axis motion is enabled, a bone can move along the X-or Y-axis to an unlimited degree, and the length of the parent bone changes to accommodate the motion.

1 Insects make perfect Bone tool examples because of their segmented body styles. Here I have applied an armature using the Bone tool to one of the legs.

2 In its current state, the bone chain will allow each segment to rotate 360 degrees without any constraints or limitations. From an anatomical perspective, this may not be the desired behavior.

6 Repeat the same procedure for the opposite direction.

7 You may want to set different constraints for each bone within the same armature. For accuracy's sake, it might be a good idea to do a little research and find out just how an insect like this one actually moves in the real world.

3 Select the root bone and in the Properties panel check the "Enable" and "Constrain" options in the Joint: Rotation category. Use the hot text sliders to change the value based on the amount of constraint you want for the root bone.

4 Rotational constraint is represented graphically by an arc at the end of the bone. Any adjustment to the value of the constrain will effect the arc and how how much the bone can move in either direction.

5 You will likely decide through trial and error how much constrain to apply. Change the value, rotate the bone in 1 direction and check to see if the right amount of constrain has been applied.

HOT TIP

To limit the speed of motion of a selected bone, enter a value in the Joint Speed field in the Property inspector. Joint speed gives the bone the effect of weight. The maximum value of 100% is equivalent to unlimited speed.

8 With 4 different segments per leg, it can get complicated quickly. Setting rotational constraints should help keep each movement under control.

9 In addition to rotation constraints, you can also set constraints to the X and Y translation of each bone. This will set limitations on the amount of movement the bone has along the X and Y axes. In some situations you may want to set the value(s) to "0" to eliminate any movement along these axes.

SHORTCUTS
MAC WIN BOTH

Bone tool easing basics

E ASING IS ALWAYS the icing on the cake for me when I am producing animations. It's usually the final step in my process. Once all key poses are created and Motion tweens applied, the final step is applying easing for that extra touch of realism. Easing is usually applied in 2 ways: *easing in* and *easing out*. Easing in calculates the rate of each frame so that the animation starts slow and gradually increases speed. Easing out is the opposite where the rate of speed is reduced as the animation plays. A perfect example of easing is when a ball is thrown towards the sky. Gravity's constant force gradually slows the ball down until it changes direction, returning to Earth with a gradual increase in speed. With easing, you can adjust the rate of change to the values for more natural or more complex animation.

1 Using an image of a crane is about as basic as it gets. The armature consists of only 2 bones since all we need to move is the cable with the ball attached. The animation requires that the ball travels back and forth much like a pendulum. To imply gravity we need to apply an ease in and an ease out for each direction the ball moves. Position the ball to the far right or far left in the first keyframe. Move the playhead to the middle of the span and position the ball in the opposite direction. *ctrl* ⌘ + click the first keyframe, right-click and select Copy Pose. *ctrl* ⌘ + click the last frame and right-click and select Paste Pose. You now have a swinging ball on a crane that loops back and forth seamlessly.

To add the easing, select any frame between the first 2 keyframes. In the Properties panel use the Ease drop-down menu to select Slow and Stop (Slow). Adjust the easing strength to -100 using the hot text slider. You can also click on this value to select it and type in "-100". Repeat this same procedure for the 2nd half of the armature span.

2 Here's a slightly more complex Bone armature involving a cartoon figure with a head and 4 limbs. I used an extra symbol that was not a part of the character's design for the root bone to be attached to. You can see this root bone start between the character's feet. The concept here was to assign the root bone to an object not integrated into the character's design. This allows for all of the character's symbols to be assigned non-root bones, allowing more articulation.

Once all the key poses have been created, all that is left to do is to add some easing from pose to pose. This helps create a more natural movement for the character. Just like with the crane example, select any frame between the keyframes and in the Properties panel use the Ease drop-down menu to select a preset ease. Adjust the easing strength to -100 or 100 depending on your needs. If you want the preset to ease in, then use a negative value. A positive value will apply easing out to the animation. The value refers to the strength of the ease.

HOT TIP

The Motion Editor does not support Armature spans. Therefore, you can not apply custom easing to armatures. The only easing for armatures is the presets available in the Properties panel. Having the ability to create custom eases and possibly edit the property curves of an armature span may be a valid feature request for a future version of Flash.

SHORTCUTS
MAC WIN BOTH

305

Bones and shapes

BONES ARE NOT LIMITED TO symbols. You can apply a bone armature to a single shape. The difference between symbols and shapes when working with the Bone tool is, you can add multiple bones to the interior of a single shape. This is different from symbols because you can have only one bone per instance. Once bones are added to the selection, Flash converts the shape and bones into an IK shape object and moves the object to a new pose layer. Once a shape is converted to an IK shape, it can no longer merge with other shapes outside the IK shape.

Manipulating a shape with an armature can produce more organic looking animation. Case in point, here I need to animate the tail of a cat waving back and forth. With the Bone tool I am able to quickly and easily produce a very natural and realistic looking tail-like motion.

1 Before applying a bone structure to the tail, it is best to start with the tail drawn without any curves. The reason is, if we start with a curved tail and apply the bone armature, then it becomes much more difficult to curve the tail in the opposite direction without the integrity of the shape becoming compromised. A straight position is neutral and can be easily manipulated in either direction. For this animation we will make the tail move from left to right in a whip-like fashion.

2 We want the tip of the tail to have the most flexibility and the bottom of the tail to be the most rigid. The root bone is the very first bone created in the chain and all subsequent bones are its children. Select the Bone **X** tool and drag inside the tail shape from the very bottom in an upward direction. Once the root bone has been applied, Flash will automatically place the shape in a container called an *IK shape object*. This new object is automatically moved to a new *pose layer*.

5 Insert several frames in the armature pose layer and then move the play head somewhere in the middle of the span. Articulate the tail in the opposite direction, simulating an "S" curve again. Use your best judgement as to how much curve you want your tail to have. There are no rules here when it comes to artistic license.

3 Continue adding bones to the shape, working your way upwards until the entire armature spans the entire tail. What may be the most important detail of this technique is making each bone slightly shorter than the previous bone moving up the tail. The reason for this is to allow the tail to become more articulate towards the tip. If you were to create longer bones towards the tip, articulation would suffer and you would end up with severe 90 degree bends instead of several softer bends representing a more curvy tail overall.

4 Once the armature is complete, position the tail in the desired starting shape in frame 1. Here I have grabbed the tip of the tail and articulated it into an "S" curve.

6 The key to creating a realistic wavy tail is to add a little secondary animation. Place the playhead a few frames after the initial starting pose and curl the tip of the tail in the opposite direction it is traveling in. This provides more of a "whip" effect as the tail begins to change direction.

7 To make this tail loop seamlessly, *ctrl* ⌘ + click frame 1 and then right-click over it. Select Copy Pose.

Bones and shapes (cont.)

8 *ctrl* ⌘ + click the last frame in the armature span and right-click again. This time select Paste Pose.

9 Next, add the secondary animation as we did in step 6 by placing the playhead a few frames before the last frame and creating a more dramatic curve in the opposite direction the tail is moving.

12 Create a new symbol in the Library using the drop-down menu in the upper right corner of the Library panel. The symbol can be a movie clip or a Graphic symbol but for this example I recommend Graphic behavior so you can see the animation inside the Flash authoring environment.

13 Once the symbol is created you will be inside this symbol and ready to add the armature you copied earlier. Right-click over the stage area and select Paste. The entire armature and its animation will now be nested inside your new symbol.

10 Without easing, the tail feels too rigid and mechanical. Select any frame between the first 2 keyframes and from the Properties panel select an ease preset using the drop-down menu in the Ease category. To ease in and then out between these 2 keyframes, set the strength of the ease to a negative value using the hot text slider. Repeat this step for each keyframed pose.

11 In most situations you could consider the animation complete. For all intents and purposes it is, but for this particular character I want to make sure the tail animation is as visible as possible. Therefore I want to Motion tween it back and forth along the X-axis. To do this, it is best to tween the entire tail animation inside a symbol. Right-click over the tail armature and select *Copy*.

14 Navigate back to the main timeline and create a new layer below your character. Drag an instance of the symbol containing the animated tail to the stage and position it relative to the character. The tail animation starts with the tail pointing to the left, so favor the left side of the character when positioning the symbol. Right-click over the symbol and select Create Motion Tween.

15 Scrub the timeline and watch the tail animation reach the half-way point where the tail is pointing to the right. Hold down *Shift* *Shift* and use the right arrow key to position the tail symbol towards the right side of the character. Copy the first frame of this Motion tween and paste it into the last frame creating a seamless loop. Now the tail is comprised of 2 simultaneous animations.

Bind tool

WORKING WITH VECTORS has many advantages. Vectors are resolution independent and help maintain small file sizes suitable for the Web. They are also easy to edit using control points and Bezier handles. But even vectors are not without their imperfections. If you have ever attempted a shape tween you probably have experienced inexplicable anomalies with shapes behaving in unexpected ways. In that situation we have Shape Hints to help correct the problem.

In Flash CS4, shapes can be manipulated by using the Bone tool and, like shape tweens, there can be some hits and some misses. That's where the Bind tool comes to the rescue. The Bind tool allows us to fine tune how control points are affected by the armature.

1 As with any Armature, designating where the root bone should be assigned is the first step. This particular object, being a single flat shape, makes that decision relatively easy. I chose the mid-torso area for the root bone.

2 From the root bone continue building the armature by adding bones to the upper arm, the forearm and then the hand.

5 If your shape has a large number of vector points, it may be worth it to optimize `ctrl` `alt` `Shift` `C` `⌘` `⌥` `Shift` `C` the shape as much as possible to eliminate any unneeded points.

6 An optimized shape will have a lower number of points. As a result, your Bone armature should work better because there will be less deformation within the shape itself.

3 Manipulate the armature by grabbing the last bone in the chain (in this case the hand) and moving it around the stage. In the above example you can clearly see some unwanted deformation below the arm along the side of the body. This is where the Bind **Z** tool comes in handy.

4 Select the Bind **Z** tool and then select a bone in the armature. The control points assigned to the selected bone are highlighted in yellow. To add points to a bone, *Shift* *Shift* + click an unhighlighted control point. To remove points from a bone, *ctrl* ⌘ + click a highlighted control point.

7 An optimized shape retains its integrity a lot more than an unoptimized shape. But as you can see here, there's still no guarantee there will not be any imperfections.

8 Use the Bind tool to assign or unassign control points for each bone along the armature to correct any anomalies with the shape. It's much easier to work with fewer points associated with an optimized object.

9 Add more bones to the armature to accommodate the entire shape. The same process applies to each limb: manipulate the armature, check for deformations and imperfections (if any) and adjust using the Bind tool.

The History of Flash

SOME OF YOU MAY RECALL the various incarnations of the Flash authoring tool over the past several years. Adobe Systems celebrated the 10-year anniversary of Flash in 2006, and this being the 13th year of Flash, I thought I'd take a trip down Flash memory lane. I assure you my age does qualify me to write about this topic, the proof being every time I find myself perpetually scrolling for the year I was born when filling out online registration forms.

1996: Known as FutureSplash, it was a bare-bone basic graphics editing tool with a simple timeline. Macromedia bought it and called it Flash 1.0

1997: Flash 2 was released with the addition of the Library and Symbols (just graphic behavior – the world actually rotated without Movie Clips up to this point).

1998: Flash 3 introduced Move Clips, dot-syntax style actionScript, javaScript plug-in integration and the stand-alone player. Transparency was also added at this point if I remember correctly.

1999: Flash 4 - holy streaming MP3s Batman!

2000: Flash 5 gave us big advancements in actionScript, smartclips and HTML text formatting.

2002: Flash MX came with not only the beginning of what would prove to be 2 years of confusion surrounding its name (why not "Flash 6?"), but also components, streaming video and XML support to name a few.

2003: Flash MX 2004 should have shipped with aspirin due to the headaches we all got trying to explain the meaning behind the name and its version number (and why it was called MX 2004 and not "Flash 7"?) to newbies over and over and over again. On the flip side it did give us actionScript 2.0, behaviors, OOP, Media Playback components and more. But then again it did give us the first and only update due to a massive amount of bugs and instability (version 7.2).

2005: Flash 8 brought back the ever-popular numerical naming convention. A collective sigh of relief was heard around the world. It also included filters, blend modes and a higher quality video codec.

2007: Flash CS3 Professional (acquired by Adobe Systems Inc. and integrated into their Creative Suite). The new features added consisted of Adobe Photoshop® and Illustrator® importers (huge!), the ability to convert animation to actionScript, the Adobe Creative Suite user interface, actionScript 3.0, an advanced debugger, Device Central, additional drawing tools, interface components, Quicktime exporter and more video and coding tools.

2008: Flash CS4 Professional has revolutionized Flash with a brand new Motion tween model that has finally unshackled us from the now antiquated frame-based Classic tween. We march onward into the future, armed with editable motion paths and an integrated Motion Editor that provides us the ability to animate position, scale, skew, rotation, and color effect properties of a single object individually. We have been granted the power to save our animations as custom presets that can be easily reused and shared with the Flash design community. Complex armatures that can be manipulated with Inverse Kinematics will rise and fall on our command as will large carniv... Oops. I got a bit carried away.

I'll admit my excitement with Flash CS4 is difficult to bridle. Adobe has really listened to the pleas from designers and animators alike and delivered, in my opinion, the strongest version Flash in over a decade. I tip my hat to the entir Flash team over at Adobe Systems. Thank you giving us these great tools.

I leave you with some Flash-related humor:

Q: Why did two keyframes stop arguing in the middle of a timeline?

A: They didn't want to create a *scene*.

2dcgi.com website, 148
2.5D animation:
  advanced, 108–9
  description, 106–7
  monkey, 110–11
3D animation:
  motion tweens, 294–5
  perspective animation, 204–5
  position and view, 295, 296–7
  Rotation tool, 39, 48–9, 50, 225,
    294–5
  Transformation tool, 39, 75, 225, 294

A

Action-safe zone, 162–3
ActionScript 2.0:
  cue points, 233
  dragging, 240–1
  events, 238–9
  Flash history, 312
  focus, 69
  interactivity, 235
  loading images, 246–7
  objects concept, 253
  timeline, 242–3
  toggling sound, 246–7
ActionScript 3.0:
  cue points, 233
  dragging, 240–1
  dynamic sounds, 222–3
  events, 237–8
  Flash history, 313
  focus, 69
  interactivity, 235
  JPG files, 244–5
  loading images, 244
  objects concept, 253
  timeline, 242–3
  toggling sound, 248–51
ActionScript:
  animation, 224–5
  billiard ball, 90
  blur filter, 90

classes, 252–3
color changes, 195
fire, 200
Flash interface, 36
Flash Video, 230
focus, 68–9
movies, 164
objects concept, 252–3
page turn, 180–1
skill level, 153
sound, 222
Soundbooth CS1 software, 216
Adjust color filters, 194–5
Adobe:
  Acrobat website, 155
  adobe.com website, 1, 154–5, 225,
    233
  Audition 3.0 software, 217, 218–19
  Bridge software, 233
  Illustrator, 6, 225
  Media Encoder CS4, 232
  Photoshop see Photoshop
  Soundbooth CS1 software, 216–17
Ajar extensions, 266–7
AKG Perception 400 microphone, 212
American Flag, 136
Animate software, 274–5
Animation:
  3D perspective, 204–5
  ActionScript, 224–5
  bees, 118–19, 178–9
  Between the Lions, 228–9
  billiard ball, 90–1
  Bone and Spray, 206–7
  bouncing ball, 52–3
  butterfly wings, 50–1
  career, 152–5
  chicken, 144–5
  coin spinning, 294–5
  color adjustments, 194–5
  cowboys, 98–9
  cranes, 304
  dogs, 120–1
  filters, 186–7
  fire, 200–1
  fireworks, 188–9

flag waving, 60–1
globe, 58–9
graphics, 94–5
gulls, 204–5
hand writing, 64–5
helicopters, 298–9
hula hoop, 56
insects, 302–3
iris transition, 62–3
motion, 74–81, 82–3
page turn, 180–1
petals, 28–31
rain, 198–9
smoke, 182–3, 184–5
snow, 202–3
soft reveal, 190–1
sounds, 211
"Star Wars" text, 192–3
steam, 186–7
storage, 53
super text, 178–9
tail, 306–9
vertigo, 196–7
see also character animation
animonger.com website, 264
AnimSlider Pro extension, 264–5
Anticipation in character animation,
  142–3
Ape Escape (Sony Playstation), 160–1
Armatures, bone, 126–7, 298–9, 300–1
Audacity® software, 214–15
Audio see sound
Audition 3.0 software, 217, 218–19
Automation see presets

B

Backgrounds:
  blurring (motion), 100–1
  looping, 146–7
Bamboo graphics tablets, 175
Bee animation, 118–19, 178–9
Belushi, John, 71

Index

Between the Lions television series, 228–9
beveled edges, 271
Bezier handles, 310
Billiard ball animation, 90–1
Bind tool, 310–11
Bitmaps:
    animation (Jib Jab), 130–1
    distortion, 40–1
    "Grotto" character, 14–15
    texture, 12–13, 14–15
Blues Brothers, 71
Blur effects in Photoshop, 96
Blur filter:
    billiard ball, 90–1
    excessive use, 183
    hazy effect, 31
    text, 96–7
Blurring:
    background, 100–1
    selective, 98–9
Bone tool:
    armatures, 126–7, 207, 298–9, 300–1
    Bone and Spray, 206–7
    bones and shapes, 306
    character animation, 126–7
    complex bone armature, 300–1
    easing, 304–5
    Flash innovation, 225
    hinging body parts, 122
    inverse kinematics, 124–5
    joint rotation and constrain, 302–3
    shapes, 310
    Spray Brush tool, 206–7
Bones and shapes, 306–9
Bouncing ball animation, 52–3
Breeze presentation, 154
Bridge software, 233
Brush tool, 6–7, 24, 225, 257
Bucket tool, 12, 21
Bush, George W., 130, 132–5
Butterfly wings animation, 50–1

C

Cameras in Flash, 296–7
Caplin, Steve, 131
"Caps" (gaps), 128–9

Card flip, 46–7
Career in animation, 152–5
CD icons, 1
Cell shading, 20, 22
Character animation:
    2.5D, 106–7, 108–9, 110–11
    anticipation, 142–3
    Ape Escape, 160–1
    bitmap animation (Jib Jab), 130–1
    Bone tool, 124–5, 126–7, 300
    Breeze presentation, 154–5
    chicken, 144–5
    classic tweens, 118–19
    design, 109
    drawing upon oneself, 144–5
    Evil Mime, 128–9
    gaps, 128–9
    George W. Bush, 130, 132–5
    "Grotto", 14–15
    hinging body parts, 122–3
    lip syncing, 112–13, 114–15, 116–17
    looping backgrounds, 146–7
    marionette style, 76–9
    monkey, 110–11
    motion blur, 100–1
    motion guides (Jib Jab), 134–5
    motion tweens, 120–1
    PSD animation (Jib Jab), 132–3
    tradigital animation, 148–51
    tweening, 106
    walk cycle, 136–7, 138–9, 140–1
    Yahoo! Super Messengers, 72
chicken animation, 144–5
Classic tweens:
    3D rotation, 48
    character animation, 118–19
    CS4, 282–3
    motion paths, 288
    Queasy tools, 267
Clay analogy in drawing, 208–9
Coin spinning animation, 294–5
Color:
    adjustments for animation, 194–5
    contrast, 27
    Easy Palette, 263
    Kuler panel, 166–7
    mixing, 8–9
    NTSC safe palette, 264
    palette management, 263
Combining effects in motion, 94–5
Constrained drag and drop, 241

Contrast and color, 27
Convert timeline to symbol extension, 267
Cowboys and selective blurring, 98–9
Crane animation, 304
Creator software, 272–3
CS3/CS4 comparison (Flash), 224–5
CS4 new features:
    Bind tool, 310–11
    bone armature, 298–9, 300–1
    Bone tool easing, 304–5
    bones and shapes, 306–9
    Classic tweens, 282–3
    custom easing, 292–3
    joint rotation and constrain, 302–3
    Motion Editor, 290–1
    Motion paths, 288–9
    Motion Presets, 280–1
    Motion spans, 286–7, 290
    Motion tweens:
        3D, 294–5
        Classic tweens, 282–3
        creation, 284–5
        editing paths, 288–9
    tweening, 278
Curves, 83
Custom easing, 292–3

D

De Visser, Martijn, 232, 233
Deco tool, 34–5
Design:
    bitmaps, 12–13, 14–15
    Brush tool, 6–7
    characters, 109
    color mixing, 8–9
    Deco tool, 34–5
    gradients, 10–11, 28–31
    monkeys, 10–11
    Pen tool, 16–17, 28–9
    petals, 28–9, 30–1
    shading, 20–1, 22–3, 24–5, 26–7
    shapes, 4–5
    Spray brush tool, 32–3
    styles, 2–37
    texture, 12–13, 14–15
    Trace Bitmap, 18–19

Digimator term, 1, 208
Disney:
    films, 20
    lip syncing, 112
Distortion:
    bitmaps, 40–1
    butterflies, 50–1
    tool, 43
    see also transformation
Dogs animation, 120–1
Drawing:
    clay analogy, 208–9
    Drawing upon oneself, 144–5
    style simplification, 102–3
Dreamworks, 70, 102
Drop Shadow, filter, 31, 86–8
Dynamic sounds, 22–3

E

Easing:
    animations, 304–5
    custom, 292–3
Easy Palette (color management system),
    263
ECMAScript standard, 256
edges:
    beveled, 271
    roughening, 266
elbow caps, 128–9
Envelope modifier tool, 42
Envelope tool, 42–3, 44–5
Events and interactivity, 236, 237–9
Evil Mime character, 128–9
Extending Flash MX 2004, 263
extensions:
    Ajar, 266–7
    AnimSlider Pro, 264–5
    beveled edges, 271
    Convert timeline to symbol, 267
    Flashjester, 272–3
    FrameSync, 266
    Guide Maker, 267
    iK'motion, 268–9
    JSFL, 256–7, 258–63
    Motion Preset Preview, 267
    Queasy tools, 267
    roughen edges, 266
    swift 3D Xpress, 270–1

Toon Boom Animate, 274
Eyedropper tool, 8

F

Fernandez, Ibis, 148
Fill Transform tool, 14–15
Film speed, 158
Filters:
    Adjust color, 194–5
    animation, 186–7
    Blur, 31, 90–1, 96–7, 183
    drop shadow, 86, 88
    effects, 89
    Gaussian Blur, 69
    steam, 186–7
Fire animation, 200–1
Fireworks animation, 188–9
FLA *see* Flash
Flag:
    American, 136
    waving animation, 60–1
Flash:
    cameras, 296–7
    CS3/CS4 comparison, 224–5
    customization, 276–7
    extensions, 254–75
    file, 1
    Forward Film Festival, 71
    history, 312–13
    interactivity, 236–51
    interface, 36–7
    JavaScript, 255, 256–7
    media applications, 156–7
    Objects concept, 252–3
    sound, 220–1
    Tools panel, 37
    Trace Bitmap, 18–19
    video, 226–31, 232–3
    see also Flash to video conversion
Flash + After Effects, 202–3
Flash JavaScript *see* JSFL
Flash to video conversion:
    Ape Escape, 160–1
    Quicktime Exporter, 170–1
    safe colors, 164–5
    safe colors (Kuler), 166–7
    SWF2Video software, 172–3
    sync, 168–9

Title and Action safety, 162–3
Flash video (FLV):
    Encoder, 230, 232, 233
    Soundbooth CS1 software, 216
    tools and articles, 232–3
    video editing, 230–1
    websites, 233
flashants website, 172
Flashjester extensions, 272–3
flashjester.com website, 272
Flat card rotation, 46–7
FLV *see* Flash video
Flying text, 92–3
Focus, 68–9
For loop control flow statement, 262
FrameSync software, 266
Free Transform tool:
    3D rotation, 48
    cube, 38
    Evil Mime character, 129
    hinging body parts, 122
    lip syncing, 117
    monkey animation, 111
    Motion tween, 75
    perspective shadow, 88
    raw vector objects, 42–3
    squash and stretch, 52–3
    uses, 39, 40–1
    walk cycle, 137
FTP (File Transfer Protocol), 160
Fuller, Warren, 264
"Future Flash Animator", 36, 225

G

Gaps in character animation, 128–9
Gaussian Blur filter, 69
GIF files, 18
Glass filter, 69
Globe, rotating, 58–9
Gradients:
    design, 10–11
    monkey animation, 111
    realism, 28–9
    smoke, 182–3
    Transform tool, 16
Graphics:
    animation, 94–5
    tablets, 6, 174–5

"Grotto" character, 14–15
Guide Maker extension, 267
Gulls animation, 204–5

H

Hand writing, 64–5
Helicopter hovering, 298–9
Hinging body parts, 122–3
History of Flash, 312–13
Hope, Jarred, 277
"*How did I get here?*", 152–5
How to Cheat in Photoshop, 131
Hue, saturation and brightness (HSB), 8–9
Hula hoop animation, 56

I

iheartvector.com website, 298
IK *see* inverse kinematics
iK' motion tool set, 268–9
Illustrator software, 6, 225
Images, loading, 244–5, 246–7
Ink Bottle tool, 5, 16, 26
Insect animation, 302–3
Interactivity:
    ActionScript 2.0, 238–9, 240–1, 246–7
    ActionScript 3.0, 237–8, 240–1, 244–5
    constrained drag and drop, 241
    dragging, 240–1
    events, 236, 237–9
    Flash, 236–51
    loading images, 244–5, 246–7
    timeline pausing, 242–3
    toggling sound (AS 3.0), 248–51
Inverse Kinematics (IK), 124–5, 126–7,
        224–5, 268–9, 306
Iris transition, 62–3

J

Jackson, Chris, 202
JavaScript (JSFL):
    customization, 276
    keyboard shortcuts, 257
    language, 255, 256–7

Trace Bitmaps, 258–63
Jib Jab media:
    bitmap animation, 130–1
    motion guides, 134–5
    PSD importer, 132–3
    Spiridellis brothers, 71, 130
Joint rotation and constrain, 302–3
JPG files, 244–5
JSFL *see* JavaScript
Jshapor tool, 273
Jugglor software, 272–3

K

Kerry, John, 130
Keyboard shortcuts:
    JavaScript, 257
Keyframe:
    definition, 285
    Motion Editor, 290
    motion tweens, 285
keyframer.com website, 1
knee caps, 128–9
Kuler Panel (colors), 166–7

L

Lego building blocks, 4
Light source, 25
Line tool, 44, 148
Lion King, 201
Lip syncing:
    nesting method, 114–15, 287
    swap method, 112–13
    syncing decisions, 116–17
Loading images, 244–5, 246–7
Logan, Dave, 263, 277
Logitech USB microphone, 212
Looping backgrounds, 146–7
"Loopology" musical instruments, 219

M

M-Audio FireWire Solo audio interface,
    213
Macromedia, 153–4, 224–5

Marionette animation, 76–9
martijndevisser.com website, 232–3
Masking:
    flag waving, 60–1
    focus, 68–9
    handwriting, 64–5
    introduction, 56–7
    iris transition, 62–3
    rotating globe, 58–9
    spotlight, 66–7
Media Encoder CS4, 232
Merge layers option, 149
Michelangelo, 103
Microphones, 212–13
MIDI editing, 218
Mineaulr, Patrick, 277
"Moment of clarity", 54
Monkeys:
    2.5D animation, 110–11
    gradient design, 10–11
Motion:
    background blurring, 100–1
    billiard ball, 90–1
    blur filter, 90–1, 96–7
    blur technique, 100–1
    combining effects, 94–5
    complex animations, 82–3
    drop shadow, 86–7
    flying text, 91–2
    Motion Editor, 78–83
    perspective shadow, 88–9
    selective blurring, 98–9
    shadows, 84–5
    tweens, 74–5, 76–81
Motion Editor, 290–1, 292–3
    armatures, 305
    complex animations, 82–3
    custom tween, 80–1
    Flash CS4, 225
    motion tweens, 79
Motion guides (Jib Jab), 134–5
Motion paths editing, 288–9
Motion Presets, 267, 280–1
Motion spans, 286–7, 292
Motion tweens:
    3D, 294–5
    creation, 284–5
    CS4, 282–3
    method, 288–9
    new/classic comparison, 76–9
    properties, 74–5

Mueller, Eric, 225
Multiple objects selection, 123

N

Newton, Isaac, 99, 143
Nolan, Dennis, 55
NTSC:
   color safe palette, 264
   standard, 158–9

O

Object Drawing Mode, 6, 20, 29
Objects concept (Flash programming), 252–3
Onionskin tool, 47, 137, 295
Oval tool, 4–5, 17, 66

P

Page turn animation, 180–1
PAL (Phase Alternating Line) standard, 158
Pausing timelines, 242–3
Pen tool, 16–17, 28–9
Perspective shadow, 88–9
Petals design, 28–9, 30–1
Peters, Keith, 263
Philips, Adam, 204, 206
Photographic images, 18–19, 68–9
Photoshop:
   American Flag, 135
   blur effects, 96
   focus, 69
   graphics tablets, 6
   How to Cheat in Photoshop, 131
   Jib Jab media, 130
   photographic images, 18, 68–9
   texture, 14
   Trace Bitmap, 18
plug-ins see extensions
Position and view in 3D, 295, 296–7

Presets:
PSD:
   animation (Jib Jab), 132–3
   importer, 68–9
   trace bitmap, 18
Putney, Justin, 266, 277

Q

Queasy tools, 267
Quicktime Exporter, 164, 170–1, 172
quip.net website, 223, 253, 276

R

Rain animation, 198–9
Raw vector objects, 42–3
Rectangle tool, 4–5, 17, 22, 190
RGB color system, 8
Rotation:
   3D, 39, 48–9, 50, 225, 295
   flat card, 46–7
   globe, 58–9
roughen edges, 266
Rubik's cube, 252

S

Safe colors:
   flash to video, 164–5
   Kuler panel, 166–7
Screensavers:
   Flashjester, 272–3
Selection tool:
   fill color, 25
   line shading, 21
   Motion tween, 74
   multiple objects, 123
   Pen tool, 16
   shape shading, 22–3
   tradigital animation, 149, 151
Selective blurring (cowboys), 98–9
Senocular website, 277
Shading:
   design, 20–7

   line tricks, 20–1
   outlines, 26–7
   paint selected, 24–5
   shaping, 22–3
Shadows and motion, 84–5
Shape tweens, 47, 313
Shapes and bones, 306–9
Shockwave website, 152–3
Simple drawing style, 102–3
Simpson, Aaron, 130
Smoke animation, 182–3, 184–5
Snow animation, 202–3
Snowflake design, 202–3
Soft reveal animation, 190–1
Sorenson Spark video codes, 232
Sound:
   animation, 211
   Audacity editing application, 214–15
   audio interfaces, 213
   Audition 3.0 editing application, 218–19
   dynamic, 222–3
   effects, 212–13
   Flash, 220–1
   microphones, 212
   Soundbooth CS1 editing application, 216–17
   toggling (AS 3.0), 248–51
Soundbooth CS1 editing software, 216–17
South Park:
   lip syncing, 112
   production, 76–9
Spiridellis brothers, 71, 130
"SPL" (Spills) format, 36
Spotlight, 66–7
Spray Brush tool, 32–3, 206–7
Squash and stretch, 52–3
"Star Wars" text animation, 192–3
Startdrag method, 240
Steam animation, 186–7
Stiller, David, 223, 253, 276
Storage animation, 53
Stylized smoke, 184–5
Subtlety, 54–5
sunchirp.blogspot.com website, 126
Super text animation, 178–9
"SWF" (Swiffs) format, 36, 235, 244
SWF2video software, 172–3, 230
swift 3D Xpress extension, 270–1
Symmetry Brush, 35

Sync option:
  classic tweens, 118–19
  Flash to video conversion, 168–9
  motion tween, 120–1
  sound, 221
  see also lip syncing

T

Tablets *see* graphics tablets
Tail animation, 306–9
Text:
  blur filter, 96–7
  flying, 92–3
Texture, 12–13, 14–15
The Animator's Survival Kit, 140
Timeline pausing, 242–3
Title-safe zone, 162–3
Toggling sound (AS 3.0), 248–51
Toon Boom Animate extension, 274–5
"Toon shading", 20, 22
toonboom.com websites, 275
Trace Bitmap command, 18–19, 258–63
Tradigital animation, 148–51
Transformation:
  3D rotation, 48–9
  3D tools, 294
  butterflies, 50–1
  card flip, 46–7
  distorting bitmaps, 40–1
  Envelope tool, 42–3
  squash and stretch, 52–3
  warping, 44–5

  see also Free Transform tool
Tubbrit, Steven J., 126
Tweens:
  character animation, 106
  classic, 267, 288
  new v. classic comparison, 74–5, 76–9
  options, 278

U

Urami, 277

V

Vectors, 310–11
Vertigo animation, 196–7
Video:
  Between the Lions television series, 228–9
  Flash animation, 226–7
  FLV (Flash Video format), 230–1, 232–3
  importing, 228–9

W

Wacom:
  Cintiq 21UX graphics tablet, 175
  graphics tablets, 6, 174–5

Walk animation, 136–7, 138–9, 140–1
Warping, 44–5
Websites:
  2dcgi.com, 148
  Adobe, 154–5
  Adobe Acrobat, 155
  animonger.com, 264
  customization, 276–7
  flash video, 233
  flashants, 172
  iheartvector.com, 298
  Jugglor, 272
  keyframer.com, 1
  Martin de Visser FLV Player, 232–3
  page turn, 180
  quip.net, 223, 253, 276
  Sunchirp, 126
  Toon Boom, 275
  Wimpy FLV Player, 233
Williams, Richard, 140
wimpyplayer.com website, 233
Wolfe, David, 149, 277
Workspace layout, 37

Y

Yahoo! Super Messengers, 72
Yard, Todd, 263

What's on the CD

ALL SOURCE FILES SHOWN are provided to you for exploratory and educational reasons. I know the value of seeing how other people build their source files and how they can often lift the veil of confusion. Keep in mind all of these source files are protected by copyright and can not be used for commercial reasons. In some cases I have used actual photographs of people or images that I shot myself. In some cases the images are from istockphoto.com®, an ever-growing independent library of royalty-free photographs, vector illustrations, Flash files, and video clips and membership is free.

I have also used images from **www. iheartvector.com**. IHeartVector.com is a database of royalty-free vector images. Many of the vector files on their website are free and won't cost you a penny. PhotoObjects.net is another great resource for royalty-free images and offers several different subscription options.

Design styles

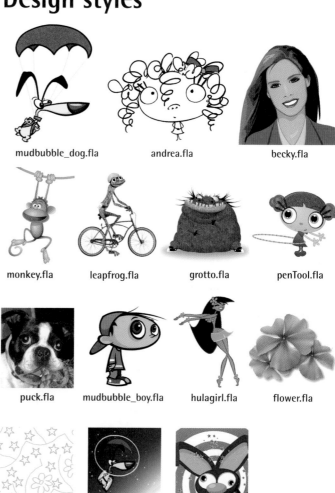

mudbubble_dog.fla   andrea.fla   becky.fla

monkey.fla   leapfrog.fla   grotto.fla   penTool.fla

puck.fla   mudbubble_boy.fla   hulagirl.fla   flower.fla

deco_tool.fla   sprayBrush.fla   sprayBrush-2.fla

Transformation & distortion

free_transform.fla   free_transform_vector.fla   evil_mime.fla

321

card_flip.fla

squash_stretch.fla

butterfly.fla

cardFlip_CS4.fla

Masking

globe.fla

flag.fla

iris.fla

writing_masked.fla

spotlight.fla

focus_image.fla

Motion tips & tricks

motion_tween_basic.fla

caveman.fla

witch.fla

mudbubble_boy.fla

hulagirl.fla

8ball.fla

flying_text.fla

keyframer_banner.fla

textblur_filter.fla

cowboy.fla

background_blur.fla

Character animation

2-3D_basic.fla

malien_headturn.fla

monkey_animated.fla

lip_sync.fla

mouths.fla

mouth_loop.fla

holiday_2006.fla

sync_on.fla

dogfood.fla

hinging.fla

chain.fla

bones_dinosaur_walkcycle.fla

caps.fla

walkcycle.fla

leg_positions.fla

leg_simulation.fla

advanced_walkcycle.fla

anticipation.fla

chicken.fla

looping_background.fla

tradigital.fla

Flash to video

NTSC.fla

NTSC.clr

Yahoo_super_
messengers.fla

SWF2Video trial

SWF2Video
Premiere plugin

Animation examples

superbusy.fla

page_turn.fla

smoke_gradients.fla

smoke_shape.fla

smoke_steam.fla

323

fireworks.fla

soft_reveal.fla

starwarstext.fla

filter_effects.fla

filter_effects_2.fla

vertigo.fla

rain.fla

fire.fla

mudbubble_
holiday_2005.fla

lightHouse.fla

grassField.fla

3Dsc_test.fla

Working with sound

Yahoo_super_
messengers.fla

dynamic_sounds_AS3.fla

Audacity (installer)

Working with video

pbs_btl.fla

cone.fla

Interactivity

event_handling_
AS3.fla

event_handling_
AS2.fla

drag_drop_AS3.fla

drag_drop_AS2.fla

constrained_drag_
drop_AS3.fla

event_handling_
AS2.fla

pause_AS3.fla

pause_AS2.fla

image_
loader_AS3.fla

image_
loader_AS2.fla

LoadAudio01.fla
(all files)

Going mobile

luv_i2fly.fla

FPS-Meter Lite2.mxp

Extending Flash

Break text into lines.mxp	SymbolCreator.mxp	drawGuide.mxp	mudbubble_FPSMeter.mxp
Unify Stroke and Fill.mxp	AutoColor.mxp	frameEdit.mxp	BitmapSmoothingMultiple.jsfl
Combine Textfields.mxp	CreateMaskingLayer.mxp	frameExit.mxp	BitmapSmoothingSelected.jsfl
Motion Preset Preview.mxp	CustomZoom.mxp	layercolor.mxp	Filter Set Selection.jsfl
FrameSync.mxp	DefaultColorsMX2004.mxp	libAppend.mxp	Filter Set All.jsfl
Guide Maker.mxp	Easy Pallette.mxp	mergeLayers.mxp	Camera.mxp
Invert Frame Selection.mxp	EnterGraphCurFrame.mxp	MultiSwap.mxp	StageCrop.jsfl
Move layers to new folder.mxp	FrameAllLayers.mxp	NewAnimClip.mxp	auto.save.mxp
Queasy Tools v_1_5_0.mxp	KeyAllLayers.mxp	TimingChart.mxp	duplicate.layer.mxp
Roughen Edges.mxp	Label Jumper.mxp	toggleGuide.mxp	paperclips.mxp
Select Empty Layers.mxp	Rotoscope.jsfl	toggleOutline.mxp	reanimatorZ.mxp
Select Frame Range.mxp	SkipAround.mxp	traceSequence.mxp	pixeltools.mxp
SelectFrames_toStartAndEnd.mxp	SquashAndStretch.mxp	tween2keys.mxp	symbolswapper.mxp
Set stage to element size.mxp	SwapColorsMX2004.mxp	Apply Motion Tween.jsfl	distributetoframes.mxp
Unify Stroke and Fill.mxp	SymbolizeFrames.mxp	Apply Shape Tween.jsfl	
AnimSlider Ltd v0.9.mxp	ViewLayer.mxp	mudbubble_Pause.mxp	

Time-saving tips youWon!.fla

What's new in CS4

BoneTool_shape.fla

catTail.fla

crane.fla

helicopter.fla

landscape.fla

mantis.fla

mime_bones.fla

car.fla

penny.fla

knight-IK.fla